ELECTING CONGRESS

NEW RULES FOR AN OLD GAME

REAL POLITICS IN AMERICA

Series Editor: Paul S. Herrnson, *University of Maryland*

The books in this series bridge the gap between academic scholarship and the popular demand for knowledge about politics. They illustrate empirically supported generalizations from original research and the academic literature using examples taken from the legislative process, executive branch decision making, court rulings, lobbying efforts, election campaigns, political movements, and other areas of American politics. The goal of the series is to convey the best contemporary political science research has to offer in ways that will engage individuals who want to know about real politics in America.

ELECTING CONGRESS
NEW RULES FOR AN OLD GAME

EDITED BY

David B. Magleby
Brigham Young University

J. Quin Monson
Brigham Young University

Kelly Patterson
Brigham Young University

PEARSON

Prentice
Hall

UPPER SADDLE RIVER, NEW JERSEY 07458

Library of Congress Cataloging-in-Publication Data

Magleby, David B.

  Electing congress: new rules for an old game/David B. Magleby, J. Quin Monson, Kelly Patterson.

    p. cm.— (Real politics in America)

  Includes bibliographical references and index.

  ISBN 0-13-243867-4

  1. United States. Congress—Elections, 2004.   2. Political campaigns—United States—Case studies.   3. United States. Bipartisan Campaign Reform Act of 2002. I. Monson, J. Quin. II. Patterson, Kelly D. III. Title. IV. Series.

  JK19682004 .M34 2007

  324.973'0931—dc22

2006015998

Editorial Director: Charlyce Jones Owen
Acquisitions Editor: Dickson Musslewhite
Associate Editor: Rob DeGeorge
Editorial Assistant: Jennifer Murphy
Marketing Manager: Emily Cleary
Marketing Assistant: Jennifer Lang
Director of Production and Manufacturing: Barbara Kittle
Managing Editor: Lisa Iarkowski
Production Liaison: Joe Scordato
Production Assistant: Marlene Gassler
Prepress and Manufacturing Manager: Nick Sklitsis
Prepress and Manufacturing Buyer: Mary Ann Gloriande
Cover Art Director: Jayne Conte
Cover Design: Kiwi Design
Cover Image: Eric Jacobson/Taxi/Getty Images, Inc.
Composition/Full Service Project Management: Karen Ettinger, Techbooks
Printer/Binder: The Courier Companies
Cover Printer: The Courier Companies

This book was set in 10/12 Palatino

Real Politics in America
Series Editor: Paul S. Herrnson

Pearson Education LTD.
Pearson Education Singapore, Pte. Ltd
Pearson Education, Canada, Ltd

Pearson Education—Japan
Pearson Education Australia PTY, Limited
Pearson Education North Asia Ltd
Pearson Educacion de Mexico, S.A. de C.V.
Pearson Education Malaysia, Pte. Ltd

PEARSON
Prentice
Hall

10 9 8 7 6 5 4 3 2 1
ISBN 0-13-243867-4

CONTENTS

PREFACE

The 2004 congressional elections were the first federal elections held under the new rules of the Bipartisan Campaign Reform Act (BCRA), which became effective the day after the 2002 election. This book continues research from three previous election cycles, beginning in 1998, which examines how political parties and interest groups affect U.S. House and Senate elections. While the long term effects of BCRA are still evolving, the 2004 elections for Congress made two things clear: First, BCRA has changed the way campaign money is raised and spent in congressional election campaigns. The congressional campaign committees, no longer able to feed at the trough of unlimited soft money that characterized their fundraising and spending through 2002, successfully increased their efforts in hard money fundraising to compensate for the absence of soft money in 2004. At least some of the soft money made its way into so-called 527 groups. Most of these were focused on the presidential election, but in a harbinger for the future, some 527 groups were focused on congressional races.

Second, while fundraising practices have changed in response to the new law, BCRA has not changed some fundamental aspects of congressional elections that were true before the passage of BCRA. Political parties and interest groups still focus the lion's share of their efforts in the districts and states perceived to be the most competitive. Due to the relatively small number of competitive contests, spending levels by parties and interest groups can meet or exceed the spending of the candidates. Furthermore, the outside money in these House and Senate races frequently buys some of the most negative advertising. Consequently, competitive races tend to see more campaign activity and the voters in those races are often deluged by a flood of negative communications.

Our book is titled *Electing Congress: New Rules for an Old Game* to communicate our sense that while BCRA has clearly changed the playing field for congressional elections in some ways, in other ways it remains largely unchanged. We will also need to wait and see what long-term effects may emerge in the future. We hope that this book at least begins to create a standard against which future developments in congressional elections can be compared.

ACKNOWLEDGMENTS

Our methodology in monitoring noncandidate electioneering efforts relies on systematic data collection and elite interviewing in a set of competitive congressional races. In 2004, our sample of competitive congressional races numbered 15, and we also observed presidential campaigns in five battleground states. This book builds on similar studies organized by the Center for the Study of Elections and Democracy (CSED) in 1998, 2000, and 2002. Across the four election cycles, we have now collected data on all forms of campaign communication in 102 contests. Our research on the 2004 election, as well as the earlier studies in 1998, 2000, and 2002, were funded by grants from the Pew Charitable Trusts, whose support in funding original research in the areas of campaign conduct and campaign finance is extraordinary. We express appreciation to Pew Program Officer Kathleen Welch and Pew President Rebecca Rimel for their trust and confidence in our work.

This kind of systematic coordinated data collection would not be possible without academics in the districts and states in our sample committing significant time and effort to this project. Our association with them on a truly collaborative effort is one of the most rewarding aspects of this research. We gratefully acknowledge the good work of Carl Shepro (University of Alaska–Anchorage) and Clive Thomas (University of Alaska–Southeast); Frederic I. Solop and Jamie I. Bowie (Northern Arizona University); Kyle Saunders and Robert Duffy (Colorado State University); Robert E. Crew (Florida State University), Terri Susan Fine (University of Central Florida), and Susan A. MacManus (University of South Florida); Charles Bullock (University of Georgia–Athens); Allan J. Cigler (University of Kansas); Lonna Rae Atkeson, Nancy Carrillo, Mekoce Walker (University of New Mexico); Steven Green (North Carolina State University) and Eric Heberlig (University of North Carolina–Charlotte); Ronald Keith Gaddie, Jennifer Christol, Charles Mullin, Katherine Thorne, and Benjamin Wilson (University of Oklahoma); Robin Kolodny, Sandra Suarez, and Justin Gollob (Temple University); Elizabeth Theiss Smith and Richard Braunstein (University of South Dakota); J. Matthew Wilson (Southern Methodist University); and Gary Bryner (Brigham Young University) and Stephen Roberds. Space did not permit us to include all of these case studies in this book. The initial version of these case studies can be found at csed.byu.edu.

We also acknowledge the hard work and professionalism of our research associates at CSED—Stephanie Perry Curtis, Kristina Gale, Betsey Gimbel Hawkins, Richard Hawkins, and Nisha Riggs. Stephanie, Kristina, Betsey, and Richard, all recent Brigham Young University (BYU) graduates, worked full time on the project for a year or more, while Nisha Riggs was involved in the project's final stages. The research associates provided assistance to the academics in the field, managed the Websites, coordinated database construction, conducted data entry and clean-up, scheduled and accompanied us on interviews, analyzed a variety of data, transcribed interviews, edited the manuscript, and much more. Their significant contribution to the overall effort is apparent to anyone familiar with the day-to-day operations of CSED. Betsey Gimbel Hawkins worked on our project from space provided us in Washington, D.C., by the Center for Public Integrity (CPI). We are most grateful to Charles Lewis and his associates at CPI for their hospitality and collegiality. BYU undergraduates Thomas Donohoe, Emily McClintock, John Baxter Oliphant, Chad Pugh, Paul Russell, and Brandon Wilson, as well as public policy graduate student Betsey Escandon, provided research assistance. Marianne Holt Viray and Jeffrey R. Makin, research associates from the previous projects, provided timely advice on this project as well. Brook Roper and Scott Cameron provided editorial assistance. We are also indebted to the Office of Research and Creative Activities at BYU, especially Gary R. Reynolds, Melvin Carr, Kathleen Rugg, and Nancy A. Davis, for helping to coordinate and facilitate our research.

To supplement our data collection directly from broadcast and cable stations, we acquired the Campaign Media Analysis Group (CMAG) data on broadcast television ads when it was available for media markets in our sample races. We gratefully acknowledge the assistance of Ken Goldstein of the University of Wisconsin–Madison and his Wisconsin Advertising Project associates Joel Rivlin and Timothy Wells. As in previous cycles, we contacted members of the League of Women Voters, Common Cause, and Brigham Young University alumni in each of the contests we monitored. Our academic partners further expanded this reconnaissance network with alumni from their own universities and others with a broad reach of interests and contacts. We express appreciation to Lloyd Leonard and Betsy Lawson of the League of Women Voters and Ed Davis of Common Cause for their assistance in this effort.

In 2004, CSED also organized a three-wave panel study of voter opinion about campaign finance. Participating in this research with us were Ken Goldstein and Charles Franklin of the University of Wisconsin–Madison. We also organized a national survey in which registered voters recorded their political phone calls and personal contacts and forwarded to us all of their political mail over a three-week period leading up to the election. The staff of the Social and Economic Sciences Research Center at Washington State University was very helpful in this major data collection effort. In particular, Don Dillman gave us sound advice on the design of the survey, and Ashley Grosse, John Tarnai, and Marion Schultz worked tirelessly to implement the data collection and coding. Bob Biersack and Paul Clark of the Federal

Election Commission (FEC) were, as always, most helpful in providing and interpreting FEC data.

Our sample selection process identifies competitive races in which outside groups and party committees are likely to mount campaigns. To help identify these races, we use data provided by Charles Cook and Stuart Rothenberg. In addition, we acknowledge the candid advice of party and interest group leaders and political reporters at various times before, during, and after the campaign. We have also been fortunate to have had access to many political professionals in the party committees, interest groups, and political consulting firms. Appendix A provides a list of all of those interviewed by CSED researchers in the 2004 studies. We are grateful that so many leaders of these organizations made time for us to interview them.

We also appreciate the insightful suggestions of Paul Herrnson, editor of this series.

Steve Rabinowitz and Adam Segal of Rabinowitz/Dorf Communications were of great assistance in organizing our Washington, D.C., press events and with media relations in general.

We are most appreciative of the careful attention and professionalism provided by Charlyce Jones Owen, Dickson Musselwhite, and Jennifer Murphy at Prentice Hall.

A project of this scope would not have been possible without the support of our spouses, Linda Waters Magleby, Kate Monson, and Jeanene Patterson. We dedicate this book to them.

ELECTING CONGRESS

NEW RULES FOR AN OLD GAME

1

INTRODUCTION

DAVID B. MAGLEBY, J. QUIN MONSON, AND KELLY D. PATTERSON
Brigham Young University

Congressional elections are often known for their predictable, even staid, nature. Incumbents generally win elections. Political action committees (PACs) donate to incumbents, and challengers are normally underfunded.[1] Open-seat races are more competitive and are often well funded. Changes occur slowly, if at all. Exogenous shocks to the electoral system, in the form of major shifts in the law or ideological realignment, can result in significant change, but those events are rare. For every election cycle where there is significant change, such as in 1994, there are dozens of cycles where business as usual prevails. The 2004 elections also presented the possibility for change; they were the first conducted under the Bipartisan Campaign Reform Act (BCRA). This legislation substantially changed some of the campaign finance rules enacted in the Federal Election Campaign Act (FECA) and its later amendments. Prominent actors in congressional elections were forced to learn a new set of rules by which to play their usual game.

The 2004 election cycle had the usual lackluster races; however, there were also some races where candidates fought bitterly and experimented with new technologies. This volume examines both types of races in light of the new BCRA regulations. An in-depth examination of specific races helps trace how the changes to the rules of the game have affected the game itself and nudged it in a different direction. This volume addresses the changes in how campaigns are financed and the role of noncandidate campaigns, such as parties and interest groups, and what parts of those changes can be reasonably attributed to the revised campaign finance law. The volume also assesses what has remained the same. Much of what scholars have learned about congressional elections in recent years holds true even in the face of major changes in campaign finance.

This introduction examines the larger context of the 2004 election cycle. Presidential cycles differ from off-year cycles. Our research shows that an intensely competitive presidential election can alter, if only temporarily, the practices of major participants in the congressional election. We then discuss BCRA and its impact on the decisions made by various participants in congressional elections. Finally, we introduce the case studies and review the general lessons they offer.

THE STRATEGIC CONTEXT: AN OVERVIEW OF 2004

Competition for control of institutions is one of the driving forces behind American democracy. Two political parties compete for control of the presidency, the two chambers of Congress, and numerous state and local offices, and this competition helps provide the accountability and responsiveness that make American democracy work.[2] Competition is also important in the behavior of parties and interest groups. Competitive races draw the attention of diverse interest groups and both political parties, while noncompetitive races are one-sided affairs. Small majorities in Congress make competitive races even more important; when only a few seats need to change hands for a party to regain control of a chamber, the parties and their allied interest groups lavish resources on seats that are up for grabs.

The last decade in American politics has witnessed intense competition for control of the presidency and Congress. The U.S. Senate has changed hands three times since 1994. Going into the 2004 elections, the Democrats were only one seat away from control of the Senate if they were to have won the vice presidency. With the exception of the open seat in Georgia, they recruited strong candidates who, in general, easily secured nomination. For a time during the cycle, their chances of winning back the Senate were taken seriously. Republicans, on the other hand, had contentious Senate primaries in Colorado, Florida, Oklahoma, and Pennsylvania in 2004. This contrasted sharply with 2002, when the White House political team succeeded in clearing the field in states such as Georgia, Minnesota, North Carolina, and South Dakota.[3]

The competitive 2004 U.S. Senate races rarely coincided with presidential battlegrounds and typically were in "red" states. Only Senate contests in Pennsylvania, Florida, and Colorado, for a time, had both major party presidential nominees mounting serious efforts. Many of the other Senate contests were in states Kerry readily conceded to Bush, such as Alaska, North Carolina, Oklahoma, and South Dakota.

Even though the Republicans controlled the U.S. House by a slim number, most observers thought that Democrats had a small chance to regain the majority. As Carl Forti, the spokesperson for the National Republican Congressional Committee (NRCC), said, "It is going to be very difficult for them to win the House back outside of some national tidal wave that right now isn't there."[4] One of the reasons for this was the redistricting following the 2000 Census, which left comparatively few competitive districts, hence comparatively few opportunities for the Democrats to pick up seats. Democrats were further weakened by the Texas redistricting, which occurred in September 2003. As we will discuss in some detail later in this book (see Chapter 7), redistricting worked well for Majority Leader Tom DeLay and the Republicans: the Texas delegation saw a net gain of six seats in the 2004 elections, from 15 Republicans and 17 Democrats to 21 Republicans and 11 Democrats.

Overall, 2004 presented a series of interesting choices for outside groups and parties. Many of the groups, when faced with the opportunity to participate in both the presidential and congressional campaigns, focused primarily on the presidential race. Others did the opposite. The lack of overlap between competitive Senate races and presidential battleground states meant that the groups would have to expend resources in different states if they wanted to influence the presidential race as well as congressional races. Political parties also had to decide how much to devote to the small number of competitive congressional races.

BCRA and the New Regulatory Framework

BCRA added another wrinkle to the strategic choices faced by parties and interest groups. Without certain forms of money and electioneering activities available to them, groups and parties had to decide not only which races to support but also how to support them. Campaign finance reformers have been concerned for several years with the efforts of some elected officials to raise large amounts of soft money, funds parties can raise in unlimited amounts, from corporations, labor unions, and wealthy individuals to bolster the coffers of party committees and indirectly finance competitive federal election contests. Of particular concern was the undue influence those donors appeared to exercise. Even some elected officials and donors expressed concern about the relationship between donors and officeholders and the unseemly appearance that resulted.[5] Some groups or individuals wanted to participate in the campaigns by running sham issue ads that purported to be only about issues but were primarily about opposing or supporting a particular candidate. Candidates often considered these groups to be disruptive to their campaign's message. BCRA dramatically modified campaign finance by banning party soft money and redefining electioneering communications.

Soft money was originally intended to fund generic party activity and infrastructure, but by 1996 soft money became a way to channel more money to congressional and presidential contests. The amount of soft money raised by the party committees in 2000 and 2002 was a little over $500 million in each election cycle (see Table 1.1). Most of this money was raised by the national parties but was spent through the state parties.

The large amounts of soft money raised and transferred thwarted the original intent of the FECA, which limited contributions in order to prevent

TABLE 1.1 HARD-MONEY, SOFT-MONEY, AND COMBINED RECEIPTS, 1992 TO 2004

Hard-Money Receipts

	1992	1994	1996	1998	2000	2002	2004
DNC	$65,790,724	$41,843,770	$108,372,562	$64,779,752	$123,997,509	$67,497,257	$404,352,278
DSCC	25,450,835	26,429,878	30,798,424	35,645,188	40,488,666	48,391,653	88,655,573
DCCC	12,815,844	19,424,492	26,623,493	25,180,286	48,394,476	46,442,229	93,168,931
RNC	85,447,469	87,392,680	193,029,129	104,048,689	212,798,761	170,099,094	392,413,393
NRSC	73,810,640	65,325,336	64,541,312	53,423,388	51,475,156	59,161,387	78,980,487
NRCC	35,272,672	26,696,951	74,224,879	72,708,311	97,314,513	141,089,250	185,719,489
Total D	163,279,568	132,786,892	221,613,028	159,961,869	362,221,908	276,500,463	747,468,322
Total R	264,915,932	244,101,180	416,513,249	285,007,168	538,144,632	485,351,179	840,058,754

Soft-Money Receipts

	1992	1994	1996	1998	2000	2002
DNC	$31,356,076	$43,923,516	$101,905,186	$56,966,353	$136,563,419	$94,564,827
DSCC	566,111	372,448	14,176,392	25,880,538	63,717,982	95,049,520
DCCC	4,368,980	5,113,343	12,340,824	16,865,410	56,702,023	56,446,802
RNC	35,936,945	44,870,758	113,127,010	74,805,286	166,207,843	113,928,997
NRSC	9,064,167	5,582,013	29,395,329	37,866,845	44,652,709	66,426,117
NRCC	6,076,321	7,371,097	18,530,773	26,914,059	47,295,736	69,677,506
Total D	36,256,667	49,143,460	123,877,924	92,811,927	245,202,519	246,061,149
Total R	49,787,433	52,522,763	138,199,706	131,615,116	249,861,645	250,032,620
DNC	$97,146,800	$85,767,286	$210,277,748	$121,746,105	$260,560,928	$162,062,084
DSCC	26,016,946	26,802,326	44,974,816	61,525,726	104,206,648	143,441,173
DCCC	17,184,824	24,537,835	38,964,317	42,046,696	105,096,499	102,889,031
RNC	121,384,414	132,263,438	306,156,139	178,853,975	379,006,604	284,028,091
NRSC	82,874,807	70,907,349	93,936,641	91,290,233	96,127,865	125,587,504
NRCC	41,348,993	34,068,048	92,755,652	99,622,370	144,610,249	210,766,756
Total D	199,536,235	181,930,352	345,490,952	252,773,796	607,424,427	522,561,612
Total R	314,703,365	296,623,943	554,712,955	416,622,284	788,006,277	735,383,799

Source: Federal Election Commission. "Party Financial Activity Summarized for the 2004 Election Cycle," press release, March 2, 2005, www.fec.gov/press/press2005/20050302party/Party2004final.html (accessed March 21, 2005).

Notes: The totals for each party do not equal the sum of the party committee receipts because the numbers provided by the Federal Election Commission have been adjusted to account for transfers between party committees so as not to double count money in the total receipts. The total also includes state and local hard-money receipts, which are not shown. Abbreviations: DNC, Democratic National Committee; DSCC, Democratic Senatorial Campaign Committee; DCCC, Democratic Congressional Campaign Committee; RNC, Republican National Committee; NRSC, National Republican Senatorial Committee; NRCC, National Republican Congressional Committee; D, Democrats; R, Republicans.

wealthy individuals or groups from exercising undue influence on a politician or in a particular contest. More important, the practice of raising and spending soft money created an appearance of corruption as elected officials, including congressional leadership, the president, the vice president, and others, directly solicited large soft-money contributions. In late 1997, Senator Fred Thompson, then Chairman of the Governmental Affairs Committee, initiated efforts to address the apparent corruption by reforming campaign finance laws.[6] The Supreme Court upheld the soft-money ban, holding that "the interests that underlie contribution limits are interests in preventing (1) the actual corruption threatened by large financial contributions, and (2) the eroding of public confidence in the electoral process through the appearance of corruption."[7]

The BCRA ban on soft money meant that the connection between large donors and party leaders was no longer direct. However, large donors are still able to influence federal elections. As the various case studies in this volume indicate, large donors were important in funding Section 527 organizations (named for the section of the Internal Revenue code that governs them), such as Citizens for a Strong Senate (CSS), in 2004. In addition BCRA permits state and local parties to raise and spend limited amounts of soft money for voter registration and get-out-the-vote (GOTV) efforts.

BCRA also changed the definition of express advocacy or an electioneering communication from "any ad that uses language such as like *vote for, elect, support, cast your ballot for, Smith for Congress, vote against, defeat,* or *reject*"[8] to a "definition of electioneering communications [that only] covers broadcast, cable or satellite advertisements that refer to a clearly identified candidate within sixty days of a general and thirty days of a primary election and are targeted to a population of 50,000 or more people in a candidate's district or state."[9] Reformers intended the new definition to eliminate the influence organizations sought by advertising for or against political candidates using innocuous names such as "Citizens for Better Medicare." The new law also required more complete and timely disclosure of electioneering communications. Nonparty entities are required to file a disclosure report within 24 hours of spending $10,000 and must continue to file reports for each $10,000 spent thereafter. BCRA also restored the longstanding ban on unions and corporations giving general or treasury funds as party soft money or for electioneering ads. Political analysts predicted that outside groups would "look for ways around the electioneering ban, perhaps by shifting to nonbroadcast communications."[10]

To compensate for the absence of soft money, BCRA doubled individual contribution limits from $2,000 per election cycle per candidate to $4,000 in most cases, it also raised the aggregate individual contribution limit per election cycle to $95,000. Reformers had long seen disclosed and limited individual contributions as preferable to unlimited soft-money contributions, whose expenditure was often hard to track.

BCRA was not intended to overhaul the campaign finance system completely; it did not change the amount that PACs could contribute to candidates. Furthermore, the new law left intact the organization of the Federal Election Commission (FEC), a development that produced serious consequences in the midst of the election season when the FEC deadlocked on the rules defining electioneering. Ultimately, the FEC allowed the 527 groups to continue unimpeded by the new law. Advocates of BCRA vehemently contended that the FEC's failure to set limits on electioneering activity circumvented the intent of the law and challenged the result in court.[11] Subsequent legislation was introduced on these matters.

BCRA AND THE CONDUCT OF CONGRESSIONAL CAMPAIGNS

It is easy to see how BCRA affected both donors and candidates. The sources of candidate funding show some signs of change, as do the political parties, which have switched from soft to hard money for many of their activities. Finally, the interest groups themselves have adapted to the new environment by using a host of new tactics. We look at each one of these in turn.

CANDIDATES

Candidates raise money from three sources: individuals, PACs, and personal funds. BCRA affected all three of these sources. First, as noted, the amount of money that candidates could raise from individuals doubled from $1,000 to $2,000 per primary, general, or run-off election. In all the Senate races of 2004, over 72% of receipts were contributions from individuals ($269.63 million), a 6.97% increase from 2002 ($188.06 million). Several of the Senate campaigns examined in this volume saw extraordinary success in raising money from individuals.[12] In South Dakota, John Thune, who was a Republican Senate candidate in both 2002 and 2004, raised over $3.5 million in 2002 and just over $14 million in 2004. While some of the increase can probably be attributed to his high-profile 2004 contest against Majority Leader Daschle, it highlights the overall importance individual contributions played in the new regulatory environment brought about by BCRA.

A similar pattern emerges for House contests. In these elections in 2004, almost 56% of contributions were from individuals, a 6.66% increase from 2002 ($347.76 million up from $269.93 million).[13] Individual contributions played a prominent role in all of the House races described in this volume.

PACs have long been an important component of how congressional candidates, especially incumbents, finance their campaigns. BCRA limited what unions and corporations could do with general treasury funds. With party soft money also banned, PACs and leadership PACs organized by senators and U.S. representatives had the potential to become more active in 2004 than they had been in 1996, when party soft money became more important. In 2004 members of Congress assisted other members by making PAC contributions to them from their leadership PACs. Members were permitted to contribute personally to the campaigns of other members, a phenomenon which has become more important in a hard-money world. Researchers predicted early on that member-to-member contributions would increase under the provisions of BCRA.[14]

Finally candidates could give their party committees money from their campaign accounts. In 2004 the following candidates gave to the Democratic Senatorial Campaign Committee (DSCC): John Kerry, $4 million[15]; Harry Reid, $1 million; and Charles Schumer, $2.5 million. Other notable transfers to the DSCC came from Senator Barbara Boxer (D-CA) ($470,000) and Senator Ron Wyden (D-OR) ($300,000). Republican office holders were less inclined to give large sums to their party committees. The exceptions were Congressman John Lewis (D-GA) who gave $1.25 million to the NRCC. Lewis later mounted a successful intra-party battle for the Appropriations Committee Chair, and for House Speaker Dennis Hastert (R-IL) who also gave $800,000 to the NRCC.

Candidates still seem to follow a national strategy for raising funds from interest groups, seeking resources from outside their districts. PACs often give to incumbents with seats on committees of concern to the PAC. Some congressional races receive an extraordinary amount of attention from groups around the nation. For example, in 2004 the U.S. Senate race in South Dakota for both parties saw fundraising "with a national focus."[16] Senate Majority Leader Bill Frist, in an unusual move, actively campaigned against Senate Minority Leader Tom Daschle.[17] GOP-allied interest groups also invested heavily and made the race a priority, including the American Medical Association (AMA), the U.S. Chamber of Commerce, and the National Rifle Association (NRA).[18] Chuck Cunningham, federal affairs director of the NRA, saw the South Dakota Senate race as his "number-one priority."[19] The Republican groups' willingness to enter the race gave them an advantage, as "there were fifteen to twenty groups against Daschle while most Democratic groups at Daschle's request stayed out."[20]

In 2004, candidates were limited in what they could give or loan their own campaigns without penalty, a change from the prior rules. BCRA requires a candidate who "spends significant amounts of his or her own personal funds on the race"[21] to notify his or her opponent of that contribution or expenditure, which automatically increases the opponent's contribution limits to between three and six times the normal amount, depending on a formula that varies from state to state. This "Millionaires' Amendment" became important in the Colorado Senate race where Republican Pete Coors personally lent his campaign over $550,000, just under the threshold that would trigger the millionaire's provision of BCRA. Late in the campaign, however, he again gave money to his own campaign[22] to counter negative advertising by the League of Conservation Voters (LCV) and CSS.[23] His

Democratic opponent, Ken Salazar, was then able to raise an additional $750,000 from people who had previously donated the maximum allowable amount to his campaign. Chapter 2, which discusses Colorado, shows that Salazar used the money to buy additional radio and television time.[24] The Millionaires' Amendment also played a key role in the Pennsylvania Thirteenth Congressional District; Democrat Allyson Schwartz developed an entire fundraising campaign around the possibility that Republican Melissa Brown would trigger the provision. Though Brown never exceeded the self-financing limit, Schwartz was prepared to both solicit new donors at the higher contribution limit and solicit contributions from those who had previously given the maximum amount.[25] This provision of BCRA had clear implications for the fundraising and strategic calculations made by the candidates in races with substantially self-financed candidates.[26]

POLITICAL PARTIES

Prior to the passage of BCRA, the national party committees (Democratic National Committee [DNC], Republican National Committee [RNC], Democratic Senatorial Campaign Committee [DSCC], National Republican Senatorial Committee [NRSC], Democratic Congressional Campaign Committee [DCCC], National Republican Congressional Committee [NRCC]) had depended on unlimited soft money, which sometimes came in large contributions or from sources otherwise prohibited from contributing to parties or candidates, such as labor union and corporate general funds. In 2000, 40 percent[27] and in 2002, 44 percent[28] of funds raised by the DNC, RNC, DSCC, NRSC, DCCC, and NRCC consisted of soft money.

The soft-money ban seems to have had some effect on spending in congressional races. The drop in party resources in 2004 occurred despite the fact that Senate Democrats had recruited strong candidates in Republican-leaning states such as Alaska, Colorado, North Carolina, and South Carolina. Senate Republicans also had more contentious primaries in 2004 than in 2002, especially in Colorado, Florida, Oklahoma, and Pennsylvania. However, the dollars spent per voter in competitive U.S. Senate races in 2004 was less than in the 1998 to 2002 period. For example, spending in dollars per voter in Florida ($3.11), Oklahoma ($6.26), and Colorado ($8.05) in 2004 lagged behind the figures in the Missouri ($11.25) and South Dakota ($37.37) races in 2002.[29] The South Dakota 2004 Senate race, however, was an exception to this trend and was likely the most expensive per-capita spending race in U.S. history, with spending reaching $86.59 per South Dakota voter.[30]

An important strategic element of soft money had been the ability to use it for competitive races or battleground states. Soft money with a hard-money match was typically transferred to state parties and then spent on the election through television ads, mail, phone banks, and GOTV activities. Total soft-money transfers in competitive U.S. Senate and House races in the

1998 to 2002 period soared: DSCC, NRSC, DCCC, and NRCC transfers saw a near fourfold increase from $41.8 million in 1998 to $159.5 million in 2002. This infusion of party soft money was important to the outcome of several competitive races like the Michigan Senate race in 2000, where Deborah Stabenow won by 1 percent of the vote after the DSCC transferred $4.7 million to the race compared to the NRSC's $3.1 million transfer. In 2002, John Sununu won New Hampshire's Senate contest by 4 percent, despite raising $2.1 million less than his opponent. The NRSC more than compensated for this gap by transferring $3,413,273 to the state, compared to $809,174 transferred from the DSCC to help Sununu's Democratic opponent.[31]

Under BCRA, the parties had to raise more hard money to make up for the soft-money ban. BCRA did not, however, prevent them from spending unlimited amounts of hard money in particular races. The parties did this through independent expenditures, a practice that a Supreme Court ruling made available to them.[32] As we discuss in the following section, party committees dramatically increased their independent expenditures in 2004. Parties can use independent expenditures, which classify as hard money made entirely independent of the candidate's campaign, to advocate the election or defeat of a particular candidate. However, in 2004, this spending fell well short of what parties had expended in soft money in 1998, 2000, and 2002. It is unlikely, given the wide margin of Bush's victory in several of these typically Republican states, that more independent spending by the DSCC would have changed the party's net loss of four seats.

The DSCC and NRSC were not able to make up for the soft-money ban with increased hard-money fundraising. Total funds available (hard money) to both senatorial campaign committees dropped about 40 percent in 2004, compared with their hard- and soft-money receipts in 2000 and 2002. The difference was substantial for the DSCC, with a drop in 2004 of $54,785,600, compared to the aggregate hard and soft dollars in 2002. For the NRSC the drop between 2002 and 2004 was $46,607,017. The DSCC, as noted, made up for some of this drop with a large infusion of money from its federal candidates.

In 2004, the DSCC raised more hard money than the NRSC (see Figure 1.1). However, the DCCC lagged well behind the NRCC (see Figure 1.2). The total GOP advantage in party-committee hard money was nearly $200 million in 2000 and 2002, representing a two-to-one advantage over Democrats that many believed would continue under BCRA.[33] In 2004, the aggregate Republican hard-money advantage dropped to about $75 million. Democrats, as shown in the soft-money section of Table 1.1, had been at or near parity with Republicans since 1994 in soft-money receipts, and the DSCC raised more soft money than the NRSC in 2000 and 2002. This meant the Democrats had a proportionately greater reliance on soft money than Republicans.

The DSCC also had noteworthy success raising money from individuals in 2004, though fundraising was slow at the beginning of the cycle.[34] In the

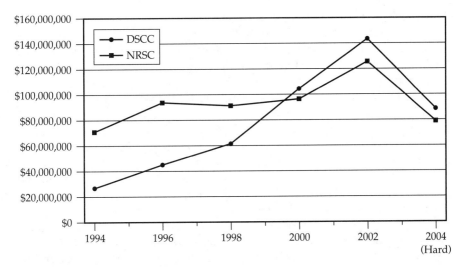

FIGURE 1.1   DSCC AND NRSC TOTAL RECEIPTS, 1994 TO 2004

Source: Federal Election Commission, "Party Financial Activity Summarized for the 2004 Election Cycle," press release, March 2, 2005, www.fec.gov/press/press2005/20050302party/Party2004final.html (accessed March 21, 2005).

Note: Abbreviations: DSCC, Democratic Senatorial Campaign Committee; NRSC, National Republican Senatorial Committee.

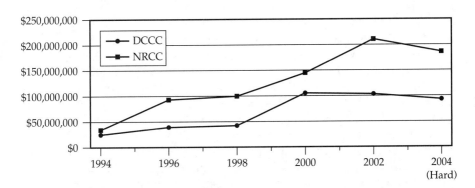

FIGURE 1.2   DCCC AND NRCC TOTAL RECEIPTS, 1994 TO 2004

Source: Federal Election Commission, "Party Financial Activity Summarized for the 2004 Election Cycle," press release, March 2, 2005, www.fec.gov/press/press2005/20050302party/Party2004final.html (accessed March 21, 2005).

Note: Abbreviations: DCCC, Democratic Congressional Campaign Committee; NRCC, National Republican Congressional Committee.

2000 and 2002 cycles, the NRSC roughly doubled the money that the DSCC raised from individuals. In 2004, the DSCC increased its gains to $57.5 million from individuals compared to $59 million for the NRSC. The DSCC, like the DNC, did much better than it had done in the past with small individual contributions and also raised $12.6 million from individuals contributing at the maximum allowable amount, compared to the NRSC's $6.3 million.

The question for Democratic committees is, Will they be able to continue their growth into 2006 and beyond? Both the DCCC and NRCC saw a net reduction in funds available to their party committees in 2004, but in proportional terms not as much as the senatorial campaign committees.

Among the Republican committees the NRCC alone continued its total receipts and individual contributions advantage over its Democratic counterpart in 2004. The House Republicans' total receipts exceeded $185 million, compared to a little over $93 million for the House Democratic committee. House Democrats lagged well behind House Republicans, their fellow Democrats in the Senate, and the DNC in matching or exceeding Republicans in individual contributions. On one positive note, the DCCC more than doubled the funds it raised from individuals in 2004 compared to 2000 or 2002 and, like the DSCC, did better than the Republicans in raising money from those who contributed the maximum possible amount.

The DCCC's underdog status might be explained partially by the opposition's preparation. The NRCC spent at least $55 million conducting new-donor prospecting with the telemarketing firm InfoCision. This work reportedly produced 500,000 new donors for the NRCC in the 2004 cycle, who the company guaranteed would contribute enough money to fund the project. Because a significant portion of the NRCC fundraising advantage was spent doing additional fundraising, the actual difference in dollars available for electioneering was much less than the aggregate totals. As a trade-off, the prospecting work may aid the NRCC in maintaining a long-term hard-money advantage in fundraising over the DCCC.[35]

The RNC, DNC, and NRSC experienced a surge in fundraising late in the campaign compared to the other party committees in 2003 and 2004. Figure 1.3 plots the proportion of total cycle receipts per party committees for each of the party committees throughout the cycle. The RNC and the NRCC had a stronger start in money raising than the other party committees. The DNC, however, shows the most dramatic surge in receipts between June 30, 2004, and October 13, 2004. That growth continued, helping the DNC surpass the RNC by November 2004. The NRCC widened its margin over the other congressional campaign committees late in the cycle, when the DSCC and DCCC took out loans of about $5 million and $10 million, respectively.[36]

When party committees were no longer able to spend hard money to match soft money in 2004, they returned to their prior patterns of contributing more hard money directly to candidates, even to candidates not in competitive races. The NRSC, for example, contributed more to candidates in 2004 than it had since 1996, and for the DSCC the 2004 amount contributed to

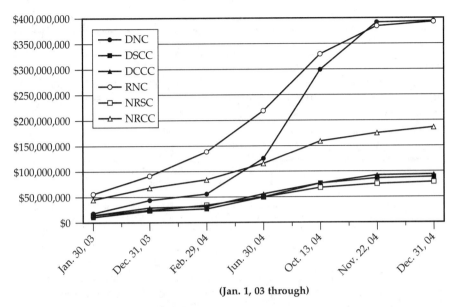

(Jan. 1, 03 through)

FIGURE 1.3   **HARD-MONEY (FEDERAL) RECEIPTS THROUGHOUT THE 2004 ELECTION CYCLE**

Source: Federal Election Commission, www.fec.gov/press/press2005/2005news.shtml (accessed March 21, 2005).

Note: Total receipts do not include monies transferred among the listed committees. Abbreviations: DNC, Democratic National Committee; DSCC, Democratic Senatorial Campaign Committee; DCCC, Democratic Congressional Campaign Committee; RNC, Republican National Committee; NRSC, National Republican Senatorial Committee; NRCC, National Republican Congressional Committee.

candidates exceeded anything it had done since 1994. Compared to 2002, the House committees were actually down in total contributed to candidates, further evidence they wanted to maximize their independent expenditures.

A national party committee and state party committees may make joint expenditures to federal candidates for the general election campaign. These expenditures, called coordinated expenditures, occur when the party committees pay for goods or services to benefit the candidate but do not give the money directly to the candidate or the candidate's committee. Coordinated party expenditures count against special limits and are not reported by the candidate.[37] Table 1.2 shows party coordinated expenditures. As with direct contributions to candidates, during the mid- to late-nineties, the DSCC and NRSC had minimized their coordinated expenditures, dropping from more than $8 million in coordinated expenditures early in the 1990s to under $10,000 in the 1998 to 2000 period. In 2004, the committees "invested a lot of money in coordinated campaigns," with coordinated expenditures growing to over $4 million from the DSCC and $8.5 million from the NRSC.[38] The same trend is evident for the NRCC and DCCC, but the extent of the expansion is less. Coordinated expenditures in 2004 nearly grew to $16 million, the maximum allowable, at the DNC, with the RNC spending the maximum in coordinated expenditures,

TABLE 1.2   COORDINATED EXPENDITURES BY PARTY COMMITTEE, 1994 TO 2004

	1994	1996	1998	2000	2002	2004
DNC	$245,011	$5,897,953	$5,849,422	$12,583,941	$346,216	$16,079,570
DSCC	12,550,478	8,476,258	8,424	127,157	181,789	4,394,396
DCCC	7,716,974	5,991,829	2,963,994	2,597,340	1,719,582	2,440,937
RNC	4,974,399	23,470,692	3,876,051	22,994,436	14,126,279	16,143,042
NRSC	8,448,136	586,197	28,513	172	553,206	8,449,099
NRCC	3,957,837	7,398,792	5,179,901	3,681,845	439,231	3,184,358

Source: Federal Election Commission, "Party Financial Activity Summarized for the 2004 Election Cycle," press release, March 2, 2005, www.fec.gov/press/press2005/20050302party/Party2004final.html (accessed March 21, 2005).

Note: Abbreviations: DNC, Democratic National Committee; DSCC, Democratic Senatorial Campaign Committee; DCCC, Democratic Congressional Campaign Committee; RNC, Republican National Committee; NRSC, National Republican Senatorial Committee; NRCC, National Republican Congressional Committee.

mostly on direct mail.[39] These coordinated expenditure figures were up substantially for the Democrats and down somewhat for the Republicans.

The parties turned to PACs and individual donors out of necessity in 2004, raising more hard money than ever before. Given the strong focus on the race for the White House, the congressional campaign committees lagged behind the DNC and RNC in total receipts and fell short of their previous total receipts (hard and soft) from 2000 and 2002.

Before the ban on soft-money spending, party committees targeted their resources to a relatively small number of competitive contests and maximized the impact of their hard money by transferring both hard and soft money to state party committees. This allowed them to target most of their resources to the most competitive contests. In 2004, party committees invested in the most competitive races by independent expenditures, funded through hard money.

To comply with the law, the expenditures by the party committees had to be independent of the candidates. This meant those managing the independent expenditures were "cordoned off from the rest of the campaign committee."[40] The detached nature of this party activity can result in the kind of misfire that occurred in Utah 2, in which the Republicans actually criticized the Democrats for backing Republican-sponsored bills. It also can mean that party committees make redundant expenditures for polls or that the timing of mail or ads may not be to the best interest of the candidate the party committee is trying to help.

Table 1.3 provides the party independent expenditures by committee for the 2004 election cycle. Overall, the party committees made $260,889,338 in independent expenditures in 2004. The DNC spent the most in independent expenditures in 2004, totaling nearly $120.5 million. The person responsible for independent expenditures at the DNC described them as oddly detached from the race: "On any given day, we felt how peripheral we were despite spending vast sums of money."[41] The RNC independent expenditures were

TABLE 1.3   INDEPENDENT EXPENDITURES BY PARTY COMMITTEE, 1994 TO 2004

	1994	1996	1998	2000	2002	2004
DNC	0	0	0	0	0	$120,333,466
DSCC	0	1,386,022	1,359,000	133,000	0	18,725,520
DCCC	0	0	0	1,916,489	1,106,113	36,923,726
RNC	0	0	0	0	500,000	18,268,870
NRSC	0	9,875,130	194,573	267,600	0	19,383,692
NRCC	0	0	0	548,800	1,203,854	47,254,064

Source: Federal Election Commission, "Party Financial Activity Summarized for the 2004 Election Cycle," press release, March 2, 2005, www.fec.gov/press/press2005/20050302party/Party2004final.html (accessed March 21, 2005).

Note: Abbreviations: DNC, Democratic National Committee; DSCC, Democratic Senatorial Campaign Committee; DCCC, Democratic Congressional Campaign Committee; RNC, Republican National Committee; NRSC, National Republican Senatorial Committee; NRCC, National Republican Congressional Committee.

more than $100 million less than the DNC's expenditures. Instead of focusing on independent expenditures, the RNC spent $45.8 million on a new strategy called 50/50 money. This strategy matches candidate expenditures with party hard money. The idea behind this joint financing is that communications advocating both Bush and members of Congress did not count as a direct contribution to a candidate or as an otherwise-limited coordinated expenditure.[42] The DNC later followed the RNC's lead. This practice had no discernable impact on the 2004 congressional races because, while the 50/50 funded advertisements mention Congress, they focused primarily on the presidential candidates. Independent expenditures by the other party committees were more evenly matched, with the NRSC and DSCC at near parity, and the NRCC spent only about $10 million more than the DCCC through independent expenditures.

Party independent expenditures in 2004 closely resembled soft-money activity from 1998 to 2002.[43] The party committees ran their own television and radio commercials, sent out direct mail, and set up phone banks. They retained their own pollsters, consultants, and attorneys and mounted their own voter mobilization efforts. While much of this ground-war activity was aimed at presidential battleground states, both parties worked at voter mobilization in the states with largely Republican-leaning Senate contests. Mobilizing Native Americans in South Dakota was a priority in 2004, for example.[44] There are substantial independent expenditures in our sample of contested U.S. Senate and U.S. House races. For example, in Senate races the DSCC spent between $2.3 and $3.7 million on the Alaska, Colorado, Florida, North Carolina, and Oklahoma Senate races. Of our sample races, the Democrats' independent expenditures fell below $1 million only in South Dakota, where they spent $938,098. The NRSC generally spent less, ranging from $4,168,203 in Florida to as little as $254,121 in Oklahoma. When looking at all House races in 2004, the Washington 8th district had the most independent expenditures, with the parties spending $6.1 million.[45]

TABLE 1.4   INDEPENDENT EXPENDITURES BY PARTY COMMITTEE FOR HOUSE AND
SENATE RACES IN THIS BOOK, 2003 TO 2004

RACE	DCCC	NRCC	TOTAL
AZ 1	$1,132,525	$1,604,272	$2,736,797
CO 7	61,850	535,864	597,714
GA 12	1,143,289	680,347	1,823,636
KS 3	694,017	608,959	1,302,976
NM 1	1,250,111	1,012,390	2,262,501
PA 13	795,643	793,956	1,589,599
SD AL	3,451,277	4,357,407	7,808,684
TX 32	1,114,511	747,483	1,861,994
UT 2	661,236	1,002,823	1,664,059

RACE	DSCC	NRSC	TOTAL
AK Sen	$2,954,847	$500,145	$2,454,992
CO Sen	2,301,264	1,139,946	3,441,210
FL Sen	3,726,182	4,168,203	7,894,385
NC Sen	2,529,622	1,853,330	4,382,952
OK Sen	2,301,293	254,121	2,555,414
SD Sen	938,098	334,864	1,272,962

Source: Federal Election Commission, ftp://ftp.fec.gov/FEC/ (accessed January 5, 2005).

Note: Abbreviations: DCCC, Democratic Congressional Campaign Committee; NRCC, National Republican Congressional Committee.

Competitive U.S. House races in our sample saw party independent ex-penditure activity achieve large differentials between the NRCC and DCCC in several cases. In the South Dakota At-Large race, the NRCC outspent the DCCC by nearly a million dollars. As noted in Table 1.3, the NRCC outspent the DCCC by more than $10 million in total independent expenditures. However, in our sample races, the difference between the two committees is much smaller. Table 1.4 summarizes party committee independent expendi-ture activity in our sample of races.

INTEREST GROUPS

Interest groups have long been major players in congressional campaign fi-nance through PAC contributions, especially to incumbents. BCRA did not change PAC contributions. PACs can give $5,000 in a primary and $5,000 in a general election. To increase their influence beyond the PAC contribution limits, some interest groups bundle contributions to candidates by asking group members to donate to particular campaigns, but to send their checks to the interest group rather than directly to the candidate. This way the group can bundle the donations together and take credit for raising the money while avoiding the PAC contribution limit. EMILY's List is one of the groups most identified with this process. The organization bundled contributions of $10.2 million in 2000 and 2002, and that number grew to $10.6 million in 2004.[46] The Club for Growth has also become an active bundler for fiscally conservative candidates, bundling approximately $7.5 million in 2004.[47]

Groups making independent expenditures were more likely to favor Democratic candidates. Prominent Democratic-leaning groups included MoveOn, unions, pro-choice groups, and environmental groups. Prominent Republican-leaning groups included medical, pro-life, and business organizations, as well as the NRA and the Club for Growth. Much of this activity focused on the ground war, which includes personal contact, mail, telephone, and e-mail. The business community, for example, had "never seen more mobilization and effort" than in the 2004 election.[48] The AMA increased its partisan communication dramatically in key Senate and House races from approximately $40,000 in 2000 and $250,000 in 2002 to $500,000 in 2004.[49] The Club for Growth saw contributions climb from $4 million in 2000 to about $10 million in 2002, reaching nearly $23 million in 2004[50] (see Table 1.5). Stephen Moore, president of the Club for Growth, believes that the elimination of party soft money did not harm his organization's activities. "Truth is, BCRA benefited us," he claimed.[51]

As with most campaign investors in 2004, groups making independent expenditures were most interested in the presidential race. Some groups making independent expenditures were active in only one or a few races. For example, You're Fired spent all its $550,400 in independent expenditures in the South Dakota U.S. Senate race.[52] Other examples of groups spending independently in congressional races included CSS and the Main Street Individual Fund.[53]

Some groups influence federal campaigns by fighting the ground war within their own constituencies. Groups that do a lot of this internal communication include labor unions, teachers associations, businesses, National Association of Realtors (NAR), the NRA, and the Sierra Club. The Associated Builders and Contractors (ABC) made a conscious decision to turn to internal communications in light of the new campaign finance restrictions. ABC used coordinators in its 23,000 member companies to contact employees approximately twelve times between Labor Day and Election Day via phone, e-mail, and mail. In addition, the coordinators distributed 890,000 voter guides in both English and Spanish in all presidential battleground states and in Alaska, Colorado, Florida, North Carolina, Oklahoma, and Washington, states with close Senate races. Even with this substantial activity, the expenditure reported to the FEC was not sufficient to show up in Table 1.6. The expenditures that the association made on internal communications targeted to the group's membership likely dwarf the association's

TABLE 1.5 INDEPENDENT EXPENDITURES BY TOP GROUPS, 2004

COMMITTEE NAME	INDEPENDENT EXPENDITURES FOR	INDEPENDENT EXPENDITURES AGAINST	TOTAL
MoveOn PAC	$10,848,932	$1,530,876	$12,379,808
NRA Political Victory Fund	5,096,563	1,917,140	7,013,703
AFSCME–PEOPLE, Qualified	6,887,872	3,714	6,891,586
United Auto Workers – VCAP	5,156,529	—	5,156,529
Service Employees International Union	4,181,956	34,191	4,216,147
National Right to Life PAC	3,652,380	9,606	3,661,986
Planned Parenthood	2,354,934	329,127	2,684,061
National Association of Realtors PAC	2,603,143	—	2,603,143
NARAL Pro-Choice America	406,317	1,722,321	2,128,638
American Medical Association PAC	1,792,655	—	1,792,655
NEA Fund for Children and Public Education	303,357	1,205,451	1,508,808
Club for Growth PAC	1,331,392	168,054	1,499,446
AFSCME, AFL-CIO (D.C.)	1,254,232	—	1,254,232
National Air Traffic Controllers Assn PAC	951,838	—	951,838
LCV Action Fund	355,357	407,847	763,204
International Association of Firefighters PAC	682,102	—	682,102
Defenders of Wildlife Action Fund	540,268	52,266	592,534
Environment 2004 Inc. PAC	—	531,509	531,509
American Neurological Surgery PAC	175,651	323,982	499,633
Sierra Club Political Committee	243,538	243,538	487,076
Other Groups	2,441,471	6,780,611	9,222,082
TOTAL FOR ALL GROUPS	51,260,487	15,260,233	66,520,720

Source: Federal Election Commission, ftp://ftp.fec.gov/FEC/ (accessed June 10, 2005).

Note: We combined expenditures for all national affiliates of an organization but excluded expenditures for the state affiliates. Abbreviations: PAC, political action committee; NRA, National Rifle Association; AFSCME, American Federation of State, County, and Municipal Employees; PEOPLE, Public Employees Organized to Promote Legislative Equality; VCAP, Voluntary Community Action Program; NARAL, National Abortion & Reproductive Rights Action League; NEA, National Education Association; LCV, League of Conservation Voters.

TABLE 1.6 INTERNAL COMMUNICATIONS BY TOP GROUPS, 2003 TO 2004

COMMITTEE NAME	INTERNAL COMMUNICATIONS FOR	INTERNAL COMMUNICATIONS AGAINST	TOTAL
AFL-CIO COPE Political Contributions Committee	$9,491,939	$138	$9,492,077
AFSCME	4,322,229	261,718	4,583,947
National Education Association	3,070,072	—	3,070,072
SEIU	2,063,780	—	2,063,780
American Federation of Teachers	2,022,338	5,482	2,027,820
National Association of Realtors	1,592,334	—	1,592,334
International Brotherhood of Teamsters	1,352,406	—	1,352,406
NRA Institute for Legislative Action	958,951	68,139	1,027,090
Sierra Club	743,792	44,151	787,943
International Association of Firefighters	558,010	—	558,010
American Medical Association	450,036	—	450,036
Laborers' International Union of North America	328,751	—	328,751
NARAL Pro-Choice America	903	185,850	186,753
Associated Builders and Contractors	124,134	14,000	138,134
National Treasury Employees Union	123,955	—	123,955
National Federation of Independent Business	111,964	—	111,964
United Food and Commercial Workers International Union	104,772	—	104,772
Other Groups	2,815,365	202,459	3,017,824
TOTAL FOR ALL GROUPS	30,235,731	781,937	31,017,668

Source: Federal Election Commission, ftp://ftp.fec.gov/FEC/ (accessed June 10, 2005).

Note: We combined expenditures for all national affiliates of an organization but excluded expenditures for the state affiliates. Abbreviations: COPE, Committee on Political Action; AFSCME, American Federation of State, County, and Municipal Employees; SEIU, Service Employees International Union; NARAL, National Abortion & Reproductive Rights Action League.

$50,000 independent expenditure made in South Dakota, asserting Daschle had taken on D.C. values and abandoned South Dakota values.[54]

LOOKING AT CONGRESSIONAL ELECTIONS

The cases in this volume were selected following a methodology used in 1998, 2000, and 2002 by the Center for the Study of Elections and Democracy (CSED) at Brigham Young University. A group of scholars organized and implemented a national study of the most competitive congressional contests, where outside group and party independent spending was most probable during the 2004 election cycle.[55] Using a case-study methodology, the research in this volume attempts to provide a full picture of the campaign communications in both candidate and noncandidate (party and interest group) campaigns. The methodology relied on academic field researchers, recruited for their knowledge of elections as well as their local political context. In 2004 the study included six U.S. Senate races and nine U.S. House races. This volume presents six of the case studies that illustrate the dynamics of a particular race in the aftermath of these changes to the law.

The sampling of competitive races CSED monitored for this study was developed based on a combination of lists of competitive races published in early spring by the *Cook Political Report*, the *Rothenberg Political Report*, and the *Congressional Quarterly Weekly Report*. This list was enhanced by interviews with current and former party and interest group professionals, reporters, and other political experts who helped identify contests in which outside money was most likely to be present.[56] In 2004, the number of potentially competitive congressional races in the published lists was small, and broad agreement on the most competitive races emerged in our interviews.[57]

The research design is based on three assumptions. First, the highest levels of campaign activity are most likely to occur in competitive races.[58] Second, because much of noncandidate campaign activity is not disclosed, it is best uncovered and understood by someone with knowledge of the local context. To this end, the academics studying each competitive race oversaw the collection of campaign communications, including the extent of mail, telephone, and personal contact; they also collected as much information as possible on broadcast advertising and monitored voter mobilization efforts conducted by candidates, parties, and interest groups. The local academics organized a network of informants to collect data on campaign communications. The informants collected their political mail and recorded other campaign communications they viewed or received. The third assumption is that political professionals are willing to be interviewed and discuss their decision making and funding allocation strategies. This elite interviewing helped "connect the dots" of our data collection efforts, both by validating what was discovered in the academics' data collection efforts and by providing new information. Academics conducting interviews in the districts or states were joined in elite interviewing by the project's principal investigators, who conducted 222 interviews in Washington, D.C. A full listing of the interviews conducted by the CSED researchers and authors of the six case studies in this volume is found in Appendix A.[59]

To uncover as much campaign activity as possible, researchers systematically collected data on campaign communications to learn about who is spending money in a particular contest. Campaign communications can be detected by examining the public files of radio and television stations for information about ads on issues of public controversy, including campaign ads; by obtaining data where possible from media monitoring firms like the Campaign Media Analysis Group (CMAG), which captures and counts ads in the largest 100 media markets; and by setting up a reconnaissance network to collect political mail, flyers, email, and to report on personal contact about the election. The study in 2004 also included a survey of a random sample of persons who were asked to forward their political mail and log telephone calls and personal appeals made to them in the last three weeks of the campaign. This book reports on this data retrieval effort in selected congressional races in 2004.

The data gathered to learn about campaign communications also include extensive interviews with candidates and their staffs, officials at party committees, interest groups, and other knowledgeable observers of congressional elections at the local and national levels. These interviews were conducted "on the record" and are cited frequently in the following chapters. Interviewing at district, state, and national levels made it possible to validate the activities of campaigns, parties and groups at the different levels.

Finally, the research relies on the disclosure requirements of federal law to learn as much as possible about the ways campaigns are financed. The activity of candidates and party committees are now more fully disclosed to the FEC, and these data are reported in this volume. In the 2004 election cycle, the Center for Public Integrity provided data on the activity of Section 527 organizations that report to the IRS and the FEC. One of the limitations of BCRA is that disclosure by Section 527 and 501(c) (named after the section of the IRS code under which they are organized) organizations is not timely or complete. To the extent possible this volume reports on the activity of these groups in competitive congressional races in 2004.

OVERVIEW OF THE BOOK

As stated at the outset, congressional elections seem to have a predictable, almost staid, nature. Yet changes do occur in their routine, and those changes occur most frequently when the system that structures these elections also changes. BCRA modified different aspects of the electoral system. In response, candidates, parties, and interest groups encountered a new environment as they waged their campaigns. The chapters in this volume examine in great detail the ways political actors responded to this new campaign environment. The book includes case studies of three Senate races and three House races.

The Senate races in 2004 offered the Democratic party its best hope of capturing control of one part of the government. Chapter 2 is a study of the Colorado Senate race. Robert Duffy and Kyle Saunders observed that the activities of interest groups and political parties do indeed matter. Candidates have a difficult time surviving a relentless pounding by well-timed and coordinated attacks. The authors also show that the Millionaire's Amendment in BCRA can level the playing field. In Chapter 3, Steven Greene and Eric Heberlig show that the South continues to be a difficult place for Democrats to win. Despite the presence of Senator Edwards on the presidential ticket, Erskine Bowles faced a difficult partisan environment. Only a couple of outside groups participated, and their impact seems to have been muted by the quality of both candidates. In Chapter 4, Elizabeth Theiss Smith and Richard Braunstein examine the South Dakota Senate race. This sparsely populated state received a tremendous amount of attention from the parties and interest groups. South Dakota offers perhaps one of the best examples of the intensity and innovation of modern high-stakes campaigns. It also illustrates how BCRA may complicate the job of political parties by making any sort of coordination with the candidate more difficult.

House races exhibit many of the same dynamics, but on a slightly smaller scale. In Chapter 5, Al Cigler looks at the 3rd district in Kansas. He shows how the incumbent advantage grows with each passing election, even when the district does not favor the incumbent's party. In Chapter 7, Matt Wilson explores the dynamics of a race where two powerful incumbents square off. The two candidates in Texas 32 had ample resources and did not need outside help to wage an intense and often negative campaign. In the last case study, Robin Kolodny, Sandra Suarez, and Justin Gollob look at the dynamics of a competitive district, the Pennsylvania 13th District, and the strategic decisions the candidates and interest groups face as the campaign unfolds. Together the Senate and House case studies provide a rich analysis of the dynamics of the campaign cycle in this new campaign regulatory environment. The final chapter of the volume pulls together the lessons learned from the case studies and the impact of BCRA. It also looks ahead to future elections and speculates about occurrences in the 2004 cycle that may develop into trends.

NOTES

1. For a discussion of the dynamics of congressional elections, see Paul S. Herrnson, *Congressional Elections: Campaigning at Home and in Washington, D.C.* 4th ed. (Washington, D.C.: Congressional Quarterly Press, 2004).
2. See Giovanni Sartori, *The Theory of Democracy Revisited* (Chatham, NJ: Chatham House, 1987).

3. David B. Magleby and J. Quin Monson, eds., *The Last Hurrah?: Soft Money and Issue Advocacy in the 2002 Congressional Elections* (Washington, D.C.: Brookings Institution Press, 2004).
4. Carl Hulse, "For House Democrats, a Whiff of Victory," *New York Times*, May 28, 2004, p. A17.
5. Peter Francia, John Green, Paul Herrnson, Lynda Powell, and Clyde Wilcox. *The Financiers of Congressional Elections: Investors, Ideologues, and Intimates* (New York: Columbia University Press, 2003).
6. Public Broadcasting Service, "Campaigns Under Scrutiny: A Tale of Two Hearings," Online News Hour, September 24, 1997, www.pbs.org/newshour/campaign/september97/hearing_9-24.html (accessed August 30, 2005).
7. *McConnell* v. *FEC*, 124 S. Ct. 619 (2003).
8. David B. Magleby, "The Importance of Outside Money in the 2002 Congressional Elections," in *The Last Hurrah?* ed. by Magleby and Monson, p. 2; *Buckley* v. *Valeo*, 424 U.S. 1, 44 n. 52 (1976).
9. David B. Magleby and J. Quin Monson, "The Consequences of Noncandidate Spending, with a Look to the Future," in *The Last Hurrah?* ed. by Magleby and Monson p. 277.
10. Michael Malbin, ed., "Thinking About Reform," in *Life After Reform: When the Bipartisan Campaign Reform Act Meets Politics* (Lanham, MD: Rowman and Littlefield, 2003), p. 16.
11. Campaign Legal Center, "Legal Center Press Release: McCain, Feingold to Support '527 Group' Lawsuit," press release, September 14, 2004, www.campaignlegalcenter.org/cases-166.html (accessed January 25, 2005).
12. Federal Election Commission, "Financial Activity of General Congressional Candidates 1992–2004," www.fec.gov/press/press2005/20050609candidate/genhistory2004.pdf (accessed November 29, 2005).
13. Federal Election Commission, "Financial Activity of General Congressional Candidates 1992–2004."
14. Michael Malbin, ed., "Thinking About Reform," p. 18.
15. "John Kerry for President" gave $3 million and then "Friends of John Kerry" gave an additional $1 million.
16. See Chapter 4 in this volume.
17. Paul Kane, "Frist's Travels Won't Include Return to S.D.," *Roll Call*, October 7, 2004, www.rollcall.com/issues/50_41/news/7090-1.html (accessed January 27, 2005).
18. Mike Cys and Jim Kwaka; director and regional political director, division of political and legislative grassroots, American Medical Association Political Action Committee, interview by David B. Magleby and Betsey Gimbel, Washington, D.C., December 15, 2004; Bill Miller, vice president public affairs and national political director, U.S. Chamber of Commerce, interview by David B. Magleby and Kristina Gale, Washington, D.C., November 9, 2004; and Chuck Cunningham, federal affairs director, National Rifle Association, interview by David B. Magleby and Kristina Gale, Washington, D.C., November 5, 2004.
19. Cunningham interview, November 5, 2004.
20. Benjamin Jones, research director, National Republican Senatorial Committee, interview by David B. Magleby and J. Quin Monson, Washington, D.C., November 10, 2004.
21. Federal Register, Vol. 68, No. 17, Monday, January 27, 2003, Rules and Regulations, p. 3970.
22. See Chapter 2 in this volume.
23. For a discussion on League of Conservation Voters and Citizens for a Strong Senate ads see Robert Duffy, Colorado State University, and Kelly D. Patterson, Brigham Young University, National Press Club event transcript, "Dancing Without Partners," (Brigham Young University, Center for the Study of Elections and Democracy, February 7, 2005), pp. 55–56.
24. See Chapter 2 in this volume.
25. See Chapter 6 in this volume.
26. See also Jennifer A. Steen, "Self-Financed Candidates and the 'Millionaires' Amendment,'" in *The Election After Reform: Money, Politics and the Bipartisan Campaign Reform Act*. ed., Michael J. Malbin (Rowman and Littlefield, forthcoming).
27. Federal Election Commission, "Party Fundraising Escalates," press release, January 12, 2001, www.fec.gov/press/press2001/011201partyfunds.htm (accessed January 26, 2005).
28. Federal Election Commission, "Party Fundraising Reaches $1.1 Billion in 2002 Election Cycle," www.fec.gov/press/press2002/20021218party/20021218party.html (accessed January 26, 2005).
29. Candidate spending per voter was calculated by dividing the sum of expenditures by the two candidates by the number of votes cast in the race as reported by the states' election

boards. Adjusted for inflation (2004 dollars) at U.S. Department of Labor, Bureau of Labor Statistics, "Consumer Price Index Home Page," www.bls.gov/cpi/home.htm (accessed January 25, 2005).

30. See Chapter 4 in this volume; See also John Bart and James Meader, "The More You Spend, The Less They Listen," in *The Last Hurrah?* ed. Magleby and Monson, pp. 159–160.

31. Data from 1998 are available at Federal Election Commission, "National Party Transfers to State/Local Party Committees," www.fec.gov/press/congst98.htm (accessed January 15, 2005). Data from 2002 are available at Federal Election Commission, "National Party Trans-fers to State/Local Party Committees," www.fec.gov/press/press2003/20030320party/congtostatesye02.xls (accessed January 25, 2005). See also Michael W. Traugott, "The 2000 Michigan Senate Race," in *The Other Campaign: Soft Money and Issue Advocacy in the 2000 Congressional Elections,* ed. David B. Magleby (Lanham, MD: Rowman & Littlefield, 2003), pp. 97–110; J. Mark Wrighton, "The New Hampshire Senate and 1st Congressional District Races," in *The Last Hurrah?* ed. Magleby and Monson (Provo, UT: Brigham Young University Press, 2003). Adjusted for inflation (2004 dollars) at U.S. Department of Labor, Bureau of Labor Statistics, "Consumer Price Index Home Page," www.bls.gov/cpi/home.htm (ac-cessed January 25, 2005).

32. *Colorado Republican Federal Campaign Committee and Douglas Jones, Treasurer, Petitioners* v. *FEC,* 518 US 604; 116 S. Ct. 2309; 135 L. Ed. 2d 795 (1996).

33. Magleby, "The Importance of Outside Money in the 2002 Congressional Elections," p. 4; Magleby and Squires, "Party Money in the 2002 Congressional Elections," in *The Last Hurrah?* ed. Magleby and Monson.

34. David Hamrick, national field director, Democratic Senatorial Campaign Committee, inter-view by David B. Magleby and Betsey Gimbel, Washington, D.C., December 15, 2004.

35. Chris Cillizza and Ethan Wallison, "NRCC Touts Alliance with InfoCision," *Roll Call,* November 29, 2004, www.rollcall.com/issues/50_55/politics/7525-1.html (accessed January 27, 2005).

36. Chris Cillizza, "Democrats Millions in Debt," *Roll Call,* November 8, 2004, www.rollcall.com/issues/50_49/news/7318-1.html (accessed January 27, 2005).

37. Federal Election Commission, "Chapter 7: Other Candidate Support Activities," www.fec.gov/info/PartyGuide/Chapter7.htm (accessed January 26, 2005).

38. Hamrick interview. See also Diana Dwyre's and Robin Kolodny's "The Parties' Congres-sional Campaign Committees in 2004," in *The Election After Reform,* ed. Malbin, p. 9.

39. Terry Nelson, political director, Bush/Cheney 2004, telephone interview by David B. Magleby and J. Quin Monson, January 5, 2005.

40. Savodnik, Peter, "Democrats cancel ad buy in Colo.-7," *The Hill,* www.hillnews.com/news/09282004/colorado.aspx (accessed November 28, 2005).

41. Ellen Moran, independent expenditure unit director, Democratic National Committee, in-terview by David B. Magleby and Betsey Gimbel, Washington, D.C., December 15, 2004.

42. Diana Dwyre and Robin Kolodny, "Learning a New Rule Book: Party Money in the Post-BCRA World," in *Financing the 2004 Election,* ed. David B. Magleby, Kelly D. Patterson, and Anthony Corrado (Brookings Institution, forthcoming).

43. See also Diana Dwyre's and Robin Kolodny's "The Parties' Congressional Campaign Com-mittees in 2004," p. 1.

44. See Chapter 4 in this volume. For more about Native American mobilization in South Dakota see Betty Smith, University of South Dakota, National Press Club event transcript, "Dancing Without Partners," (Brigham Young University, Center for the Study of Elections and Democracy, February 7, 2005), p. 60.

45. See also Diana Dwyre's and Robin Kolodny's "The Parties' Congressional Campaign Com-mittees in 2004," p. 9.

46. Karen White, political director, EMILY's List, interview by David B. Magleby and Richard Hawkins, Washington, D.C., November 5, 2004. Adjusted for inflation (2004 dollars) at U.S. Department of Labor, Bureau of Labor Statistics, "Consumer Price Index Home Page," www.bls.gov/cpi/home.htm (accessed January 25, 2005). For additional discussion see, Karen White, EMILY'S List Political Director, National Press Club event transcript, "Danc-ing Without Partners," p. 64.

47. Moore, interview.

48. Tiffany Adams, vice president of public affairs, National Association of Manufacturers, in-terview by David B. Magleby and Kristina Gale, Washington, D.C., November 5, 2004.

49. Cys and Kwaka interview.
50. Moore interview. Adjusted for inflation (2004 dollars) at U.S. Department of Labor, Bureau of Labor Statistics, "Consumer Price Index Home Page," www.bls.gov/cpi/home.htm (accessed January 25, 2005). The totals include contributions to the Club for Growth political action committee, a Section 527 organization, as well as bundled contributions then given to candidates.
51. Ibid.
52. Internal Revenue Service, "Political Organization Disclosure," forms.irs.gov/politicalOrgsSearch/search/submitBasicSearch.action (accessed January 26, 2005). For more discussion of You're Fired see Betty Smith, University of South Dakota, National Press Club event transcript, "Dancing Without Partners," p. 60.
53. Federal Election Commission, "Electioneering Communication," www.fec.gov/finance/disclosure/electioneering.shtml (accessed January 26, 2005).
54. Ned Monroe, director of political affairs, Associated Builders and Contractors, interview by David B. Magleby and Kristina Gale, Arlington, Va., November 8, 2004.
55. The generous support of the Pew Charitable Trusts funded the 1998, 2000, 2002, and 2004 projects.
56. Among others, we acknowledge the assistance in this effort of Tiffany Adams, Matt Angle, Kori Bernards, Heather Booth, Ed Brookover, Bernadette Budde, Peter Cari, Chuck Cunningham, Patrick Davis, Michael Ellis, Noe Garcia, Ed Goeas, Andy Grossman, Dan Gurley, John Guzik, Greg Hagele, Dan Hazelwood, Chris LaCivita, Jim Landry, Mark Longabaugh, Mike Lux, Bill Miller, Steven Moore, Laurie Moskowitz, Sheila O'Connell, Jack Polidori, Chuck Porcari, Amy Pritchard, David Rudd, Elizabeth Shipp, Erik Smith, Gail Stoltz, Sara Taylor, Paul Tewes, Karen White, David Williams, Sharon Wolff, and Brad Woodhouse.
57. In addition to the cases included in this volume, cases studies were also conducted in the following races: Alaska Senate, Florida Senate, Oklahoma Senate, Arizona 1st Congressional District, Georgia 12th Congressional District, New Mexico 1st Congressional District, South Dakota At-Large Congressional District, and the Utah 2nd Congressional District. Written reports of these races as well as earlier versions of the cases in this volume, can be found in David B. Magleby, J. Quin Monson, and Kelly D. Patterson, eds., *Dancing without Partners: How Candidates, Parties, and Interest Groups Interact in the New Campaign Finance Environment* (Brigham Young University, Center for the Study of Elections and Democracy, 2005).
58. In 2002, Center for the Study of Elections and Democracy studied seventeen noncompetitive races as a control group, in part, to test this assumption. We found that while some noncompetitive races have significant levels of candidate spending, the vast majority of noncandidate campaign activity occurs in competitive races. See Magleby and Monson, eds., *The Last Hurrah?* pp. 8–10.
59. The interviews for the study were conducted on the record, and with few exceptions the information from those interviews is fully attributed. During the four election cycles of similar research, very few groups declined an invitation to be interviewed. In 2004, there were only two that declined our attempts for an interview. They were National Right to Life and the National Republican Congressional Committee.

2

MONEY, MODERATION, AND MOBILIZATION IN THE 2004 COLORADO SENATE RACE

A BLUEPRINT FOR DEMOCRATIC SUCCESS IN RED STATES[1]

KYLE SAUNDERS AND ROBERT DUFFY

Colorado State University

In an open-seat senate race that attracted national attention, Democrat Ken Salazar, a two-time state attorney general, defeated GOP beer magnate Pete Coors in the most expensive statewide race in Colorado history. In addition to its cost, Salazar's run to succeed retiring Republican Ben Nighthorse Campbell was noteworthy because he was the only Democrat to win a tightly contested Senate seat in what was a disappointing year for the Democratic Party. Moreover, Salazar's win came in a state won by President George W. Bush and where Republicans hold an almost 180,000-person edge in voter registration.

Salazar ran as a moderate and won by mobilizing the Democratic base, carrying the independent vote, and picking up a larger number of Republicans than usual. Salazar fared better than Senator John Kerry, the Democratic presidential candidate, in all but two counties; he also did very well in rural areas and in the western slope, where his brother John won a very close and expensive race for the open Third District House seat. Conversely, Bush outperformed Coors in every county in Colorado. Salazar's ability to attract votes in the rural, largely Republican parts of the state was said to be a model for Democrats seeking to compete in areas outside of the Northeast and West Coast.[2]

Reflecting his political inexperience, Coors got off to a rough start in the primary, looking ill at ease in a few early appearances. Over the course of the campaign, he improved as a candidate and made only a few insignificant mistakes during the fall,[3] but in the end Coors lost because Salazar ran a better campaign.

THE ELECTORAL CONTEXT

Although Colorado is a large state, 80 percent of its estimated 4.6 million residents live in the rapidly growing urban corridor along the Front Range of the Rocky Mountains, most within a two-hour drive of Denver. Colorado's population increased 30 percent from 1990 to 2000; in fact, only 41.1 percent of current residents were born in-state. Colorado is relatively wealthy and educated, ranking seventh nationally in per capita income and second in percentage of college graduates. Like most states in the Mountain West, Colorado is disproportionately white, but Hispanics constitute 17.5 percent of the voting-age population, an important consideration given Salazar's Hispanic heritage.[4]

Voter interest in Colorado was high in 2004, with the prospects of a competitive Senate race, several tight House races and, of course, the presidential election. Voter registration exceeded 2000 figures by 230,618 or 8 percent. Going into the 2004 election, registered Republicans (1,125,374) outnumbered registered Democrats (947,866) by 177,000, but a third of the electorate (1,028,886) was registered as unaffiliated.[5] Boosted by competitive races at all levels, including a surprisingly tight presidential race, turnout in Colorado rose dramatically from 57.5 percent of the eligible voting population in 2000 to 67.4 percent in 2004, an increase of 9.9 percent.[6]

Exit poll results estimated that Salazar won the Hispanic vote by a margin of three to one. He also did much better than Coors among independents, winning that group by a margin of three to two. In addition, many more self-identified Republicans (10 percent) voted for Salazar than did Democrats defecting to Coors (4 percent).[7]

THE CANDIDATES

Ken Salazar, a fifth-generation Hispanic Colorado rancher, water lawyer, and former state natural resources chief, began 2004 in the middle of his second term as state attorney general. Although others, including Representative Mark Udall, expressed interest in seeking the Senate seat, the field cleared once Salazar announced his candidacy. Salazar had been elected statewide twice and was clearly the most popular Democrat in Colorado.

Stressing his roots in the rural San Luis Valley, Salazar ran as a moderate who understood the concerns of ranchers, farmers, and small business owners. For much of the race Salazar, wearing a white cowboy hat, campaigned in his old, green pickup truck and promised to protect Colorado's "land, water, and people."[8] Salazar's emphasis on water was of particular importance to farmers and ranchers, who were concerned about losing water rights to the rapidly growing Front Range suburbs. To reinforce his moderate, populist agenda, Salazar often talked about the struggles of the working class and promoted tax cuts for the middle class rather than for millionaires, and affordable health insurance and prescription drugs; he also reiterated his support for the death penalty and gun owners.[9]

Pete Coors, a well-known face but political neophyte whose great-grandfather founded the Colorado-based Adolph Coors Company, was drafted by GOP leaders, notably Governor Bill Owens, to run for the open Senate seat. Although Owens had promised to endorse former Representative Bob Schaffer, he was apparently concerned that Schaffer was too conservative to win a statewide election. Owens' reversal angered Schaffer and his supporters and contributed to a bruising primary. Although Coors prevailed, many conservatives never fully embraced his candidacy, which may have contributed to his loss in November: Coors did not do as well as Bush among social conservatives, who expressed concerns about his firm's racy advertising, marketing to gays, and comments Coors made about the possibility of lowering the drinking age.[10]

Coors campaigned on a platform of lower taxes, economic growth, anti-terrorism, and conservative "Colorado values."[11] At every turn he emphasized his experience as a businessman who understood how to create jobs and opportunity. At the same time though, Coors articulated a variety of "liberal" positions on social issues: for example, Coors opposed the death penalty and the company provided benefits to same-sex partners.

MONEY

CANDIDATES

Lack of money was not a problem in the race: The two candidates raised and spent record amounts for a Colorado statewide election. As indicated by Table 2.1, fundraising by the candidates approached $18 million. Despite Coors' business ties, the Salazar campaign raised $9.9 million while the Coors campaign raised only $7.9 million. Approximately 80 percent of Salazar's money came from individual donors, with PACs contributing just over 10 percent. In comparison, individual donors accounted for 64 percent of Coors' funds while PACs contributed 17 percent.[12]

Coors loaned more than $1 million to his campaign for the general election, including $500,000 in the final week. Ironically, that loan triggered the "Millionaires' Amendment" provision of BCRA. In Colorado the amendment is triggered when a candidate spends more than $571,000 of his or her own money.[13] Coors had loaned his campaign $400,000 in the primary and put another $550,000 into the campaign earlier in the general election. This allowed Salazar to raise up to $6,000 from individual donors, three times the normal amount. After learning that Coors had put yet another half million dollars into his race, Salazar's campaign immediately began contacting supporters to ask for more money, which was then used to buy an additional

TABLE 2.1   CANDIDATE RECEIPTS AND EXPENDITURES, COLORADO SENATE RACE, 2003 TO 2004

	KEN SALAZAR (D)	PETER COORS (R)
From PACs	$1,018,212	$1,301,667
From individuals	7,838,762	5,020,196
From party	40,375	50,000
From candidate	0	1,450,000
Other contributions	1,028,429	57,319
Total receipts	9,925,778	7,879,182
Total expenditures	9,886,551	7,858,598
Cash on hand (as of 12/31/04)	39,225	24,833

Source: Federal Election Commission, "2003–04 U.S. House and U.S. Senate Candidate Info," December 31, 2004, www.fecinfo.com/cgi-win/x_candidate.exe?DoFn=&sYR=2004 (accessed February 11, 2005).

Note: Abbreviation: PAC, political action committee.

$750,000 of radio and television advertising.[14] Coors had previously shied away from spending more of his own money for fear of actuating the Millionaires' Amendment but explained that the extra money was needed to counter spending by outside groups, including the LCV and CSS.[15]

Although the Salazar campaign took out a $600,000 unsecured bank loan in August, which was not disclosed until October 15, the action did not trigger the Millionaires' Amendment. In an unusual step, the bank accepted future campaign contributions and "any and all terminated media contracts" as collateral for the loan.[16] The Coors campaign asked the FEC to intervene, but the Commission declined, saying that the Millionaires' Amendment did not apply because Salazar had used his campaign's property, not his own, to secure the loan.[17]

The two campaigns combined spent $17.7 million, easily surpassing the previous state record of $10.4 million set in the 2002 Senate contest between incumbent Wayne Allard and Democrat Tom Strickland. As Table 2.1 shows, Salazar spent $9.9 million against Coors' $7.9 million; perhaps more importantly, Salazar outspent Coors by a two-to-one margin in the final weeks of the campaign.[18] According to Sean Tonner, Coors' campaign manager, the "defining factor in the race was money and weight of message," and Salazar, the DSCC, and outside groups aired three ads for every one aired on behalf of Coors.[19]

POLITICAL PARTIES

Given the Colorado seat's perceived importance to each party's hopes of controlling the U.S. Senate, it was no surprise that both senatorial campaign committees spent heavily in the state. What is surprising is that the

DSCC outspent its Republican counterpart, $2.3 million to $1.9 million (see Table 2.2), with most of the spending going to television and radio advertising (see Table 2.3). The DSCC committed to the race early and never wavered in its support for Salazar. Indeed, the DSCC spent more

TABLE 2.2   INDEPENDENT EXPENDITURES BY PARTY COMMITTEE, COLORADO SENATE RACE, 2003 TO 2004

PARTY COMMITTEE	CANDIDATE	INDEPENDENT EXPENDITURES *FOR*	INDEPENDENT EXPENDITURES *AGAINST*	*TOTAL*	PARTY TOTAL
DSCC					$2,301,264
	Pete Coors	0	0	0	
	Ken Salazar	$2,301,264	0	$2,301,264	
NRSC					1,989,181
	Pete Coors	63,890	0	63,890	
	Ken Salazar	0	$1,925,291	1,925,291	

Source: Federal Election Commission, ftp://ftp.fec.gov/FEC/ (accessed January 5, 2005).
Note: Abbreviations: DSCC, Democratic Senatorial Campaign Committee; NRSC, National Republican Senatorial Committee.

TABLE 2.3   THE AIR WAR: TELEVISION AND RADIO ADVERTISING EXPENDITURES, COLORADO SENATE RACE, 2004[a]

TYPE AND ORGANIZATION	TV	RADIO	TOTAL $ SPENT	CMAG TV
Democratic Allies[b]				
Candidates				
Salazar for Senate	$2,597,683	$106,119	**$2,703,802**	$4,549,846
Political Parties				
DSCC	1,620,975	—	**1,620,975**	1,300,240
DNC	24,400	63,750	**88,150**	2,565,565
Interest Groups				
New Democrat Network	723,590	—	**723,590**	581,988
Citizens for a Strong Senate	596,765	—	**596,765**	742,815
League of Conservation Voters	414,250	—	**414,250**	498,261
American Family Voices	298,650	—	**298,650**	239,027
JustGoVote.org	32,275	9,350	**41,625**	—
Campaign Money Watch	3,320	20,000	**23,320**	—
American Federation of Government Employees	—	1,265	**1,265**	—
Communication Workers of America	—	—	—	4,337
Stronger America Now	—	—	—	3,124

(continued)

TABLE 2.3 *(continued)*

Type and Organization	TV	Radio	Total $ Spent	CMAG TV
Republican Allies[b]				
Candidates				
Pete Coors for Senate	2,258,641	187,480	**2,446,121**	4,174,756
Political Parties				
NRSC	474,880	35,250	**510,130**	1,024,256
RNC	124,050	—	**124,050**	310,325
Interest Groups				
Americans for Job Security	382,220	—	**382,220**	655,595
Hispanics Together	—	41,440	**41,440**	—
Small Business Survival	—	36,000	**36,000**	—
Republican Leadership Council	—	7,250	**7,250**	—
United Seniors Association	4,570	—	**4,570**	534,357
U.S. Chamber of Commerce	—	—	—	110,738
National Rifle Association	—	—	—	5,980
Nonpartisan				
Interest Groups				
Americans for Better Government, LLC	—	17,265	**17,265**	—
AARP	—	—	—	130,350

[a]Please see Appendix A for a more detailed data explanation. The ad-buy data collected for this study may contain extraneous data because of the difficulty in determining the content of the ads. The parties or interest groups that purchased the ad buys possibly ran some ads promoting House, Senatorial, or presidential candidates or ballot propositions not in the study's sample but still within that media market. Unless the participating academics were able to determine the exact content of the ad buy from the limited information given by the station, the data may contain observations that do not pertain to the study's relevant House, Senate, or presidential battleground races. For comparison purposes the CMAG data is included in the table. Because of the sheer volume of television and radio stations and varying degrees of compliance in providing ad-buy information, data on spending by various groups might be incomplete. These data do not include every station in the state. This table is not intended to represent comprehensive organization spending or activity within the sample races. Television ads purchased from national cable stations that aired in this state are not reflected in this table. A more complete picture can be obtained by examining this table with Table 2.4.

[b]Certain organizations that maintained neutrality were categorized according to which candidates their ads supported or attacked or whether the organization was openly anti- or pro-conservative or liberal.

In blank cells, "—" reflects the absence of collected data and does not imply the organization was inactive in that medium.

Source: Data compiled from David B. Magleby, J. Quin Monson, and Kelly D. Patterson, "2004 Campaign Communications Database," (Center for the Study of Elections and Democracy: Brigham Young University, 2005); and Campaign Media Analysis Group (CMAG) data.

Note: Abbreviations: DSCC, Democratic Senatorial Campaign Committee; DNC, Democratic National Committee; NRSC, National Republican Senatorial Committee; RNC, Republican National Committee; AARP, American Association of Retired People.

money here than in any other Senate race. The relative lack of spending by the NRSC reflects its expectation that Coors would put more of his own money into the race, allowing the NRSC to direct its resources to other states.[20] Coors' campaign manager said of the NRSC, "We would have loved more money for TV, but understood that they had budgets, too, and other races."[21]

INTEREST GROUPS

As shown in Table 2.3, there was considerable interest group activity in the race, especially late in the campaign on the Democratic side. One 527 organization, CSS, was considered by the Coors campaign to be a front for the Association of Trial Lawyers of America and spent $921,000 on a television and mail campaign targeting Coors.[22] Overall, the LCV made close to $1.1 million in independent expenditures,[23] while the New Democrat Network (NDN) spent more than $700,000 on television ads.[24]

Interest groups spent noticeably less on Coors, perhaps because they, too, expected him to devote more of his own fortune to the race. In the 2002 Colorado Senate race, Republican-allied groups spent $6 million compared to $2 million from Democratic groups.[25] In 2004 spending by Republican groups amounted to less than $2 million. Americans for Job Security (AJS), a 501(c)(6) organization, made the biggest expenditure for the Coors' side, totaling approximately $1 million on television and mail criticizing Salazar's environmental record. The U.S. Chamber of Commerce, whose mail endorsed Coors' business background, spent approximately $500,000 on its effort.[26] The National Beer Wholesalers Association spent $140,000 supporting their fellow brewer, and the National Rifle Association Political Victory Fund (NRA-PVF) put $148,680 into the race.[27] Club for Growth made no independent expenditures in the race, but it did help with fundraising.[28]

State 527 organizations, most of which focused their efforts on state legislative races, accounted for a considerable amount of activity in this election. Many of these organizations had field staff working to boost interest and turnout in those races. This probably worked to benefit Ken Salazar, as a majority of the $7.1 million was spent by groups working to elect Democratic candidates, primarily in swing districts also targeted by the U.S. Senate candidates.[29] In fact, the biggest surprise in Colorado on election night was that the Democrats gained control of both chambers of the state legislature. According to Sean Tonner, Coors' campaign manager, "in the end, we had the national 527s going after our head, and we were getting our ankles chopped by the local 527s."[30]

THE EFFECTS OF MONEY

THE GROUND WAR

Perhaps in reaction to BCRA restrictions on broadcast issue advocacy, interest groups and 527 groups played prominent roles in the ground war on the Democratic side. The Republican Party, on the other hand, did it all "in house," focusing its ground efforts on shoring up the Republican base. The final stages of the ground war were critical to both campaigns, as they had tracked early voting and knew that Republicans were ahead by about 140,000 votes going into election day.[31]

The Salazar campaign sent four pieces of direct mail stressing the candidate's long ties to rural Colorado and understanding of the area (see Table 2.4). All mailings depicted rural images and photos of Salazar in his trademark white hat, often on horseback, and all prominently mentioned his opposition to the death tax on family farms, ranches, and small businesses. One brochure noted that Salazar's family members settled in the state in the 1850s and "have been farming and ranching here ever since." In a clear effort to appeal to moderates, the mailer also notes that "Salazar's values run deep—from the land, from his faith, from his family."

In addition to direct mail, both campaigns placed ads in Spanish-language newspapers and created Spanish-language versions of their Web sites.[32] The Salazar campaign's ground war also used telephone and e-mail extensively to contact supporters. One automated telephone message said, "Pete Coors wants to change the law to let men convicted of domestic violence buy guns." The claim was based on remarks that Coors made about supporting the repeal of the Brady Bill, which contained a provision barring people convicted of domestic violence from owning guns.[33]

The Colorado Democratic Party paid for seven direct mail pieces, three of which criticized Coors for his "extreme" positions on abortion. Two of the same pieces also noted Coors' support for lowering the drinking age to 18. The state party also sent two mailings supporting Kerry and Salazar and two generic "Vote Democratic" pieces, one timed to arrive during early voting and the other just before election day.[34] For its part, the DSCC did not make independent expenditures for direct mail, but it did send one fundraising appeal to previous contributors (see Table 2.4).

On behalf of the Coors campaign, the Colorado Republican Committee did seven unique ads and mailed more than one million pieces overall.[35] Such arrangements are typical because parties can mail at nonprofit rates, thereby reducing costs by 30 percent. One brochure contrasted the Bush–Coors team with Kerry–Salazar, depicting the latter as the arrows on a weathervane "following the prevailing political winds." Most of the other pieces reflected the campaign's "Straight Talk, Honest Answers" theme and stressed that Coors was a businessman, not a professional politician, taking a not-too-subtle dig at Salazar.

Both parties were involved in GOTV efforts. Colorado Victory 2004 (CV04) was a part of the federal coordinated campaign for the Democrats. CV04 conducted door-to-door efforts to identify and target base voters, using 11 coordinating offices statewide, hundreds of staff, and thousands of volunteers, all working only for named federal candidates. The money for CV04's phone banks came from its own fundraising and from money transferred from the DNC ($890,754), the DSCC ($450,000), the DCCC ($57,500), the state party, and some transfers of excess funds from the Salazar campaign.[36]

TABLE 2.4 Number of Unique Campaign Communications by Organization, Colorado Senate Race, 2004[a]

Type and Organization[b]	Type of Campaign Communication							
	E-mail	Mail	Newspaper/ Magazine	Personal Contact	Phone Call	Radio Ad	TV Ad	Total
Democratic Allies[c]								
Candidates								
Salazar for Senate	12	4	—	—	1	12	21	50
Political Parties								
Colorado Democratic Party	—	8	—	1	2	—	—	11
DSCC	—	1	—	—	—	—	5	6
Adams County Democratic Party	—	1	—	—	—	—	—	1
DNC	—	1	—	—	—	—	—	1
Interest Groups								
Citizens for a Strong Senate	—	6	—	—	—	—	2	8
Sierra Club	—	2	—	—	5	—	—	7
NARAL Pro-Choice Colorado	—	6	—	—	—	—	—	6
JustGoVote.org	—	5	—	—	—	—	—	5
League of Conservation Voters	—	3	—	—	—	—	2	5
Colorado Education Association	—	3	—	—	1	—	—	4
Colrado AFL-CIO	3	—	—	—	—	—	—	3
Association of Trial Lawyers of America[d]	—	1	—	—	—	—	—	2
Moving America Forward	—	1	—	—	—	—	1	2
WILD PAC	—	1	—	—	—	—	—	1
Republican Allies[c]								
Candidates								
Pete Coors for Senate	—	1	—	—	1	11	13	26
Political Parties								
Colorado Republican Committee	—	8	—	—	2	—	—	10
NRSC	—	—	—	—	—	—	3	3
Larimer County Republican Party	—	1	—	—	—	—	—	1

Interest Groups

							Total
U.S. Chamber of Commerce	—	—	—	—	1	7	8
Americans for Job Security	—	—	—	1	—	2	3
National Federation of Independent Business[e]	—	—	1	—	—	2	3
National Rifle Association	—	—	—	1	—	2	3
Coors Brewing Company	—	—	—	2	—	—	2
Focus on the Family Action	—	—	—	—	—	2	2
National Right to Life	—	—	1	—	—	1	2
Straight Talk Colorado	—	—	—	—	—	2	2
Associated Builders and Contractors	—	—	—	—	—	1[f]	1
Committee to Protect Our Families	—	—	—	—	—	1	1
National Beer Wholesalers Association	—	—	—	—	—	1	1

Nonpartisan

Interest Groups

							Total
Americans for Better Government, LLC	—	1	—	—	—	1	2

[a] See Appendix A for a more detailed data explanation. Data represent the number of unique or distinct pieces or ads by the group and do not represent a count of total items sent or made. This table is not intended to portray comprehensive organization activity within the sample races. A more complete picture can be obtained by examining this table together with Table 2.3.

[b] All state and local chapters or affiliates have been combined with their national affiliate to better render the picture of the organization's activity. For instance, League of Conservation Voters Education Fund data have been included in the League of Conservation Voters totals.

[c] Certain organizations that maintained neutrality were categorized according to which candidates their ads supported or attacked or whether the organization was openly anti- or pro- conservative or liberal. In blank cells, "—" only reflects the absence of collected data and does not imply the organization was inactive in that medium.

[d] Linda Lipson, senior director of public affairs, Association of Trial Lawyers of America, telephone interview by David B. Magleby and Betsey Gimbel, December 14, 2004.

[e] Sharon Wolff Sussin and Andrew Finka, national political director and political programs coordinator, National Federation of Independent Business, interview by J. Quin Monson and Betsey Gimbel, Washington, D.C., December 14, 2004.

[f] Ned Monroe, director of political affairs, Associated Builders and Contractors, interviewed by David B. Magleby and Kristina Gale, Washington, D.C., November 5, 2004.

Source: Data compiled from David B. Magleby, J. Quin Monson, and Kelly D. Patterson, "2004 Campaign Communications Database," (Center for the Study of Elections and Democracy: Brigham Young University, 2005).

Note: Abbreviations: DSCC, Democratic Senatorial Campaign Committee; DNC, Democratic National Committee; NRSC, National Republican Senatorial Committee.

The Democratic Party included towns in Colorado in its three-state, eleven-city "Una Nueva Esperanza" bus tour aimed at registering Latinos.[37]

The Republican side did much of its GOTV and phone banks in-house, as per national trends, recruiting up to 8,000 volunteers, walking well over 1,000 precincts, and reaching out to more than 200,000 households. Additionally, volunteers made more than 300,000 phone calls in the GOTV effort. The 96-Hour Campaign, the Republican effort in the weekend prior to election day, was a large part of this effort aimed at mobilizing core supporters.[38] The NRSC did not contribute to the federal coordinated campaign, but the RNC and NRCC transferred $819,159 and $670,000 respectively to the state party.[39]

As indicated by Table 2.4, liberal interest groups were considerably more active on the ground than conservative groups. The LCV sent three pieces of mail focusing on Coors' environmental record. One of the direct mail pieces, titled "One Fish, Two Fish, Red Fish, Doomed Fish," is an obvious reference to Dr. Seuss and criticizes Coors for "hundreds of violations of environmental laws" and for being one of Colorado's "top three toxic polluters."[40] The Rocky Mountain Chapter of the Sierra Club paid for a mailer sent only to Club members endorsing various candidates. The parent organization also worked with local groups to send mail and contact members by telephone, using live and recorded calls. The Rocky Mountain Chapter called 4,000 "frequent voters" up to four times each.[41] Other groups contacting voters by mail, telephone, or e-mail included the Colorado Education Association and the Colorado American Federation of Labor-Congress of Industrial Organizations (AFL-CIO).[42]

National Abortion and Reproductive Rights Action League (NARAL) Pro-Choice Colorado distributed three issue ad mailers all dealing with privacy and reproductive rights. None of the mailers referenced the election or any candidate. That was not the case, however, with NARAL Pro-Choice Colorado Fund, a 527 group established by the parent organization, which sent three pieces of mail criticizing Coors on the abortion issue. One depicting a young woman gazing out a window read, "Pete Coors has some interesting ideas about helping rape victims"; the tag line for the mailer was, "He's opposed to it."

In addition to sending mail, a number of organized groups were present on the ground in the Senate race. LCV was very active on the ground in Jefferson County, going door-to-door every day for seven weeks in the heavily targeted towns of Aurora, Arvada, Wheat Ridge, and Lakewood. This group contacted more than 50,000 households, some as many as four times.[43] LCV's internal polling suggested that their "Polluter Pete" ground campaign, which delivered the same message at the same time as its television ads and Web site, broke through the campaign clutter and reinforced its advertised attacks on Coors. The goal of the synchronized campaign was to "create a brand" that encapsulated the group's message, enabling it to build negative perceptions of Pete Coors. According to LCV, a full 25 percent of voters remembered the "Polluter Pete" label.[44]

As part of the effort by state 527 organizations, the Colorado AFL-CIO engaged in an intensive voter identification, education, and mobilization campaign beginning in March. In addition to polling in the state races, union volunteers knocked on "a ton" of their members' doors, primarily to discuss the state candidates. If the voter seemed receptive, the volunteer would sometimes push federal candidates as well, especially Salazar. The organization also encouraged absentee voting and drove activists to different state Senate districts to encourage early voting. In the last four days, the organization had 2,500 volunteers helping in a "very targeted" GOTV effort, using information obtained from county clerks to focus on union members who had not yet voted.[45]

Many newly formed organizations were involved in voter registration and GOTV activities that likely benefited Democratic candidates up and down the ticket. MoveOn was very active, registering thousands of new voters and working to turn them out during the election. The New Voters Project was active in Colorado, with the goal of registering 265,000 18- to 24-year-olds in six states, as was Moving America Forward, which focused on Hispanic GOTV.[46] JustGoVote.org, a nonprofit, ostensibly nonpartisan organization engaged in education, outreach, and registration activities, sent five GOTV mailers aimed at likely Democratic voters, and People for the American Way participated in a voter protection project, mostly in minority precincts.[47]

Conservative groups were more active in the ground war than on television or radio with efforts mostly confined to direct mail, e-mail, and telephone. In addition to endorsing Coors during the primary, the U.S. Chamber of Commerce spent $500,000 on seven direct mail pieces. Several of the mail pieces targeted women ages 18 to 29 and addressed issues that had tested well with this group, such as medical liability reform and escalating health care costs. The Chamber also sent 2.5 million e-mails directing people to its Web site.[48] The National Beer Wholesalers PAC spent $140,000 on an independent expenditure campaign involving direct mail, coasters, and a phone bank.[49] In addition to direct mail, the NRA-PVF supported Coors with two Web ads and a plastic bag containing the Sunday newspaper that had "Vote for Freedom First; Pete Coors for Senate" written on it. AJS sent two pieces of direct mail, one assailing Salazar on taxes, the other repeating the charges made in TV ads connecting the Summitville Mine cyanide spill with Salazar's tenure as head of the Department of Natural Resources. Finally, the ABC distributed a voter's guide.[50]

Social conservative groups were not a major presence in the race: Focus on the Family Action sent two small mailers on abortion and gay marriage, and National Right to Life sent one mailer comparing the presidential and Senate candidates on a range of issues. A state-based 527 organization called

Straight Talk Colorado also sent two mailings: The first attacked Salazar for being a flip-flopper; the other featured Salazar, Hillary Rodham Clinton, Ted Kennedy, and Tom Daschle in cowboy hats and argued that these "liberal lawmakers" would soon have Salazar supporting "abortion on demand," "big government health care," and "liberal judges."

THE AIR WAR

The air war in the Colorado Senate race involved a concentrated set of actors: the two candidates' campaigns, the two parties' senatorial campaign committees, AJS, NDN, the LCV, and CSS. The parties' advertising, which was rather negative on both sides, was largely indistinguishable in content and style from the candidates' own negative ads. The themes and images used by the candidates and parties in their broadcast ads reinforced those that appeared in their mail.

TV ad spending in the Denver market topped $40 million, five times the amount spent in 2000.[51] As a result, advertising rates in the Denver market shot up, driven by the demand for time. Thirty seconds of advertising in the Denver market usually costs about $140 per point, but in September and October it cost three times that amount. Even this price tag was discounted; costs were as high as $1,000 per point for interest groups who bought time in the final week of the campaign.[52] In addition to driving up the cost, both campaigns noted after the election that the combined effect of the competitive presidential and Senate races had been to "suck the air out of the room" with respect to media coverage, making it much harder to get attention.

Both sides also spent heavily on radio advertising. The Salazar campaign in particular used the unique character and the relatively cheap production and broadcasting costs of radio to "narrowcast" to certain target audiences, especially outside the Denver market. All told, the campaign produced 12 unique radio ads.[53] The Coors campaign aired 11 mostly positive radio ads, which essentially mirrored those on television with the exception of one ad featuring former New York Mayor Rudy Giuliani.[54]

The Salazar campaign aired 21 unique television ads and was the only campaign to air Spanish language ads.[55] In a gamble that nearly bankrupted the campaign, Salazar bought television time for late October on August 11, taking advantage of the lower rates and effectively blocking out Coors and other campaigns. To make the buy, the campaign spent $2 million, which included the $600,000 loan noted previously.[56]

Salazar's first ad began airing two days after the primary and was typical of the many positive ads it would run in the general election. As mentioned earlier, this first ad stated that Ken Salazar's values "run deep, from the land, from his faith, and from his family" and went on to tout his record as attorney general when "he took on criminals who prey on seniors and those who pollute the land and water that he loves." The ad concluded with a promise that "in the Senate, he'll always be a champion of the people."

Salazar also ran several ads criticizing Coors as a millionaire who was out of touch with ordinary people. Several ads used a creatively edited sound bite of Coors saying, "I don't know what a common man is" to contrast with Salazar's humble beginnings and his understanding of middle-class concerns. In other ads, Salazar hit Coors hard on environmental violations by the Coors brewery and for advocating tax cuts for the rich.

The Coors campaign aired thirteen television ads during the general election, some positive and some negative.[57] The positive ads portrayed Coors as an honest family man and businessman who had done good things for the state. In these ads Coors vowed to end the "Washington, D.C. spending spree" and advocated lower taxes and stronger federal efforts against terrorism. In other ads, Coors said that he was "not a politician or a lawyer" and lamented attacks from people who "have never created a job or had to meet a payroll."

Coors' negative ads were primarily contrast ads. One highlighted Salazar's "tax agenda" and linked Salazar to Kerry's tax-and-spend liberalism. The ad concluded with Coors looking directly into the camera and saying, "Ken Salazar wants to raise taxes. I don't." An ad featuring a "Keystone Kops" theme detailed "John Kerry and Ken Salazar's tax plan" and told Coloradans to "hang on to their wallets." A number of Coors' ads noted that he was not a lawyer, which, of course, Salazar was. Among the charges leveled in these ads were that Salazar was a pawn for the trial lawyer lobby and that "lawsuit abuse" was "killing jobs, hurting families, and putting doctors out of business."

Both senatorial campaign committees aired television ads, but the DSCC outspent the NRSC. This relative imbalance, as well as the synergy with the ads from the interest groups and the campaign, benefited Salazar. The DSCC ran five attack ads that emphasized one theme: "Good for Pete Coors, bad for Colorado." Several of the ads linked Coors to his company's poor record on the environment and job outsourcing. Another began with an audio clip of Coors saying "I don't think there's anything wrong with being self-serving" and then proceeded to mention Coors' expressed desire to eliminate corporate taxation and establish a national sales tax that would harm ordinary Coloradans. A humorous ad featured grainy black and white footage of "bad ideas," including a plane with 10 wings and a man crashing on a winged bicycle. Meanwhile, the voice-over detailed a litany of criticisms of Coors' support for a national sales tax, the privatization of Social Security, and lowering the drinking age "to make bigger profits."

The NRSC aired three attack ads; most criticized Salazar as a tax-and-spend liberal tied to Kerry. One analysis found that Kerry was attacked in 42 percent of the ads run by Coors and the NRSC between September 24 and October 7.[58] The NRSC's first ad, which began airing the first week of October, linked Salazar to Kerry on cuts in military spending and limits on the investigative tools needed to capture terrorists. The NRSC's final ad detailed the "scary ideas that will hurt Colorado," including Kerry and Salazar's plans for higher taxes. The ad concluded by suggesting "We cannot afford Ken Salazar in Washington."

Largely because of Denver's high advertising rates, only three interest groups bought significant television time. The first to go on the air was AJS, which ran an ad shortly after the primary, attempting to connect Salazar, as former head of the Department of Natural Resources, with a cyanide spill at the notorious Summitville Mine. The ad blamed Salazar's "lax oversight" of the Department for the disaster and alleged that as attorney general, Salazar had cut a deal with the company responsible for the spill, leaving Colorado taxpayers to pick up the $230-million bill. The ad generated considerable media attention and prompted Salazar to demand that Coors renounce the ad. Even though Coors had nothing to do with it, his campaign had to answer a lot of questions about the AJS ad, diverting attention from his own message.

The LCV aired two television ads at a combined cost of almost $800,000.[59] The first ad was a response to the AJS ad criticizing Salazar's environmental record. LCV spent much more to air its "Polluter Pete" ad, which received national attention. The ad discussed an incident in which the Coors Brewery, one of the "top three" polluters in Colorado, illegally dumped 77,000 gallons of waste into Clear Creek, killing 50,000 fish. Coors, the ad claimed, helped shape a law that made it easier for polluting businesses to escape penalties. The ad ended by directing viewers to a special Web site criticizing Coors' environmental record, www.polluterpete.com.

CSS paid almost $1 million to run two ads, including one in the final week of the campaign, when advertising costs were at their peak.[60] This later ad featured repeated images of severe automobile accidents while the announcer criticized Coors for advocating lowering the drinking age to 18 and claimed that "overnight" Coors would have 200,000 more customers in Colorado. The ad concluded by claiming that for Coors it does not matter that a lower drinking age is bad for kids, as long as it is really good for business. According to Sean Tonner, the ad hurt Coors badly; the campaign's internal polling showed that it resonated with voters.[61] The ads, which stressed issues also featured in ads by the DSCC, LCV, and in the primary by the Colorado Conservative Voters, may have been particularly effective in rural Colorado and among social conservatives, who never quite embraced the beer millionaire.[62]

CONCLUSION

While the Colorado Senate contest illustrated many of the characteristics of a competitive senate race, especially reflected in the inordinate amount of money that was raised and spent, there were some differences. The most striking difference was that the forces on the left outraised and outspent the forces on the right by a sizeable margin, whether at the level of candidates, parties, or interest groups. The second important difference was that Coors' campaign triggered the Millionaires' Amendment to BCRA, which enabled Salazar to raise even more money at a crucial time in the campaign. The third difference was the critical role played by the many interest groups and state-based 527 organizations whose efforts in state legislative races drove up the Democratic turnout, which, in turn, helped Salazar.

Salazar won the race in Colorado because he offered a moderate populist message and had more resources at his disposal. On the other hand, Coors won the Republican primary because he was seen as a moderate by voters and as more electable by party leaders. Ironically, Coors lost support because conservative Republicans thought he was too liberal, and Democrats and a majority of independents thought he was too conservative. In short, Coors was effectively "whipsawed" by the attacks from the left and less-than-needed support from the right, while Salazar was able to capture a large enough portion of the middle to win the election.

NOTES

1. The authors would like to thank John Straayer for his wise counsel and expertise, as well as Andrew Kear, Matt Buttice, and Michael Roloff for their research assistance in putting this chapter together.
2. Gwen Florio, "Rural Roots Appeal," *Rocky Mountain News*, November 5, 2004, p. 4A.
3. Coors also fared poorly in his appearance with Salazar on NBC's *Meet the Press*, for example, but, because he was well known to most Coloradans, it seemed that any damage was fleeting.
4. Michael Barone and Richard E. Cohen, *The Almanac of American Politics, 2004* (National Journal Group, 2003: 302–03).
5. Colorado Secretary of State, "October 2004 Voter Registration Numbers: Voter Recap by Party," www.sos.state.co.us/pubs/elections/oct2004.htm (accessed November 25, 2004).
6. United States Election Project, "2004 Voting-Age and Voting-Eligible Population Estimates and Voter Turnout," elections.gmu.edu/Voter_Turnout_2004.htm (accessed November 29, 2004).
7. CNN, "U.S. Senate/Colorado/Exit Polls," www.cnn.com/ELECTION/2004/pages/results/states/CO/S/01/epolls.0.html (accessed November 19, 2004).
8. M. E. Sprengelmeyer, "For Last Sprint, Salazar Heads Home," *Rocky Mountain News*, November 1, 2004, p. 6A.
9. Mark P. Couch and Karen E. Crummy, "Senate Seat Goes Blue as Salazar Ices Coors," *Denver Post*, November 3, 2004, p. 1A.
10. Gwen Florio and Lynn Bartels, "Coors' Fizz Sapped by Ads," *Rocky Mountain News*, November 4, 2004, p. 34A.
11. Couch and Crummy, "Senate Seat Goes Blue as Salazar Ices Coors," November 3, 2004.
12. The Center for Responsive Politics, "Ken Salazar," www.opensecrets.org/politicians/-summary/newmems.asp?CID (accessed December 30, 2004).
13. The Millionaires' Amendment in Bipartisan Compaign Reform Act (BCRA) allows for spending that exceeds the standard limits and amounts set by a formula that takes into account population and personal spending by the opponent.
14. Burt Hubbard and M. E. Sprengelmeyer, "Salazar Topped Coors in Spending," *Rocky Mountain News*, December 3, 2004, p. 5A.

15. Sean Tonner, campaign manager, Coors for Senate, personal e-mail communication to Robert Duffy, January 3, 2005.
16. Karen Crummy, "Coors' Open Wallet," *Denver Post*, October 25, 2004, p. A1.
17. Sean Tonner, campaign manager, Coors for Senate, telephone interview by Robert Duffy, November 12, 2004.
18. Hubbard and Sprengelmeyer, "Salazar Topped Coors in Spending," p. 5A.
19. Tonner, interview, November 12, 2004.
20. Patrick Davis, political director, National Republican Senatorial Committee, interview by J. Quin Monson and Richard Hawkins, Washington, D.C., November 11, 2004.
21. Tonner, interview, November 12, 2004.
22. Ibid.
23. Andy Schultheiss, southwest regional director, League of Conservation Voters, telephone interview by Robert Duffy, November 9, 2004.
24. M. E. Sprengelmeyer, "Dems Hitting Airwaves," *Rocky Mountain News*, October 6, 2004, p. 20A.
25. Ibid.
26. Bill Miller, vice president and national field director, U.S. Chamber of Commerce, interview by David B. Magleby and Kristina Gale, Washington, D.C., November 9, 2004.
27. Gwen Florio and Burt Hubbard, "Coors Gets $1.65M in Two Weeks," *Rocky Mountain News*, October 22, 2004, p. 6A.
28. Tonner, interview, November 12, 2004.
29. Burt Hubbard, "Outsiders Fueled Election," *Rocky Mountain News*, January 3, 2005, p. B5.
30. Tonner, interview, November 12, 2004. Tonner may have overstated the case, as later reports showed that Democratic 527s outspent their Republican counterparts by just over $1 million. Democratic groups got off to an early start, but Republican 527s spent $1.8 million in the last two weeks of the race. In fact, one of the biggest spending 527s was Americans for Better Government, an organization headed by Mike Ciletti of Phase Line Strategies, a political consulting firm of which Tonner is president. The group bought voter registration lists in many counties and did several mailings, spending a total of $946,333 in the 2004 race. See Hubbard, "Outsiders Fueled Election," p. B5.
31. Tonner, interview, November 12, 2004; and Jim Carpenter, campaign manager, Salazar for Senate, interview by Kyle Saunders, Denver, CO, December 13, 2004.
32. Javier Erik Olivera, "Family's Table Talk Turns to Politics," *Rocky Mountain News*, October 23, 2004, p. 26A.
33. Gwen Florio, "No Let-up in Senate Slugfest," *Rocky Mountain News*, October 29, 2004, p. 30A.
34. Chris Gates, chair, Colorado Democratic Party, telephone interview by Kyle Saunders, November 10, 2004; Carpenter, interview, December 13, 2004.
35. Tonner, interview, November 12, 2004.
36. Gates, interview, November, 2004; Carpenter, interview December 13, 2004; spending figures from the Center for Responsive Politics, "National Party Transfers: Colorado," www.opensecrets.org/states/type20.asp?states=CO&year=2004 (accessed December 30, 2004).
37. The phrase translates to "A New Hope." See Susan Greene, "Latinos on a Drive for Dems," *Denver Post*, September 21, 2004, p. B4.
38. David Wardrop, executive director, Colorado Republican Party, interview by Kyle Saunders, Denver, CO, December 10, 2004.
39. The Center for Responsive Politics, "National Party Transfers: Colorado," www.opensecrets.org/states/type20.asp?states=CO&year=2004 (accessed December 30, 2004). Also of note, the Wyoming Republican State Committee shifted $165,000 to its Colorado counterpart.
40. One novel development was the decision by the Coors Brewing Company, at the end of the campaign, to take out full-page ads in most of the state's newspapers. The ads, which did not mention the candidate or the election, touted the firm's commitment to Colorado's people and environment and stressed its contributions to the state's economy, as well as its charitable giving. A company spokesman explained the unusual action as a necessary response to attacks on the company's environmental record and citizenship by the LCV and others. Although it is impossible to say for certain at this point, it seems that the ads did not cause the firm any lasting harm.

41. Susan LaFever, director, Rocky Mountain Chapter of the Sierra Club, telephone interview by Robert Duffy, December 3, 2004.
42. Most of the mail pieces by League of Conservation Voters, Citizens for a Strong Senate, U.S. Chamber of Commerce, and Americans for Job Security were 8.5-by-11.5-inch color "billboards"; mail from National Abortion and Reproductive Rights Action League Pro-Choice Colorado, Straight Talk Colorado, Focus on the Family Action, and National Right to Life was smaller (6 inches by 11 inches).
43. Andy Schultheiss, southwest regional director, League of Conservation Voters, telephone interview by Robert Duffy, November 9, 2004.
44. Mark Longabaugh, senior vice president for political affairs, League of Conservation Voters, interview by David B. Magleby and Betsey Gimbel, Washington, D.C., November 10, 2004.
45. Steve Adams, political director, Colorado AFL-CIO, telephone interview by Robert Duffy, December 6, 2004.
46. Ivan Frishberg, director, New Voters Project, interview by J. Quin Monson and Richard Hawkins, Washington, D.C., November 11, 2004.
47. JustGoVote.org, "About Just GoVote 2004," www.JustGoVote.org/about.htm (accessed December 13, 2004); and Kimberly Robson, deputy national field director, People for the American Way, interview by David B. Magleby and Kristina Gale, Washington, D.C., November 5, 2004.
48. Miller, interview, November 9, 2004.
49. Linda Auglis and David Rehr, political affairs director and president, National Beer Wholesalers Association, interview by Kelly D. Patterson and Betsey Gimbel, Alexandria, VA, November 8, 2004.
50. Ned Monroe, political affairs director, Associated Builders and Contractors, interview by David Magleby and Kristina Gale, Arlington, VA, November 8, 2004.
51. Chris Walsh, "Political Spots Fill TV's Pots," *Rocky Mountain News*, November 6, 2004, p. 1C.
52. Tonner, interview, November 12, 2004; this point was also substantiated by a review of the available per point data. For example, on KCNC, the Denver CBS affiliate, an ad during "Dr. Phil" cost $185 per point when purchased on September 15. By October 18, the cost was $450 per point.
53. Carpenter, interview, December 13, 2004.
54. Tonner, interview, November 12, 2004.
55. Carpenter, interview, December 13, 2004; see also Walsh, "Political Spots Fill TV's Pots," November 6, 2004, p. 6C.
56. Mark P. Couch, "Savvy Fund-Raising, Publicity Fueled Salazar's Senate Drive," *Denver Post*, November 4, 2004, p. A19.
57. Tonner, interview, November 12, 2004.
58. John Aloysius Farrell, "Colorado Among Top TV Ad Targets," *Denver Post*, October 13, 2004, p. A14.
59. Schultheiss, interview, November 9, 2004.
60. Burt Hubbard and Tillie Fong, "$17 Million For Ads: Outside Groups Spend a Fortune to Influence Races," *Rocky Mountain News*, November 6, 2004, p. 4A.
61. Tonner, interview, November 12, 2004.
62. Florio and Bartels, "Coors' Fizz Sapped by Ads," November 4, 2004, p. 34A.

3

THE SOUTHERN TICKET-SPLITTER
SHALL RISE AGAIN

THE 2004 NORTH CAROLINA SENATE CAMPAIGN[1]

STEVEN GREENE AND ERIC HEBERLIG

North Carolina State University and University of North Carolina–Charlotte

North Carolina has become a competitive two-party state over the last 30 years. Like much of the South since 1952, it has consistently voted for Republicans in presidential elections and Democrats in state elections. In 2004, this pattern was likely to recur; President Bush was expected to win North Carolina despite John Kerry's selection of North Carolina Senator John Edwards as the Democratic vice presidential nominee and despite Democratic Governor Mike Easley's reelection efforts. The outcome of the Senate campaign between Republican U.S. Representative Richard Burr and Democrat Erskine Bowles would be determined by whether more Bush presidential or Easley gubernatorial voters split their tickets.

North Carolina Senate races have shown similar political divisions in the past. Since U.S. Senator Sam Ervin retired in 1974, his seat has consistently switched back and forth between the parties every six years. Republican Jesse Helms held the other Senate seat throughout that period by consistently winning close elections with a coalition of Republicans and "Jessecrats," the culturally conservative Democrats from rural eastern North Carolina. Following Helms's retirement in 2002, the seat went to former Reagan cabinet secretary and Republican presidential candidate Elizabeth Dole. Her opponent in 2002 was former Clinton chief of staff Erskine Bowles.

THE ELECTORAL CONTEXT

In 2004, the implementation of BCRA changed the context of the campaign from 2002. Outside spending, particularly Democratic and Republican Senate campaign committees soft-money spending, had played a prominent role in the 1998 and 2002 North Carolina Senate campaigns.[2] BCRA's limitation on soft money spending by national parties was expected to expand the role of 527 organizations, which could collect unlimited contributions to spend on behalf of favored candidates.[3] BCRA's new definition of electioneering communications was expected to accelerate a trend of interest groups doing less broadcast advertising and more grassroots mobilization, particularly by mail, phone, and person-to-person contact.

The broader electoral context also changed from 2002 to 2004. Though Bowles entered the 2004 race with a clear advantage in name recognition, he faced an obstacle that was not there in 2002—George W. Bush, the Republican President. No Democrat had won a U.S. Senate race in North Carolina in a presidential election year since Sam Ervin in 1968. In a state that last gave its electoral votes to a Democrat, Jimmy Carter, in 1976, Bowles would be facing a tougher context, if not a tougher candidate, in 2004.

THE CANDIDATES

Erskine Bowles seized another opportunity to run for the Senate when John Edwards vacated his Senate seat to run for the Democratic presidential nomination. Bowles started the 2004 campaign with name recognition from his 2002 Senate run and personal wealth to supplement his fundraising. Bowles was determined to run a better campaign in 2004 than he had in 2002. He vowed to select his own campaign issues rather than run on the generic national Democratic Party agenda.[4] However, his key weaknesses—association with Bill Clinton, residence in Charlotte, and a "geeky" appearance—were largely out of his control in both elections. Swing voters in eastern North Carolina generally perceive Charlotteans as elitist, and Bowles was especially hurt by this stereotype due to his wealth and his connection to Bill Clinton.[5]

The Republicans had a quality candidate, too. Representative Richard Burr of Winston-Salem had been viewed by many as a rising star in the Republican Party. The White House signaled early that Burr was its candidate of choice and helped clear the field of potential competitors in the primary.[6] Burr was a candidate from central casting: good hair, a nice smile, and an energetic and personable demeanor. He was also a serious legislator who had made his mark in health care legislation from his seat on the House Committee on Energy and Commerce. This committee assignment also gave Burr early access to contributions and support from corporate PACs.[7] Such support proved to be a double-edged sword: Bowles and allies spent much of the campaign accusing Burr of being the largest recipient of special interest groups' cash in the House and a sellout to their agenda. Burr's key weakness at the start of his campaign, however, was his lack of name recognition and previous experience running for statewide office.

THE CAMPAIGN

Both campaigns considered the socially conservative registered Democrats in the eastern part of the state the key to winning the race. These are classic swing voters, tending to vote their partisanship in state and local races but regularly supporting Republicans in presidential and Senate elections. With the goal of keeping these voters in the Democratic column, Bowles set out to run a campaign based on ideological moderation and pragmatism. He consistently focused on his many "plans" for helping North Carolinians and emphasized his experience in the executive branch, finding solutions and building consensus across parties. In the September 27 debate, he explicitly noted that he disagreed with national Democrats regarding Bush's tax cuts and the war in Iraq, supported English as the official language, and opposed gay marriage.

With regard to issues, the campaign focused on jobs and health care. North Carolina has been hard hit by the loss of textile and manufacturing jobs.[8] Bowles wanted to run an upbeat campaign focusing on his positive, pragmatic solutions for North Carolina's problems. He rejected calls from within his campaign to define Burr negatively until September, when Burr began to run negative ads.[9]

As part of his strategy of emphasizing his independence, Bowles kept the national Democratic Party at arm's length. Although he did attend a July rally in Raleigh with Edwards and Kerry, he avoided all other such opportunities, including the Democratic convention. The Bowles campaign felt it was essential to run significantly ahead of the national Democratic ticket. Going into the race, they thought they could do at least four points better than Kerry.[10] In that sense Bowles did his part, winning 47 percent of the vote in North Carolina, as opposed to Kerry's 43 percent.

Burr campaigned as he had in his House races: He would climb in his car without staff or schedule and find people to chat with.[11] Before entering politics, Burr had been a traveling salesman and was most comfortable campaigning this way. His plan for the first two-thirds of the campaign was to amass resources and to introduce himself to voters, saving the money for advertising until after Labor Day, when he thought voters would be paying attention. Burr felt he would not have enough money to compete with Bowles in the last weeks of the campaign if he spent early to increase his name recognition.[12]

George W. Bush, Dick Cheney, Laura Bush, and other administration officials made appearances at Burr's rallies and fundraisers. Burr consistently noted that Bush needed a Republican Senator to help achieve his goals in national security, to confirm Court appointments, and to make the tax cuts permanent. In the debate, Burr defended the Bush administration's record more than he presented his own agenda. When Bowles accused him of toeing the line for the administration in Congress, Burr retorted, "I'm not embarrassed by voting with the president 96 percent of the time. He's right that often."[13]

The passage of federal buyout of tobacco quotas was a critical event during the campaign.[14] Farmers said they needed a buyout of the Depression-era allotments to survive in a time when tobacco companies are increasingly buying cheaper leaves overseas. Republican congressional leaders appointed Burr to the conference committee overseeing the legislation, positioning him to claim credit for its passage. Douglas Heye, communications director of the Burr campaign, argued that this event shifted the momentum of the campaign by allowing Burr to run on his specific accomplishments for the state.[15]

MONEY

Both candidates were concerned about the role of money in the campaign. Burr was concerned that Bowles would use his personal wealth to outspend him, and Bowles worried that national Republican Party organizations and interest groups would outspend his national Democratic allies. In the end, it was the Bowles campaign that outspent Burr's campaign $13.4 million to $12.9 million (see Table 3.1).

CANDIDATES

The two candidates both raised the majority of their funds from individual contributors, but otherwise the sources of their funds differed. Burr raised 22 percent of his funds from PACs (79 percent from corporate PACs), while only 6 percent of Bowles's contributions were from PACs (44 percent labor, 26 percent corporate).[16] The real estate and health care industries were substantial contributors to Burr, while the banking industry, lawyers, and

TABLE 3.1   CANDIDATE RECEIPTS AND EXPENDITURES, NORTH CAROLINA
SENATE RACE, 2003 TO 2004

	ERSKINE BOWLES (D)	RICHARD BURR (R)
From PACs	$822,974	$2,800,484
From individuals	8,505,712	6,731,312
From party	34,300	58,058
From candidate	3,757,012	0
Other contributions	285,745	3,361,372
Total receipts	13,405,743	12,951,226
Total expenditures	13,357,851	12,853,110
Cash on hand (as of 12/31/04)	76,803	98,114

Source: Federal Election Commission, "2003–04 U.S. House and U.S. Senate Candidate Info," December 31, 2004, www.fecinfo.com/cgi-win/x_candidate.exe?DoFn=&sYR=2004, (accessed February 17, 2005).

Note: Abbreviation: PAC, political action committee.

TABLE 3.2   INDEPENDENT EXPENDITURES BY PARTY COMMITTEE, NORTH CAROLINA
SENATE RACE, 2003 TO 2004

PARTY COMMITTEE	CANDIDATE	INDEPENDENT EXPENDITURES FOR	INDEPENDENT EXPENDITURES AGAINST	TOTAL	PARTY TOTAL
DSCC					$2,517,622
	Erskine Bowles	$2,517,622	0	$2,517,622	
	Richard Burr	0	0	0	
NRSC					2,433,945
	Erskine Bowles	0	$2,331,279	2,331,279	
	Richard Burr	102,666	0	102,666	

Source: Federal Election Commission, ftp://ftp.fec.gov/FEC (accessed January 5, 2005).
Note: Abbreviations: DSCC, Democratic Senatorial Campaign Committee; NRSC, National Republican Senatorial Committee.

miscellaneous groups were Bowles's top sources of contributions. Bowles's personal wealth accounted for 15 percent of his contributions, whereas Burr made no personal contributions to his campaign.

POLITICAL PARTIES

The parties' Senate campaign committees also made substantial independent expenditures to this campaign, about $2.5 million each (see Table 3.2). Consistent with Bowles's desire to run a positive campaign, the DSCC used expenditures to advocate for him. On the other hand, the NRSC spent only a small amount to promote its candidate and used most of its funds to oppose Bowles.

THE EFFECTS OF MONEY

THE AIR WAR

The data in Table 3.3 indicate a considerable parity in the ad war.[17] The Burr campaign outspent the Bowles campaign on television and radio ads $6.3 million to $5.5 million, and the two national senatorial campaign committees were within $200,000 of each other in ad spending (see Table 3.3, "Total $ Spent"). Total spending was dominated by the two candidate campaigns; their combined spending on broadcast advertising, nearly $12 million, accounted for close to 46 percent of all spending in this race. Spending by Burr and the NRSC exceeded spending by the DSCC, but spending by the CSS, a 527 organization against Burr equalized overall spending by the two sides. The $1.2 million that the CSS spent dwarfed the spending of the next closest outside group, $338,421 from the 501(c) organization, AJS. All other interest-group players spent less than $300,000 in ad buys (see "Total $ Spent", Table 3.3).

Advertising followed the standard progression of ads in competitive campaigns.[18] The candidates started with biographical ads painting a positive image of their own character, while discussing their commitment to widely shared values. After Labor Day, weeks of attack ads by the candidates and the parties followed. The attacks largely focused on the other candidate's inconsistencies in policy positions and votes and their disreputable allies (Bill Clinton versus "special interests"). Mail from the parties and candidates reinforced the same themes and images as their television and radio ads.

The first television ad came from AJS. It was a pro-Burr issue ad, praising the work of "Republican congressmen" to pass a prescription drug plan and urging viewers to call Burr. Bowles responded with an offer to bar ads from outside groups, but no agreement was reached.[19]

Bowles's early ads attempted to reintroduce him as a pragmatic moderate. His first television ad appeared in mid-June and pictured Bowles incredulously shaking his head while discussing Congress' spending for "a rainforest in Iowa!" In another early ad, Bowles shared that he "prays hard" about diseases that have afflicted family members and asserted that affordable health care is a "moral responsibility." Burr's more limited early ads featured a variety of ordinary people saying, "Thanks, Richard," for his legislative accomplishments, such as promoting jobs and job training and

TABLE 3.3   THE AIR WAR: TELEVISION AND RADIO ADVERTISING EXPENDITURES, NORTH CAROLINA SENATE RACE, 2004[a]

TYPE AND ORGANIZATION[b]	TV	RADIO	TOTAL $ SPENT	CMAG TV
Democratic Allies[c]				
Candidates				
Erskine Bowles for Senate	$5,181,759	$278,257	**$5,460,016**	$7,339,060
Political Parties				
DSCC	2,488,235	—	**2,488,235**	1,453,253
North Carolina Democratic Party	246,517	58,147	**304,664**	—
Interest Groups				
Citizens for a Strong Senate	1,202,058	—	**1,202,058**	607,291
League of Conservation Voters	234,425	14,750	**249,175**	166,826
Stronger America Now	199,600	—	**199,600**	376,235
NARAL Pro-Choice North Carolina	—	9,600	**9,600**	—
Communication Workers of America	6,000	—	**6,000**	2,118
American Federation of Government Employees	—	—	—	29,098

(continued)

TABLE 3.3   THE AIR WAR: TELEVISION AND RADIO ADVERTISING EXPENDITURES,
NORTH CAROLINA SENATE RACE, 2004[a] *(continued)*

TYPE AND ORGANIZATION[b]	TV	RADIO	TOTAL $ SPENT	CMAG TV
Republican Allies[c]				
Candidates				
Richard Burr for Congress	5,867,192	416,144	**6,283,336**	5,732,963
Political Parties				
NRSC	2,548,736	143,300	**2,692,036**	1,561,901
Interest Groups				
Americans for Job Security	338,421	—	**338,421**	495,409
American Medical Association	258,571	—	**258,571**	287,347
United Seniors Association	216,060	—	**216,060**	358,287
National Rifle Association	73,125	—	**73,125**	43,093
National Right to Life	—	10,065	**10,065**	6,249
Small Business Survival Committee	—	8,568	**8,568**	—
National Association of Realtors	—	—	—	220,639
U.S. Chamber of Commerce	—	—	—	175,435
National Right to Work Committee	—	—	—	7,168
Nonpartisan				
Interest Groups				
AARP	—	—	—	119,306

[a]Please see Appendix A for a more detailed data explanation. The ad-buy data collected for this study may contain extraneous data because of the difficulty in determining the content of the ads. The parties or interest groups that purchased the ad buys possibly ran some ads promoting House, Senatorial, or Presidential candidates or ballot propositions not in the study's sample but still within that media market. Unless the participating academics were able to determine the exact content of the ad buy from the limited information given by the station, the data may contain observations that do not pertain to the study's relevant House, Senate, or Presidential battleground races. For comparison purposes the Compaign Media Analysis Group data are included in the table. Because of the sheer volume of TV and radio stations and varying degrees of compliance in providing ad-buy information, data on spending by various groups might be incomplete. These data do not include every station in the state. This table is not intended to represent comprehensive organization spending or activity within the sample races. Television ads purchased from national cable stations that aired in this state are not reflected in this table. A more complete picture can be obtained by examining this table with Table 3.3.

[b]All state and local chapters or affiliates have been combined with their national affiliate to better render the picture of the organization's activity. For instance, National Rifle Association Political Victory Fund data have been included in the National Rifle Association.

[c]Certain organizations that maintained neutrality were categorized according to which candidates their ads supported or attacked or whether the organization was openly anti- or pro- conservative or liberal.

In blank cells, "—" only reflects the absence of collected data and does not imply the organization was inactive in that medium.

Source: Data compiled from David B. Magleby, J. Quin Monson, and Kelly D. Patterson, "2004 Campaign Communications Database," (Center for the Study of Elections and Democracy: Brigham Young University, 2005); and Campaign Media Analysis Group data.

Note: Abbreviations: DSCC, Democratic Senatorial Campaign Committee; NARAL, National Abortion and Reproductive Rights Action League; NRSC, National Republican Senatorial Committee; AARP, American Association of Retired Persons.

getting medications for women and children approved more quickly by the Food and Drug Administration.

Bowles maintained a 10-point lead in the polls throughout the summer, but the margin closed in late September with the initial round of attack ads and the candidate debate.[20] Burr's attack ads and those run by the NRSC consistently pictured Bowles with Bill Clinton and included a clip of Bowles introducing Clinton as "a man I respect and admire." The ads also accused Bowles of "negotiating" trade deals with Mexico and China that sent North Carolina jobs abroad. In one, the flag of communist China provided the backdrop to an unflattering photo of Bowles.

The ads linking Bowles to Clinton were especially effective and played a key role in Burr pulling ahead.[21] Bowles' field representative Stefanos Arethas concluded, "Once Burr started with the Clinton attacks, we couldn't stop the bleeding."[22]

In eastern North Carolina, Burr targeted radio ads on the tobacco buy-out. Former Senator Jesse Helms and Representative Walter Jones taped ads praising Burr for his moral values and for helping to protect farmers.[23] Burr also ran radio ads in the east in which a female voice asserts, "It's a shame that Erskine Bowles doesn't have the courage to stand up for traditional marriage."[24]

The main theme of the television ads and mail by Bowles, the DSCC, and the North Carolina Democratic Party was that Burr was a sellout to special interests. They accused Burr of siding with nursing home operators over patients, employers over workers in denying overtime pay, and, in a prominent and controversial series of ads, insurance companies over breast cancer patients.[25]

Advertising from outside groups played a mixed role in the campaign. DSCC and NRSC ads were very important and largely indistinguishable in content and style from the candidates' ads. Interest group broadcast advertising played a minor role, however, perhaps as a result of BCRA's restrictions on issue ads (Table 3.3). In addition to AJS's summertime ads for Burr, only two other groups ran television ads in his behalf. The AMA PAC ran ads for two weeks in September explicitly endorsing Burr, and the NRA ran ads in the last weekend of the campaign, praising Burr for protecting gun rights.

The groups supporting Bowles clearly decided to jump on the bandwagon of Burr's ties to special interests. CSS, a pro-Democratic 527 organization headed by former staffers of Senator John Edwards, ran ads similar in theme to those of the Bowles campaign and the DSCC.[26] These ads, however, had a more strident tone—one ad crowned Burr the "King of Special Interests"; another showed a man's back, claiming Burr had "turned his back on North Carolina." The LCV ran ads in Raleigh and the eastern part of the state, criticizing Burr for choosing special interests over the environment.

TABLE 3.4 NUMBER OF UNIQUE CAMPAIGN COMMUNICATIONS BY ORGANIZATION, NORTH CAROLINA SENATE RACE, 2004[a]

TYPE AND ORGANIZATION[b]	TYPE OF CAMPAIGN COMMUNICATION							
	E-MAIL	MAIL	NEWSPAPER/ MAGAZINE	PERSONAL CONTACT	PHONE CALL	RADIO ADS	TV ADS	TOTAL
Democratic Allies[c]								
Candidates								
Erskine Bowles for Senate	—	1	1	—	8	6	42	58
Political Parties								
North Carolina Democratic Party	—	9	—	1	2	—	2	14
DSCC	—	—	—	—	—	—	7	7
Mecklenburg County Democratic Party	—	2	—	—	—	—	—	2
DNC	—	—	—	—	—	—	1	1
Interest Groups								
Citizens for a Strong Senate	—	5	—	—	1	—	2	8
AFL-CIO	—	3	—	—	2[d]	—	—	5
Issues Matter	—	—	—	—	2	—	1	3
National Education Association	—	2	—	—	1[e]	—	—	3
North Carolina Association of Educators	—	2	—	—	1	—	—	3
American Federation of Teachers	—	2	—	—	—	—	—	2
League of Conservation Voters	—	—	—	—	1[f]	—	1	2
Sierra Club	—	—	—	—	2	—	—	2
Black Political Caucus of Charlotte-Mecklenburg	—	1	—	—	—	—	—	1
Democracy North Carolina	—	1	—	—	—	—	—	1
Healthy Kids PAC	—	—	—	—	1	—	—	1
Rock the Vote	—	—	—	—	1	—	—	1
SEIU	—	1	—	—	—	—	—	1
Teamsters Union	—	—	—	—	1	—	—	1
United Auto Workers Union[d]	—	1	—	—	—	—	—	1
Voices for Working Families[g]	—	—	—	—	—	—	—	1

Republican Allies[c]

Candidates

Richard Burr for Senate	4	1	3	1	3	7	35	54
Political Parties								
NRSC	—	3	—	—	4	—	14	21
North Carolina Republican Executive Committee	3	9	—	—	9	—	—	21
RNC	—	—	—	—	—	—	2	2
Johnston County Republican Party	1	—	—	—	—	—	—	1
Mecklenburg County Republican Party	—	1	—	—	—	—	—	1
Interest Groups								
National Association of Realtors	—	9	—	—	—	—	—	9
American Medical Association	—	3	—	—	—	—	5	8
National Rifle Association	—	3	3	—	—	—	2	8
U.S. Chamber of Commerce	—	7	—	—	1[h]	—	—	8
United Seniors Association	—	3	—	—	—	—	2	5
Focus on the Family Action	—	3	—	—	—	—	—	3
Freedom Works[i]	1	—	—	1	1	—	—	3
Americans for Job Security	—	—	—	—	—	—	2	2
Associated Builders and Contractors	—	2[j]	—	—	—	—	—	2
National Federation of Independent Business	—	1[k]	—	—	—	1[l]	—	2
National Right to Life	—	2	—	—	—	—	—	2
Susan B. Anthony List	—	—	—	—	2	—	—	2
Club for Growth[m]	—	1	—	—	—	—	—	1
Council for Government Reform	—	1	—	—	—	—	—	1
Greater Greensboro Republican Woman	—	—	1	—	—	—	—	1
North Carolina Citizens for a Sound Economy	—	1	—	—	—	—	—	1
Retire Safe	—	1	—	—	—	—	—	1
Small Business Survival Committee	—	—	—	—	—	1	—	1
Triangle Republican Women	—	1	—	—	—	—	—	1

(continued)

TABLE 3.4 NUMBER OF UNIQUE CAMPAIGN COMMUNICATIONS BY ORGANIZATION, NORTH CAROLINA SENATE RACE, 2004[a] (continued)

TYPE AND ORGANIZATION[b]	TYPE OF CAMPAIGN COMMUNICATION							
	E-MAIL	MAIL	NEWSPAPER/ MAGAZINE	PERSONAL CONTACT	PHONE CALL	RADIO ADS	TV ADS	TOTAL
Nonpartisan								
Interest Groups								
AARP	—	—	—	—	1	—	—	1
American Manufacturing Trade Action Coalition	—	—	1	—	—	—	—	1
National Council of Textile Organizations	—	—	1	—	—	—	—	1
National Textile Association	—	—	1	—	—	—	—	1

[a]See Appendix A for a more detailed data explanation. Data represent the number of unique or distinct pieces or ads by the group and do not represent a count of total items sent or made. This table is not intended to portray comprehensive organization activity within the sample races. A more complete picture can be obtained by examining this table together with Table 3.4.

[b]All state and local chapters or affiliates have been combined with their national affiliate to better render the picture of the organization's activity. For instance, National Rifle Association Political Victory Fund data have been included in the National Rifle Association.

[c]Certain organizations that maintained neutrality were categorized according to which candidates their ads supported or attacked or whether the organization was openly anti- or pro-conservative or liberal.

[d]Ray Riffe, Committee on Political Education director, North Carolina American Federation of Labor and Congress of Industrial Organizations, telephone interview by Eric Heberlig, November 12, 2004.

[e]Eddie Davis, president, North Carolina Association of Educators, telephone interview by Steven Greene, November 30, 2004.

[f]Randy Davis, North Carolina contractor, League of Conservation Voters, telephone interview by Steven Greene, November 21, 2004.

[g]Arlene Holt Baker, president, Voices for Working Families, interview by Kelly D. Patterson and Betsey Gimbel, Washington, D.C., October 3, 2004.

[h]Bill Miller, vice president, U.S. Chamber of Commerce, interview by David B. Magleby and Kristina Gale, Washington, D.C., November 9, 2004.

[i]Rob Jordan, national director of federal and state campaigns, Freedom Works, interview by J. Quin Monson and Richard Hawkins, Washington, D.C., November 11, 2004.

[j]Ned Monroe, director of political affairs, Associated Builders and Contractors, telephone interview by Steven Greene, November 8, 2004.

[k]Dave Boyer, Political Director, Richard Burr for Senate, interview by Eric Heberlig, Winston-Salem, NC, November 4, 2004.

[l]Sharon Wolff Sussin and Andrew Finka, national political director and political programs coordinator, National Federation of Independent Business, interview by J. Quin Monson and Betsey Gimbel, Washington D.C., December 14, 2004.

[m]Unspecified race involvement. Stephen Moore, president, Club for Growth, interview by David B. Magleby and Richard Hawkins, Washington, D.C., November 5, 2004. In blank cells, "—" only reflects the absence of collected data and does not imply the organization was inactive in that medium.

Source: Data compiled from David B. Magleby, J. Quin Monson, and Kelly D. Patterson, "2004 Campaign Communications Database," (Center for the Study of Elections and Democracy: Brigham Young University, 2005).

Note: Abbreviations: DSCC, Democratic Senatorial Campaign Committee; DNC, Democratic National Committee; AFL-CIO, American Federation of Labor and Congress of Industrial Organizations; PAC, political action committee; SEIU, Service Employees International Union; NRSC, National Republican Senatorial Committee; RNC, Republican National Committee; AARP, American Association of Retired Persons.

THE GROUND WAR

Turning out voters involved extensive efforts on the part of the candidates, the parties, and a variety of interest groups. Several groups worked on each side, though only a handful appeared to make a major push (see Table 3.4).

Both campaigns had similar grassroots strategies: They combined public databases on voter registrations and magazine subscription lists to "microtarget" narrow sectors of the electorate with contacts. This process created demographic profiles of voters to target mail, phone, door knocking, and candidate appearances. Both campaigns focused their attention on swing votes, which meant spending most of their time and effort in eastern North Carolina. They relied on the political parties to mobilize their core supporters in the rest of the state.

The microtargeting process identified the ticket-splitters, those who were likely to vote for Republican President Bush and Democratic Governor Easley. The Burr campaign identified key ticket-splitters in two groups of people: unaffiliated women and Democratic men over age 50.[27] Burr's basic message to the ticket splitters was, "You agree with the president. Richard agrees with the president. Shouldn't you have a Senator who agrees with the president?"[28]

The geographic region east of I-95 and south of New Bern was the key battleground for split-ticket voters. The Burr campaign also spent a lot of effort on the "ex-urban" areas of the counties surrounding Charlotte and Raleigh, while Bowles and the Democrats attempted to mobilize African Americans statewide.[29] The Bowles campaign credits the Republican margins in ex-urban counties with counterbalancing Bowles's less-than-expected margins in the cities.[30]

Both parties focused on turning out their base with extensive mail, phone bank, and door-to-door contacts and responded to BCRA by placing considerably more resources into their grassroots and GOTV efforts.[31] There was considerable coordination between the state Democratic Party and the Bowles campaign in this effort and less on the Republican side.[32]

According to both campaigns, having Senator Edwards on the presidential ticket was helpful. Scott Falmlen, executive director of the North Carolina Democratic Party, believed it had a positive impact on the energy and enthusiasm of Democratic supporters and increased support for all statewide Democratic candidates.[33] On the Republican side, the Bush campaign reacted to Edwards's selection by building an infrastructure for their field operation in North Carolina and leaving four staff members and their grassroots plan with the state party when they pulled out in mid-September.[34] This improved Republican GOTV efforts.

Interest groups also played a major role in grassroots mobilization for Burr. The NAR and the NRA did "tons of work; everyone else was secondary."[35] These two groups sent a dozen unique mailers (see Table 3.4) and deployed their members door-to-door on behalf of Burr. The NRA bought pro-Burr ads on hundreds of thousands of newspaper sheaths across the state on the Saturday before the election.[36] They also held two workshops to train grassroots activists[37] and a rally for Burr at a major NASCAR race. The NAR featured Burr in articles in the September and October editions of the *Tar Heel Realtor*.

ABC made repeated contacts to owners and managers, encouraging them to talk to their workers on behalf of Burr. They strongly encouraged their membership to volunteer for Burr's campaign and spent nearly $1 million on ostensibly nonpartisan voter guides that were included in the paycheck envelopes of thousands of construction workers the Friday before the election.[38] Other business organizations, the National Federation of Independent Businesses (NFIB) and the U.S. Chamber of Commerce, were also active on Burr's behalf but mainly confined their participation to mass mailings.

Religious conservatives participated largely through the mail and voter guides distributed in churches. Focus on the Family Action and the National Right to Life Committee both sent out multiple mailers across the state (Table 3.4). Burr's father, a retired minister, sent letters to over 10,000 pastors urging support for his son.[39]

The most visible grassroots effort to benefit Bowles was the nonpartisan "All Souls to the Polls" campaign to educate African Americans on North Carolina's early vote option and to recruit churches to provide transportation to the polls after services on October 24. They distributed 130,000 pamphlets, featuring Martin Luther King, Jr., through churches in Charlotte and other mostly urban counties.[40]

Perhaps in reaction to BCRA restrictions on what money can be spent on broadcast electioneering communications, mail and phone calls from 527 organizations played a prominent role on the Democratic side. CSS mailed a series of bright yellow flyers featuring a variety of dogs begging for treats, accusing Burr of being a lap dog for special interests, to reinforce their television and radio advertising. Issues Matter targeted Democrats with GOTV calls, and in addition to their television ads, the LCV spent about $200,000 on automated voice recordings called "robocalls."[41] The Sierra Club provided staff assistance to Bowles in the final days of the campaign and made 10,000 robocalls and personal calls to infrequent voters on their membership list.[42]

Organized labor relied on internal communications to promote Bowles. They used mail and phone calls, as well as distributing leaflets at worksites to reach their members.[43] North Carolina is one of the least unionized states in the country, so efforts by organized labor had less of an effect than in many other places. Eddie Davis, president of North Carolina Association of Educators, felt that BCRA led to moderate curtailment of union activities due to uncertainty about new regulations. The interest group mentality became "when in doubt, play it safe."[44]

On the whole, the groups assisting the Republican ground game seemed to be more effective.[45] The efforts of the NRA, NAR, and ABC were all prominently mentioned by the Burr campaign as particularly valuable in the ground war. On the Democratic side, the campaign did not give particular value to any interest groups in interviews regarding the ground effort.

CONCLUSION

On November 2, Burr won the election 52 percent to 47 percent as part of a Republican sweep of Southern Senate seats. Bush's commanding 13-point victory in North Carolina was too great for Erskine Bowles to overcome. Bowles's polls had found he could win only if Bush's margin in North Carolina was less than 8 points.[46] It seemed that Burr's strategy of tying himself closely to Bush and tying Bowles to Clinton was highly effective.

Another major factor in Burr's victory may have been the success of the Republican ground game in North Carolina. In a state where Democrats have a roughly 14-percent advantage in party registration, the party identification of voters on election day was 40 percent Republican and 39 percent Democratic.[47] Despite earlier concerns that socially conservative Democrats would split their tickets, it seems that Bowles was defeated mainly by the sheer numbers of Republicans voting. Bowles actually did well within his party, garnering the votes of 89 percent of Democrats, a figure not far below Burr's 93 percent of Republicans.

Geographically, Burr accomplished what he needed to, and Bowles did not. Burr won the eastern part of the state convincingly. His association with the tobacco buyout had a "huge" influence in this region.[48] Meanwhile, Bowles's winning margins in the Raleigh/Durham and Charlotte areas were just not enough to offset losses elsewhere. For example, in Wake County, home to Raleigh and one of the "ideopolises" in John Judis and Ruy Teixeira's *The Emerging Democratic Majority*, Bowles only managed a three-point margin (51 percent to 48 percent).[49]

BCRA certainly had an impact on how the campaigns were run. Rather than parties contributing millions to soft-money ads, one little-known 527 emerged on each side to spend significant dollars on television. However, the amount spent by these 527s was probably less than what would have been spent had party soft money still been allowed. The party and interest group leaders interviewed generally suggested that more of their resources were invested in phone and mail efforts due to these legal changes. BCRA likely did not affect the intensity and amount of resources that parties and groups put into the campaign, but it did certainly affect how those resources were allocated.

In the end, Bowles could have run the perfect campaign and still lost. It is probably asking too much for a non-incumbent Democrat with close ties to Bill Clinton to win a Senate seat in a state that voted 56 percent to 43 percent for Bush. One should not discount the importance of the campaign, though. Both candidates ran an expensive, professional campaign with considerable support from parties and interest groups. Had Burr not been a strong candidate with considerable resources, Bowles could have captured the race, as the success of Democrats in other statewide elections demonstrated. Given the very different issue context in Senate races, the prospect for Democrats in future Senate races remains an open question. Ultimately, however, this election may simply be part of the larger pattern of Southern Senate seats moving into the Republican column.

NOTES

1. The authors would like to thank John Willingham, Geoff Luxenberg, and Emily Hovis for all their assistance in putting this chapter together.
2. Thad Beyle and Ferrel Guillory, "North Carolina Senate," in *Outside Money: Soft Money and Issue Ads in Competitive 1998 Congressional Elections*, eds. David B. Magleby and Marianne Holt (The Center for the Study of Elections and Democracy: Brigham Young University), pp. 53–62; Jim Morrill and Mark Johnson "From End to End, N.C. Elects Its First Woman to the U.S. Senate After Bruising, Costly Campaign," *Charlotte Observer*, November 6, 2002, p. 1A.
3. On predictions regarding Bipartisan Campaign Reform Act effects, see Michael J. Malbin, ed., *Life After Reform: When the Bipartisan Campaign Reform Act Meets Politics*. (Lanham, MD: Rowman and Littlefield, 2003).
4. Mark Johnson, "Same Man, New Approach," *Charlotte Observer*, March 21, 2003, pp. 1B, 13B.
5. Stefanos Arethas, field representative, Erskine Bowles for Senate, interview by Eric Heberlig, Charlotte, NC, November 15, 2004.
6. Mark Johnson, "Senate Hopeful Has GOP Support," *Charlotte Observer*, September 10, 2003, pp. 1B, 5B; Tim Funk, "GOP Heavyweights Backing Senate Bid," *Charlotte Observer*, February 11, 2003, pp. 1B, 3B; Rob Christensen, "Burr Carries Bush Torch," *Raleigh News and Observer*, May 2, 2004, p. A1.
7. Dave Boyer, political director, Richard Burr for Senate, interview by Eric Heberlig, Winston-Salem, NC, November 4, 2004.
8. Rob Christensen, "Trade is Central, Slippery," *Raleigh News and Observer*, September 30, 2004, p. A1.
9. Gary Pearce, political consultant, Erskine Bowles for Senate, interview by Steven Greene, Raleigh, NC, November 22, 2004.
10. Ibid.
11. Mark Johnson, "At the Wheel of His Campaign," *Charlotte Observer*, April 11, 2004, p. 1B; Political director Dave Boyer estimated that he traveled with Burr only ten days during the campaign. Boyer, interview, November 4, 2004.
12. Boyer, interview, November 4, 2004; Douglas Heye, communications director, Richard Burr for Senate, interview by Eric Heberlig, Winston-Salem, NC, November 4, 2004.
13. WSOC-TV, 2004 U.S. Senate Debate, September 27, 2004.
14. Tim Funk, "Senate Advances Tobacco Buyout," *Charlotte Observer*, October 11, 2004, pp. 1A, 8A.
15. Heye, interview, November 4, 2004.
16. Center for Responsive Politics www.opensecrets.org (accessed November 11, 2004).
17. We report actual ad buy data from North Carolina's largest media markets in this paragraph. The Campaign Media Analysis Group estimates differ somewhat but confirm the conclusions reported with regard to the general parity in spending among the campaigns, the parties, and the interest group allies of each campaign.
18. Paul S. Herrnson, *Congressional Elections*, 4th edition (Washington, D.C.: CQ Press, 2003), p. 213.
19. "Editorial: A Lost Chance," *Charlotte Observer*, June 4, 2004, p. 8A. Burr thought that Bowles would have the advantage in this scenario due to his greater personal wealth. Such an agreement would be unenforceable anyway. Heye, interview, November 4, 2004.
20. Mark Johnson, "Poll Says U.S. Senate Race Narrows," *Charlotte Observer*, October 1, 2004, p. 8B.

21. Rob Christensen, "State Displays Its Dual Nature," *Raleigh News and Observer,* November 3, 2004, p. AA2.
22. Arethas, interview, November 4, 2004.
23. Jim Morrill, "Helms Praises Burr on Tobacco Buyout," *Charlotte Observer*, October 15, 2004, p. 7B; Boyer, interview, November 4, 2004.
24. Jason Zengerle, "At the Helm," *The New Republic*, November 1, 2004, p. 16; Jim Morrill, "Burr Ad Criticizes Bowles's Position on Gay Marriage," *Charlotte Observer*, October 12, 2004, p. 3B.
25. Jim Morrill, "Senate Hopefuls' Backers Defend Record on Cancer," *Charlotte Observer*, October 30, 2004, p. 4B.
26. Jim Morrill, "Outside Backers Include California Billionaires," *Charlotte Observer*, October 28, 2004, p. 5A.
27. Ryan Rankin, Charlotte field representative, Richard Burr for Senate, interview by Eric Heberlig, Charlotte, NC, October 22, 2004.
28. Boyer, interview, November 4, 2004.
29. Rankin interview, October 22, 2004.
30. Arethas interview, November 15, 2004.
31. Bill Peaslee, Executive Director, North Carolina Republican Party, interview by Steven Greene, Raleigh, NC, December 7, 2004.
32. Scott Falmlen, executive director, North Carolina Democratic Party, interview by Steven Greene, Raleigh, NC, December 1, 2004; Peaslee, interview, November 7, 2004.
33. Falmlen, interview, December 1, 2004.
34. Boyer, interview, November 4, 2004.
35. Ryan Rankin, Charlotte field representative, Richard Burr for Senate, interview by Eric Heberlig, Charlotte, NC, November 10, 2004; Boyer, interview, November 4, 2004.
36. Jim Morrill, "Newspaper Wrappers Will Carry Political Ad," *Charlotte Observer*, October 29, 2004, p. 7B.
37. Glen Caroline, director, Institute for Legislative Action Grassroots Division, National Rifle Association, interview by J. Quin Monson and Richard Hawkins, Fairfax, Va., November 10, 2004; Rankin interview, October 22, 2004.
38. Ned Monroe, director of political affairs, Associated Builders and Contractors, telephone interview by Steven Greene, November 8, 2004.
39. Heye, interview, November 4, 2004; Nancy Kraft, pastor, Advent Lutheran Church, personal communication to Eric Heberlig, October 24, 2004.
40. The organizations included: Democracy North Carolina, National Association for the Advancement of Colored People, black fraternities and sororities, black Masons, and local black political organizations, such as the Mecklenburg Black Political Caucus and the Mecklenburg Voter Coalition. Danielle Obiorah, chair, Mecklenburg Black Political Caucus, telephone interview by Eric Heberlig, October 26, 2004; Adam Sotak, organizer, Democracy North Carolina, telephone interview by Eric Heberlig, November 12, 2004.
41. Randy Davis, North Carolina contractor, League of Conservation Voters, telephone interview by Steven Greene, November 21, 2004.
42. Molly Diggins, state director, Sierra Club, e-mail communication to Eric Heberlig, November 19, 2004.
43. Ray Riffe, Committee on Political Education, director, North Carolina American Federation of Labor and Congress of Industrial Organizations, telephone interview by Eric Heberlig, November 12, 2004; Scott Thrower, political coordinator, for International Brotherhood of Electrical Workers Local #379, telephone interview by Eric Heberlig, October 24, 2004.
44. Eddie Davis, president, North Carolina Association of Educators, telephone interview by Steven Greene, November 30, 2004.
45. Rob Christensen, reporter, *Raleigh News and Observer*, telephone interview by Steven Greene, December 13, 2004.
46. Arethas, interview, November 15, 2004.
47. CNN.com, "Election 2004," www.cnn.com/ELECTION/2004/pages/results/states/NC/S/01/epolls.0.html (accessed December 13, 2004).
48. Rankin interview, October 22, 2004.
49. John Judis and Ruy Teixeira, *The Emerging Democratic Majority* (New York: Scribner, 2002).

4

THE NATIONALIZATION OF LOCAL POLITICS

THE SOUTH DAKOTA U.S. SENATE RACE

ELIZABETH THEISS SMITH AND RICHARD BRAUNSTEIN

University of South Dakota

The 2004 South Dakota U.S. Senate election pitted Democrat Tom Daschle, a 26-year veteran of both houses of Congress and Senate minority leader, against Republican John Thune, who served three terms in South Dakota's At-Large House seat before running for the Senate and narrowly losing to incumbent Tim Johnson in 2002.[1] Both candidates had statewide name recognition and a political base in every county. The election was the most expensive in the nation, and the vast majority of the money spent was from out-of-state donors. While the defeat of a powerful Senate leader is rare on a national level (and has not happened since 1952), South Dakota has a history of tossing out Senators after three terms, including George McGovern in 1980.

The election's outcome can be understood only in terms of South Dakota's unique political environment of prairie populism. The context presented an interesting dilemma for South Dakota voters in 2004: either return Daschle with his seniority and reputation for constituent service or support the George W. Bush administration by electing Republican Thune. Voters that supported the Bush administration's war on terrorism, the war in Iraq, and generally conservative values were reminded that Daschle had obstructed the Bush agenda, strongly criticized the Iraqi invasion, and filibustered conservative nominees to the federal judiciary.[2]

Daschle, a proven vote getter, was also known to have secured federal government support for the state and, in his position as minority leader, held the promise to continue to do so. The tension between support for a conservative president who shared the same values as most of the electorate and a skilled and effective local politician was a persistent theme throughout the election. John Thune had developed his own popular base in the state. In his first successful bid for the U.S. House, Thune promised to serve only three terms. His fulfillment of this pledge resonated well with the populist South Dakota electorate. In his 2002 campaign against Tim Johnson he ran on a national agenda and lost.[3] He did not make that mistake in 2004, but rather emphasized South Dakota values and interests.

THE ELECTORAL CONTEXT

South Dakota's political culture is bifurcated by the Missouri River. West River is sparsely populated by ranchers and is deeply conservative with a substantial dose of libertarianism; East River is more densely populated by farms and population centers that hug the I-29 and I-90 corridors and is more likely to elect Democrats. The state also contains nine Native American reservations, which vote overwhelmingly Democratic.

South Dakota also has a strong populist tradition. It was the first state in the nation to have an active Populist party and the first state in the nation to give its citizens the right to initiate and refer laws; South Dakota holds true to these traditions in its contemporary politics.[4] It is also a deeply religious community, and this combination of populism and religiosity provides the broad context in which campaign issues, strategies, and politics must be understood.

THE CANDIDATES

John Thune presented himself as a man of conservative values. He supported a constitutional amendment to ban gay marriage, while Tom Daschle sidestepped the moral concerns of the issue, stating that it was a matter for states to decide.[5] In response, bumper stickers that said "Vote Daschle & Vote for SODOMY" were sent as mass mailings to churches across the state with the Daschle campaign's headquarters as the return address. An enclosed flyer asked churches to place notices in church bulletins telling parishioners to urge Daschle to support the Federal Marriage Protection Act, the House of Worship Free Speech Restoration Act, and the Pledge Protection Act; and to vote for him only if he supported these bills. Daschle had already publicly voiced his opposition to the Federal Marriage Protection Act, making this virtually a moot point.

The candidates also took opposing positions on abortion, with Thune taking a strong pro-life stance and Daschle supporting a woman's right to choose. Pro-life groups played a large role in the campaign, recruiting volunteers, making phone calls, and distributing and mailing persuasive literature comparing the candidates' positions. The abortion issue had great traction in South Dakota churches, many of which handed out a "Voter's Guide" put out by the South Dakota Family Policy Council in the weeks leading up to the election. This same guide was also handed out door-to-door in many communities. The guide detailed candidate positions on abortion, gay marriage, school vouchers, and tax cuts among other issues. Ministers and priests spoke from the pulpit abut the importance of "voting your conscience," which many parishioners translated as voting pro-life. One member of this study's reconnaissance network said, "The homily stated that we could consider it 'serious sin' to knowingly vote for candidates that were known to have a pro-choice voting record." Such homilies were documented in Catholic, Methodist, and Lutheran churches. James Dobson, the vice president of government public policy for the pro-life group Focus on the Family, was featured at mass rallies in Rapid City and Sioux Falls.[6]

Bishop Carlson of the Catholic Diocese of Sioux Falls stopped just short of calling a Democratic vote a sin, which, according to Daschle campaign manager Steve Hildebrand, was far enough. In an interview with KELO anchor Steve Hemmingsen, Hildebrand noted that while a lot of things contributed to Senator Tom Daschle's defeat, "the churches pushed it over the edge, and not just one religion, making it plain that abortion was not an issue but the issue."[7]

Thune supported ending the 10-year-old ban on assault weapons when it expired, saying that he taught his daughters to fire a semiautomatic handgun for their own protection. In this case, he parted ways with President Bush, who said that he favored extending the ban, though he took no steps to urge Republicans in Congress to do so. Daschle, however, was able to use Bush for cover on this issue by telling the media that he agreed with the president on this matter and would vote for an extension if given the opportunity.

THE CAMPAIGN

The principal strategy of the Thune campaign was to make the case that Daschle had become more liberal than his constituency and was out of touch with South Dakotans, especially as a Democratic leader. In that role, Thune argued, Daschle had obstructed legislation that South Dakotans would have supported. Thune promised to vote consistently with South Dakota values in mind.

Daschle ran a classic incumbent's campaign centered on his clout as Democratic minority leader and his record of producing important projects and programs for South Dakota. Compared to Daschle, who began running ads on July 5, 2003, Thune delayed the start of his 2004 campaign. Daschle's ads were upbeat and positive, presenting an affirmative spin on issues. Early ads highlighted his support for tax credits for building ethanol plants in the state, claiming "no soldier has to fight overseas to protect it, and no foreign power can turn off the spigot."[8] He also targeted several localities in the state with large-format color postcards and radio ads highlighting his specific contributions to those areas.

These early ads established a major theme of the Daschle campaign, but they did not have an appreciable impact on polling numbers. After Thune entered the fray with radio and television spots a full year later, the heat would increase as would the pressure for attack ads. Thune's first radio ad addressed the need for a constitutional amendment to ban gay marriage so that liberal judges could not force South Dakota to recognize them—a popular position in this conservative state and a contrast to Daschle's position that decisions on gay marriage should be left to the states to decide. Thune's ads tried to paint Daschle as an out-of-touch liberal who cared more about the Democratic caucus in Washington and special interest issues than South Dakota values. His early ads suggested that Daschle was not as strongly pro-ethanol as he had claimed, pointing to his failure to get Democratic support for the Bush administration's energy bill that included ethanol provisions. Both of these Thune ads cast Daschle as an obstructionist. Thune defined himself as the honest kid from Murdo, South Dakota, a community of just over 600 residents, dedicated to the South Dakota values of family, church, and public service.

Thune had a particularly effective ad entitled "Daschle in His Own Words," which appeared toward the end of the campaign. This ad provided three brief video clips of Daschle praising Hillary Clinton, claiming D.C. residency, and promising to protect a woman's right to choose. Ultimately, according to Steve Hildebrand, Daschle's campaign manager, the simple words, "I'm a D.C. resident," were the most effective tool used by the Thune campaign. The fact that Daschle was caught saying this and that the Thune campaign took good advantage of it made it difficult for the Daschle campaign to respond. Hildebrand noted, "There was no practical way to beat that perception."[9]

In addition to the ad war, Republican activists launched a cluster of blogs in an effort to start a "populist prairie fire" to shape the campaign agenda and public opinion.[10] Republicans had long complained that the state's major daily newspaper, the *Sioux Falls Argus Leader,* lacked objectivity, especially its political columnist, David Kranz. The blogs aimed to curb the *Argus*'s perceived bias by publicizing the newspaper's failure to report negative news about Daschle. The blog SouthDakotaPolitics.blogs.com initiated a "Kranz Watch" section that focused on news its creator believed Kranz wrongfully ignored. The Thune campaign placed two of the most prominent bloggers, Jon Lauck and Jason Van Beek, on the payroll as research consultants.[11]

The bloggers' success had repercussions beyond the Internet as well. Reporters at a number of news outlets described a pattern that began in the summer of 2004: The blogs would pounce on a particular story, conservative radio talk shows would pick it up, then Thune operatives would weave the issues into their attacks on Daschle. Many of these themes were also echoed in a paperback book entitled *The Other Side of Tom Daschle*, which highlighted the Thune campaign's "two Daschles" storyline.[12] In the closing days of the campaign, blogs pushed two particular stories: Daschle's wife's lobbying activities in the House and Daschle's claim of D.C. residency in order to receive a special tax credit. These stories were published in the *Argus*, were discussed on conservative radio talk shows, and became the subject of Thune campaign ads. According to media sources and bloggers, this concerted effort permitted Republicans to amplify the Thune campaign's themes.[13] In all, the cyber war was extremely important to South Dakota, where low population densities and long distances between population centers present challenges for political organizers.

MONEY

CANDIDATES

In part because of his status as Democratic leader, Daschle's campaign was highly successful in fundraising. In the end, Daschle raised $3,242,662 more than Thune (see Table 4.1), apparently expecting to offset Thune's third-party assistance with hard-money contributions. However, Daschle was unable to benefit from visits by nationally prominent Democrats because the majority of South Dakota voters held a negative view of them.

Daschle's funding constituency reached beyond South Dakota to Washington, D.C. and elsewhere. The campaign's most successful fundraising strategy was buying national fundraising lists from other political committees

TABLE 4.1   CANDIDATE RECEIPTS AND EXPENDITURES, SOUTH DAKOTA SENATE RACE, 2003 TO 2004

	TOM DASCHLE (D)	JOHN THUNE (R)
From PACs	$2,807,562	$1,183,602
From individuals	16,017,216	14,046,445
From party	35,950	62,195
From candidate	0	0
Other contributions	484,957	810,781
Total receipts	19,345,685	16,103,023
Total expenditures	19,993,497	14,666,225
Cash on hand (as of 12/31/04)	767,334	1,444,545

Source: Federal Election Commission, "2003-04 U.S. House and U.S. Senate Candidate Info," December 31, 2004, www.fecinfo.com/cgi-win/x_candidate.exe?DoFn=&sYR=2004 (accessed February 11, 2005).
Note: Abbreviation: PAC, political action committee.

and sending out fundraising letters signed by nationally prominent Democrats. A direct-mail appeal signed by James Carville brought in $160,000 over one weekend. Bill Clinton and John Edwards also wrote fundraising letters.[14] All told, the Daschle campaign spent $787,000 on direct mail in 2003 alone, much of it for identifying national donors.[15]

The Internet also proved to be a productive way for the campaign to solicit funds with minimal financial investment and immediate results. Howard Dean sent an e-mail solicitation to his 600,000-member list that yielded impressive results. He also linked his blog directly to Daschle's contributions page, as did the Daily Kos, Act Blue, Blog for America, and other liberal Internet sites. The DSCC and the DNC sent several fundraising e-mails for the campaign as well.[16] Further contributions came almost by accident: according to Daschle Campaign Finance Assistant Lindsey Dorneman, "People would wander on to our Web site and find out that they could contribute. In the last month, we received about $250,000 in contributions off the Web, much of it unsolicited."[17]

Daschle also received strong support from the Native American community, particularly out-of-state Native American gaming interests. Gaming is an important revenue source for South Dakota Democrats because many South Dakota tribes that typically support Democratic candidates do not have substantial economic resources and tend to go to wealthier out-of-state Native American communities to support their interests.

Although John Thune raised $3.24 million less than Daschle (see Table 4.1), he enjoyed a number of advantages that negated his opponent's financial edge. First, Thune's campaign spent most of the money it raised on media and mail because, as noted in the following section, the South Dakota Republican party's coordinated campaign took responsibility for getting out the vote.[18] Second, Thune's refusal to sign a pledge to ban third parties from campaigning meant that outside groups would have a significant presence in the state, and this represented considerable media exposure. Finally, Thune did not begin spending significant funds until July 2004, when Daschle had already been advertising for a year. This allowed Thune to concentrate campaign spending during the last critical months of the campaign.

POLITICAL PARTIES

The South Dakota Republican party had a record-breaking fundraising year, raising approximately $3 million, 500 percent more than what had been raised before (see Table 4.2). Contributions came largely from individual donors, with an average contribution of $35 per person. The party began national fundraising in July 2003 with only 400 out-of-state donors. By the end of the campaign, there were over 50,000 out-of-state donors. The party rented, bought, and exchanged lists, which it used for telemarketing and direct-mail solicitations focused on Daschle. The Internet was also a powerful

TABLE 4.2 INDEPENDENT EXPENDITURES BY PARTY COMMITTEE, SOUTH DAKOTA SENATE RACE, 2003 TO 2004

PARTY COMMITTEE	CANDIDATE	INDEPENDENT EXPENDITURES FOR	INDEPENDENT EXPENDITURES AGAINST	TOTAL	PARTY TOTAL
DSCC					$952,132
	Tom Daschle	$952,132	0	$952,132	
	John Thune	0	0	0	
NRSC					3,256,329
	Tom Daschle	0	$3,158,465	3,158,465	
	John Thune	97,864	0	97,864	

Source: Federal Election Commission, ftp://ftp.fec.gov/FEC (accessed January 5, 2005).

Note: Abbreviations: DSCC, Democratic Senatorial Campaign Committee; NRSC, National Republican Senatorial Committee.

fundraising tool for the Republican party and netted over $100,000 with very few associated costs.[19]

Because of Daschle's status as Senate Democratic leader, fundraising was nationalized for both candidates. Former mayor of New York City Rudy Giuliani and Senator George Allen, chairman of the National Republican Senatorial Committee, hosted fundraising events at the Republican National Convention and urged GOP senators to give the maximum amount allowed to the GOP senatorial committee.[20] Thune also received help from a number of GOP stars who traveled to South Dakota to raise money and stump for him, including Vice President Dick Cheney, Elizabeth Dole, and a highly unusual visit from Senate Majority Leader Bill Frist of Tennessee.[21] Senate leaders do not often campaign actively against the other party's leader, and by way of explanation, Frist noted that his visit "may be rare, but these are rare times," and it is "rare to have the leader of a party . . . not be very strongly supported by the people in their home state."[22] The state Democratic party, weakened by persisting debt from the 2002 election, relied on Daschle's national supporters for its own financial support rather than acting as a source of funding.

INTEREST GROUPS

Ads by interest groups seeking to unseat Tom Daschle began running in January 2002, nearly three years before Daschle ran for office. The Club for Growth, with major agenda items including tax cuts and smaller government,[23] attacked Daschle as an obstructionist in an early 2002 ad. This ad had the strategic intent to soften support for him and to undercut Democratic U.S. Senator Tim Johnson's 2002 reelection campaign by challenging the benefits for South Dakota from Daschle's leadership. The Club returned in August 2003 with an ad that incorporated photographs of Daschle's $2-million home in D.C. with a voiceover noting the Senator's opposition to tax relief.

Both campaigns addressed the themes of campaign tone and spending. Daschle ran a series of inoculation ads calling on Thune to run a positive campaign because, according to one ad, "South Dakota deserves no less." Thune challenged Daschle to sign a pledge agreeing to limit his campaign spending to $10 million while Thune would limit himself to $6 million. This challenge was made well before the election when Daschle had already spent nearly $9 million and Thune's campaign was just ramping up; Daschle did not agree to Thune's proposed spending limit. Instead, Daschle challenged Thune to accept a third-party ad-ban pledge, which Daschle unilaterally signed, asking outside groups to refrain from advertising in the race. Thune had drafted and signed this same pledge in his 2002 race, but Thune declined to sign the pledge in 2004.

Daschle kept his promise and requested that third parties stay out of the election. In contrast, electioneering by outside groups seeking to defeat Daschle or elect John Thune were an important part of the campaign. You're Fired, Inc. sponsored the first interest-group ad of the general election on television and radio during the week of July 26, 2004. According to Daschle campaign e-mails, the group was run by a California businessman who was also a Thune campaign donor.[24] The ad was a parody of the NBC show *The Apprentice;* in it a paid actor imitating Donald Trump "fires" Daschle for spending more time helping other Democrats than helping South Dakotans. The ad was reported in both print and electronic media, an indication of its success.

The U.S. Chamber of Commerce also played an important role in the election, making the South Dakota U.S. Senate race its highest priority in 2004. According to an interview with the Chamber's political director Bill Miller, the Chamber committed $1 million to unseating Daschle,[25] saying that Daschle was "more of an obstacle than an ally."[26] The Chamber noted where Thune was weak, particularly in the area of television and radio spots, and targeted $410,000[27] to ad buys to help the Thune campaign.[28] The U.S. Chamber of Commerce also spent at least $590,000 for ground war and other efforts.[29] The AMA PAC also invested heavily against Daschle, who had not been supportive of the organization's lobbying. Club for Growth, as noted previously, came into the race early and stayed throughout, contributing or directing contributions of an estimated $237,000 to the overall effort to unseat Daschle.[30] The National Right to Life was also instrumental, along with a host of other third-party Republican allies (see Table 4.3 and Table 4.4).[31] Other groups active for Thune or against Daschle included Families for a Secure America and the NRA. Overall, interest groups supporting Thune or the Republicans outspent those supporting Daschle or the Democrats nine to one ($927,062 to $103,710).

TABLE 4.3 THE AIR WAR: TELEVISION AND RADIO ADVERTISING EXPENDITURES, SOUTH DAKOTA SENATE RACE, 2004[a]

TYPE AND ORGANIZATION	TV	RADIO	TOTAL $ SPENT
Democratic Allies[b]			
Candidates			
A Lot of People Supporting Tom Daschle	$2,745,618	$214,589	$2,960,207
Political Parties			
DSCC[c]	623,963	—	623,963
DNC	—	10,000	10,000
Interest Groups			
The Media Fund	100,542	—	100,542
Sierra Club	1,887	—	1,887
Daschle Democrats	1,101	—	1,101
American Federation of Government Employees	—	180	180
Republican Allies[b]			
Candidates			
Thune for U.S. Senate	1,969,523	335,769	2,305,292
Political Parties			
NRSC	2,131,073	71,565	2,202,638
Interest Groups			
You're Fired	188,362	39,564	227,926
Families for a Secure America	183,876	—	183,876
U.S. Chamber of Commerce[d]	144,073	17,545	161,618
Club for Growth[e]	121,762	—	121,762
NRA Political Victory Fund	85,748	29,857	115,605

United Seniors Association	34,595	—	34,595
Ave Maria List	—	29,081	29,081
American Medical Association	—	25,111	25,111
National Right to Life	—	8,128	8,128
Family Research Council	—	7,200	7,200
America's PAC	—	6,120	6,120
National Right to Work Committee PAC	4,310	—	4,310
NRA Institute for Legislative Action	—	1,730	1,730

Nonpartisan

Interest Groups

Taxpayers for Common Sense	—	14,217	14,217

[a]Please see Appendix A for a more detailed data explanation. The ad-buy data collected for this study may contain extraneous data because of the difficulty in determining the content of the ads. The parties or interest groups that purchased the ad buys possibly ran some ads promoting House, Senatorial, or presidential candidates or ballot propositions not in the study's sample but still within that media market. Unless the participating academics were able to determine the exact content of the ad buy from the limited information given by the station, the data may contain observations that do not pertain to the study's relevant House, Senate, or presidential battleground races. Because of the sheer volume of television and radio stations and varying degrees of compliance in providing ad-buy information, data on spending by various groups might be incomplete. These data do not include every station in the state. This table is not intended to represent comprehensive organization spending or activity within the sample races. Television ads purchased from national cable stations that aired in this state are not reflected in this table. A more complete picture can be obtained by examining this table with Table 4.4.

[b]Certain organizations that maintained neutrality were categorized according to which candidates their ads supported or attacked or whether the organization was openly anti- or proconservative or liberal.

[c]Democratic Senatorial Campaign Committee; the Democratic Senatorial Campaign Committee spent $800,000 in broadcast advertising. Benjamin Jones, research director, Democratic Senatorial Campaign Committee, interview by David B. Magleby and J. Quin Monson, November 10, 2004.

[d]The U.S. Chamber spent $410,000 on television and radio combined. Bill Miller, vice president, U.S. Chamber of Commerce, interview by David B. Magleby and Kristina Gale, Washington, D.C., November 9, 2004.

[e]Club for Growth spent $200,000 on television. Stephen Moore, president, Club for Growth, interview by David B. Magleby and Richard Hawkins, Washington D.C., November 5, 2004.

In blank cells, "—" only reflects the absence of collected data and does not imply the organization was inactive in that medium.

Source: Data compiled from David B. Magleby, J. Quin Monson, and Kelly D. Patterson, "2004 Campaign Communications Database," (Center for the Study of Elections and Democracy: Brigham Young University, 2005).

Note: Abbreviations: DSCC, Democratic Senatorial Campaign Committee; DNC, Democratic National Committee; NRSC, National Republican Senatorial Committee; NRA, National Rifle Association; PAC, political action committee.

TABLE 4.4 NUMBER OF UNIQUE CAMPAIGN COMMUNICATIONS BY ORGANIZATION, SOUTH DAKOTA SENATE RACE, 2004[a]

TYPE AND ORGANIZATION	E-MAIL	MAIL	NEWSPAPER/ MAGAZINE	PERSONAL CONTACT	PHONE CALL	RADIO AD	TV AD	TOTAL
			TYPE OF CAMPAIGN COMMUNICATION					
Democratic Allies[b]								
Candidates								
A Lot of People Supporting Tom Daschle	17	38	17	2	14	2	31	121
Political Parties								
DSCC	—	4	—	—	—	—	3	7
South Dakota Democratic Party	1	2	—	—	—	—	—	3
Interest Groups								
Focus South Dakota	—	5	8	—	—	—	—	13
MoveOn	3	—	—	—	—	—	1	4
New House PAC	—	—	—	—	3	—	—	3
Sierra Club	1	2	—	—	—	—	—	3
Democracy for America	2	—	—	—	—	—	—	2
JustGoVote.org	—	—	—	—	2	—	—	2
Clean Water Action	—	1	—	—	—	—	—	1
NARAL Pro-Choice America	—	1	—	—	—	—	—	1
National Education Association	—	1	—	—	—	—	—	1
South Dakota AFL-CIO	—	1	—	—	—	—	—	1
Republican Allies[b]								
Candidates								
Thune for U.S. Senate	4	20	31	1	4	3	33	96

Political Parties								
South Dakota Republican Party	18	13	—	1	4	—	—	36
NRSC	—	8	—	—	1	3	22	34
Interest Groups								
U.S. Chamber of Commerce	—	13	1	2	1[c]	—	—	17
National Rifle Association	—	2	2	—	—	1	4	9
Americans for Job Security	—	2	2	—	2	—	1	7
Individuals	—	1	3	—	—	—	—	4
You're Fired	—	—	—	—	—	2	2	4
Club for Growth	—	—	1	—	—	—	2	3
National Federation of Independent Business	—	2	—	—	—	1[d]	—	3
National Right to Life	—	3	—	1	—	—	—	4
Susan B. Anthony List	—	1	—	—	2	—	—	3
60 Plus	—	2	—	—	—	—	—	2
Associated Builders and Contractors PAC	—	2	—	—	—	—	—	2
Ave Maria List	—	1	1	—	—	—	—	2
Council for Government Reform	—	2	—	—	—	—	—	2
Focus on the Family Action	—	1	1	—	—	—	—	2
Thanksgiving 2004 Committee	—	—	2	—	—	—	—	2
American Conservative Union	—	—	1	—	—	—	—	1
BPI Technologies	—	—	1	—	—	—	—	1
Campaign for Working Families	—	—	1	—	—	—	—	1
Christian Voter Project	—	1	—	—	—	—	—	1
Heritage Fund	—	1	—	—	—	—	—	1

(continued)

TABLE 4.4 NUMBER OF UNIQUE CAMPAIGN COMMUNICATIONS BY ORGANIZATION, SOUTH DAKOTA SENATE RACE, 2004[a] *(continued)*

TYPE AND ORGANIZATION	TYPE OF CAMPAIGN COMMUNICATION							
	E-MAIL	MAIL	NEWSPAPER/ MAGAZINE	PERSONAL CONTACT	PHONE CALL	RADIO AD	TV AD	TOTAL
National Right to Work Committee PAC	—	1	—	—	—	—	—	1
Progress for America Voter Fund	—	—	—	—	—	—	1	1
South Dakota Mothers, Daughters, and Grandmothers for John Thune	—	—	1	—	—	—	—	1
South Dakota Pro-Life Committee	—	—	1	—	—	—	—	1
Nonpartisan								
Interest Groups								
TrueMajority.org	4	—	—	—	—	—	—	4
AARP	1	—	—	—	—	—	—	1
Families for a Secure America	—	—	—	—	—	—	1	1

[a]See Appendix A for a more detailed data explanation. Data represent the number of unique or distinct pieces or ads by the group and do not represent a count of total items sent or made. This table is not intended to portray comprehensive organization activity within the sample races. A more complete picture can be obtained by examining this table together with Table 4.3.

[b]Certain organizations that maintained neutrality were categorized according to which candidates their ads supported or attacked or whether the organization was openly anti- or pro- conservative or liberal.

[c]U.S. Chamber did phone banking in South Dakota. Bill Miller, vice president, U.S. Chamber of Commerce, interview by David B. Magleby and Kristina Gale, Washington, D.C., November 9, 2004.

[d]Sharon Wolff Sussin and Andrew Finka, national political director and political programs coordinator, National Federation of Independent Business, interview by J. Quin Monson and Betsey Gimbel, Washington D.C., December 14, 2004.

In blank cells, "—" only reflects the absence of collected data and does not imply the organization was inactive in that medium.

Source: Data compiled from David B. Magleby, J. Quin Monson, and Kelly D. Patterson, "2004 Campaign Communications Database," (Center for the Study of Elections and Democracy: Brigham Young University, 2005).

Note: Abbreviations: DSCC, Democratic Senatorial Campaign Committee; PAC, political action committee; NARAL, National Abortion and Reproductive Rights Action League; AFL-CIO, American Federation of Labor and Congress of Industrial Organizations; NRSC, National Republican Senatorial Committee; AARP, American Association of Retired Persons.

THE EFFECTS OF MONEY

THE GROUND WAR

As in 2002, the Thune campaign relied on the Republican Victory operation to provide grassroots organization for both state and federal candidates, including voter registration, voter identification, persuasion, and GOTV. However, the tactics had to become more proactive, given the nature of the race and changes wrought by BCRA. While Jason Glodt, executive director of the South Dakota Republican party, reported that BCRA had crippled the state party's ability to raise money, the party actually increased the number of donors dramatically due to more aggressive fundraising and national interest in South Dakota's Senate race. Glodt said that the state GOP had to fund the grassroots effort in its entirety and was unable to rely on support from the national party committees as in years past. In earlier campaigns state party ground war efforts were supported largely by contributions from national party organizations, but in 2004 the BCRA soft-money ban meant the state party had to rely on hard money. Despite these limits, both the Republican Party and the Thune campaign managed to fill the financial void by expanding their donor networks.

In addition to financial restraints, BCRA also prevented party staffers from volunteering for other campaigns and state parties from talking to candidates about mail or ads prior to deployment. These rule changes meant that both the state party and the Thune campaign had to change their fundraising tactics and learn to operate with less coordination with the NRSC. This is not to say that the NRSC stayed clear of this campaign. The NRSC actively supported the Thune campaign, contributing $2.2 million to the air war and a total of 34 unique campaign communications.

The Republican party set up 12 Victory field offices around the state, expanding to 17 toward the end of the campaign. The offices hired 40 full-time staff and 500 to 600 part-time staff who worked up to 30 hours a week on voter registration, voter identification, persuasion, and GOTV. During the final 72 hours, they deployed approximately 6,000 volunteers as poll watchers, phone callers, door-to-door canvassers, and drivers.[32] The Victory program changed its voter identification method and used phone calls, door-to-door contacts, and yard-sign acceptance contacts to link voters to issues. They kept meticulous notes on voters and cross-tabulated issues and Bush supporters. Identification data were used to target 12 groups for persuasion, including women, pro-life, pro-gun, business, soft Republicans who voted for Johnson in 2002, conservative Democrats, seniors, youth, self-identified Bush–Daschle and Bush–Herseth voters, and the Republican base. Volunteers were assigned to call voters who "matched" their political concerns. For example, pro-life supporters called pro-life voters, veterans called veterans, and women called women. South Dakota's Republican party managed to fund and coordinate an aggressive ground war despite concerns about the impact of BCRA.

The Daschle campaign, long known for its competence and efficiency in field operations, relied on its own operatives to staff its field operation and did not coordinate the campaign with the state party, which began the election cycle with a $350,000 debt from 2002. Daschle's 2004 campaign opened 29 field offices across the state, including one on every Indian reservation. State party involvement was largely confined to the final two weeks when the Democratic party spent $1 million federal dollars, including $100,000 transferred by Senator Chuck Schumer (D-NY) to the South Dakota Democratic party for GOTV operations. They paid canvassers, phone callers, and drivers and chartered two jets from Dulles International Airport to bring 1,000 people to South Dakota from Washington, D.C., for the week before election day.[33]

Organizations active in the state, mostly Republican allies of the Thune campaign, also aided in the ground war with numerous campaign communications, including e-mail, mail, newspaper, magazine, personal contact, phone calls, radio, and television. In total unique campaign communications for Democratic allies and Republican allies (see Table 4.4), Republican efforts exceeded Democratic efforts 240 to 162. The greatest difference between the two campaigns was the level of party communication support: Republican party organizations contacted voters at seven times the rate of Democratic party organizations. While Daschle's candidate committee raised and spent more money than Thune's, Thune enjoyed more support from political parties and interest groups. Consider the efforts of the U.S. Chamber of Commerce as a case-in-point. In addition to purchasing ads, it dispatched an emissary to meet with local chambers across the state to convince them to support the U.S. Chamber's preferred candidate. Their considerable efforts to minimize defections to the Daschle camp will not show up in Federal Election Commission reports; however, they cannot be ignored in the larger picture of third-party activities in this election.

A final point of interest in the 2004 ground war concerns the candidates' treatment of Native American issues and voters. Until 2002, neither party expended much effort on Native Americans. Historically, Republicans have conceded the Native American vote to the Democratic party and have not spent time campaigning on reservations. Democrats assumed that the Native American vote would be overwhelmingly Democratic and generally spent little time on persuasion, although they always included reservations in the party's GOTV efforts. Turnout in reservation counties was always strikingly low in a state known for its high voter turnout. But the Native American vote was seen as decisive in the 2002 Senate race and became a source of continuing controversy throughout the 2004 contest.

In 2002, the incumbent U.S. Senator Tim Johnson (D) won over challenger John Thune (R) by a margin of 524 votes. Among the last counties to report results were two reservation counties that provided the final votes necessary for Johnson's win. Republicans charged voter fraud, though these charges were later dismissed. In the wake of the fraud allegations, the Republican-controlled state legislature passed a new law requiring voters to show photo identification at the polls or sign an affidavit concerning their identity. The June 1, 2004, special congressional election was the first test of this new voter requirement.

In response to the new law, the Four Directions Committee, a nonprofit 501(c)(4) organization, was created "to ensure fair treatment for Native American voters."[34] It was funded by out-of-state Indian tribes and staffed by the former executive director of the South Dakota Democratic party, Brett Healey. During the 2004 general election, the Four Directions Committee worked to educate voters about the process and their rights, ensure that auditors were available for early voting, and help people get to the polls by paying those with vehicles to drive others to the polls. They coordinated their work with tribal chairs and councils to ensure their support. Finally, they trained lawyers and poll watchers prior to election day.

The Northern Plains Tribal Voter Education Project, a nonpartisan 501(c)(3) organization working to increase Native American turnout by 10 percent regionally through personal contact, was also active in areas populated by Native Americans. It was funded with a grant from the Center for Community Change in Washington, D.C. At the end of September, the group allied with the United Sioux Tribes, another 501(c)(3) with similar aims. Strategies included deploying hundreds of largely Native American canvassers to solicit votes on the reservations and in Rapid City, taking people to vote early and giving rides to the polls on election day. As Chas Jewett of the Northern Plain Tribal Voter Education Project said, "When a brown face walks up to a brown face, a different kind of communication takes place."[35] The project also targeted women who were eligible to vote in 2002 but failed to do so. True Majority, a liberal organization, bolstered late volunteer recruitment efforts by asking for volunteers through its extensive national e-mail list on October 29 to help on reservations during the last few days of the campaign.

Democrats focused more attention on the reservations in 2004 than they did in 2002. Daschle had field offices on every reservation and set up a registration office on the populous Pine Ridge Reservation eight months before the election. Instead of bringing in political staff from off the reservation, the Daschle campaign hired local Native Americans to canvass, persuade, and GOTV. Daschle visited each reservation in the state and won the endorsement of all the tribal governments.[36]

Thune's 2004 campaign and the Republican party courted Native American voters in response to Thune's close 2002 loss. That year Thune received only 8 percent of the Native American vote, which had, as in previous years, been written off by the Republican party.[37] This year would be different. Republicans set up an office in a prime location on Pine Ridge

Reservation near the gas station and taco stand. Bruce Whelan, a Lakota Sioux who is chair of the Shannon County Republican party and is employed by the Republicans, said that "most" Native Americans are really Republicans because of their belief in limited government, family values, and empowerment,[38] and that reservations are Catholic and pro-life. The Republican party responded to this demography by pushing a pro-life message and the need for change after 26 years of empty promises from Daschle. The party went to every powwow and sponsored voter registration, as well as other events.[39] Thune visited Shannon County six times, played basketball in Eagle Butte, and attended the Black Hills Powwow, where the state Republican party sponsored a "chili feed."[40] In a postelection interview, Thune's campaign manager Dick Wadhams noted, "Thune always did well on reservations as a House member. Our argument is that Daschle's been here for 26 years. Has your life gotten better? We included this message in our debates, in radio interviews, in ads in Indian publications, and in special brochures for reservations."[41] Although Daschle benefited from his normal majority of the Native American vote and a high voter turnout that increased his votes in Native American counties significantly, Thune increased the proportion of his Native American vote to 13 percent in 2004. In two important Native American counties he more than doubled his votes: In Shannon County votes went from 248 in 2002 to 564 in 2004, and from 464 to 776 in Todd County.[42]

THE IMPACT OF BCRA

According to Dick Wadhams, Thune's campaign manager, "BCRA has made the process less accountable and more confusing . . . As a practical matter, BCRA encourages outside activity that's not accountable to campaigns. Groups throw ads up there independent of the campaigns. The 'You're Fired' ads were so poorly done. We hated them . . . you never knew who would come in and say something for which the campaign would be held accountable by the voters."[43] However, issue ads were a part of this pre-BCRA world and had the same reaction from campaign managers. Jason Glodt, executive director of South Dakota GOP, noted that "(t)he law is too complex. It is hard to know what can be coordinated, what federal money can be spent on. There are two different rulebooks for state and federal campaigns. The NRSC had to pay a firm with a blank check and had to trust them. They couldn't see the ad. Campaigns were not allowed to see non-allocable mail. They couldn't coordinate ads."[44] These observations about party independent expenditures are not unique to South Dakota. In all, Glodt felt that the law takes power away from the parties, making it harder to raise money and run ground-war efforts because resources go to special interest groups with more radical approaches. He made a point to note that influence and power have "shifted to these more radical groups."[45] This seems to contradict one of the main conclusions of this study, however, as candidates and parties raised more money than ever before.[46]

The concern of state party leadership is the perceived marginalization of the political parties in the electoral arena at the state level. In all, it is interesting that Thune's campaign manager and the director of the South Dakota Republican party hold such negative views of BCRA, because we estimate that the outside groups had a positive impact for their candidate. This sentiment was echoed by the executive director of the South Dakota Democratic party, Jason Schulte, who felt that under BCRA the state party was "inherently less relevant." He pointed out that "money that used to go to the parties now goes to 527s. Five-twenty-sevens are bigger players. The challenge now is to raise money in an off year. It's going to be harder to keep the institution of the party going." Parties will have to "become more creative in fundraising."[47] The fundraising experience of South Dakota's parties this year is arguably unique to a high profile race. The concerns of party leadership are clearly future oriented and reflect a preference for unfettered political parties over interest groups.

CONCLUSION

Given that Thune, the winner, received assistance from outside groups and Daschle refused it, the perception that these groups are extremely influential in contemporary elections will likely be strengthened. The election was a referendum on Daschle's performance in office. The "gone Washington" or "two Daschles" theme stuck, and the Daschle campaign's clout argument was not strong enough to counteract the ideological fit. Thune also enjoyed a considerable push from his framing of moral issues. Clearly he came out on the right side of many in the South Dakota religious community and was aided by the assertive role of state and national church groups. These factors contributed to Thune's improved performance in the more liberal East River communities and helped maintain his large lead in conservative West River communities. Thune did somewhat better among Native Americans than in 2002 and held down his losses in the populous Minnehaha County. He also did generally well along the I-29 corridor in the eastern part of the state. These gains were enough to provide the margin of victory that had eluded him two years earlier. Daschle was unable to break through the negative role of "chief obstructionist" or the perception that he had drifted from being a local South Dakotan.

It appears that BCRA may serve to make face-to-face voter contact by the state parties more difficult by de-funding that element of the state campaign system that (1) exists from election to election and therefore has institutional memory; (2) is the basic voter mobilization system; and (3) has a long-term stake in the electoral system. Either state parties will have to find new independent funding mechanisms, or they will wither and be replaced by large national nonprofit and 527 organizations as a primary intermediary system for voters.

A closing thought that should not be overlooked is the increasing nationalization of key federal campaigns. South Dakota's 2004 Senate race provides plenty of evidence of this nationalization through the use of blogs, Internet sites, and coordinated efforts to direct campaign contributions and locate and place volunteer resources. This trend seems a bit ironic given the state electorate's strong preference for local politics. This election, however, showed that national players using new online technologies to direct resources to key races can and will play the local politics game.

NOTES

1. John Bart and James Meader, "The More You Spend, the Less They Listen: The South Dakota U.S. Senate Race," in *The Last Hurrah?: Soft Money and Issue Advocacy in the 2002 Congressional Elections*, eds. David B. Magleby and J. Quin Monson (Washington D.C.: Brookings Institution Press, 2004), pp. 159–180.
2. Many would come to agree with the *Wall Street Journal*'s characterization of the "Daschle Dead Zone," meaning his obstruction of the president's agenda.
3. Bart and Meader, "The More You Spend, the Less They Listen."
4. Richard Braunstein, *Initiative and Referendum Voting: Governing Through Direct Democracy in the United States* (New York: LFB Scholarly Publishing, 2004), pp. 1, 38.
5. Jennifer Sanderson, "Thune Backs Amendment Banning Gay Marriages," *Sioux Falls Argus Leader*, July 9, 2004, p. 1B.
6. Tom Minnery, vice president of government public policy, Focus on the Family, telephone interview by David B. Magleby, J. Quin Monson, and Betsey Gimbel, December 16, 2004.
7. Steve Hemmingsen, "My Name is Steve and I'm a Polito-holic," Keloland.com, www.keloland.com/News/WeighingIn/NewsDetail4731.cfm?ID=22,36483 (accessed December 9, 2004).
8. South Dakota produces over 400 million gallons of ethanol each year.
9. Steve Hildebrand, quoted in Hemmingsen, "My Name is Steve and I'm a Polito-holic."
10. John Stanton, "Lobbying and the Law: Bloggers Targeted Daschle and the Press," *National Journal*, November 20, 2004, p. 3540.
11. SouthDakotaPolitics.com, southdakotapolitics.blogs.com/south_dakota_politics/kranz_watch/index.html (accessed May 10, 2006).
12. Talmage Ekanger, *The Other Side of Tom Daschle*, (Ottawa, IL: Green Hill Publishers, 2004).
13. Ibid.
14. Lindsey L. Dorneman, finance assistant, A Lot of People Supporting Tom Daschle, telephone interview by Elizabeth T. Smith, January 6, 2005.
15. Chris Cillizza, "Daschle's Five-Year, $9.5M Spending Spree," *Roll Call*, February 26, 2004, www.rollcall.com/issues/49_83/news/4506-1.html (accessed January 18, 2005).
16. Andrew Golodny, director of Internet operations, A Lot of People Supporting Tom Daschle, telephone interview by Elizabeth T. Smith, January 6, 2005.
17. Dorneman, interview, January 6, 2005.
18. Dick Wadhams, campaign manager, John Thune for U.S. Senate, interview by Elizabeth T. Smith, Sioux Falls, SD, November 22, 2004.
19. Jason Glodt, executive director, South Dakota Republican party, interview by Elizabeth T. Smith, Pierre, SD, November 16, 2004.
20. Mike Madden, "Thune Attacks Daschle Record at Convention," *Sioux Falls Argus Leader*, August 31, 2004, p. A1. See also Chris Cillizza, "Thune to Get Star Billing This Week" *Roll Call*, August 30, 2004.

21. Stephen Dinan, "South Dakota Becomes Turf War," *Washington Times*, May 23, 2004, p. A2.
22. Sheryl Gay Stolberg, "The 2004 Campaign: The Senate; Daschle Has Race on His Hands and Interloper on His Turf," *New York Times*, May 23, 2004, p. A20.
23. Club for Growth, "Why Is the Club for Growth Necessary," www.clubforgrowth.org/why.php. (accessed August 3, 2004).
24. Steve Hildebrand, "Wealthy California Conservatives Try to 'Fire' Daschle," campaign e-mail (July 26, 2004) Information on contributions and expenditures confirmed on the Internal Revenue Service Web site at 'YOU%27RE+FIRED,' forms.irs.gov/politicalOrgsSearch/search/gotoSearchDrillDown.action?pacId='22728'&criteriaName= (accessed December 15, 2004).
25. Bill Miller, vice president and political director, U.S. Chamber of Commerce, interview by David B. Magleby and Kristina Gale, Washington D.C., November 9, 2004.
26. Brody Mullins, "Chamber Targets Daschle," *Roll Call*, February 2, 2004, www.rollcall.com/issues/49_71/vested/4162-1.html (accessed January 18, 2005).
27. We realize that the figure of $410,000 for ad-buys is higher than the $161,618 noted in Table 4.3 and expect that the difference can be explained by either deficiencies in the record-keeping system of the stations where the data were collected and/or by the data collection methodology employed for this study. In any case, we are confident from the interview given by Bill Miller that his statement of $410,000 expended in this area is correct.
28. Miller, interview, November 9, 2004.
29. Table 4.3 provides ad-buy data only, and not total expenditures from groups, which are likely greater. Ad buys do not include what was actually spent on the ground war. The U.S. Chamber spent $410,000 on TV and radio combined. Miller, interview, November 9, 2004.
30. Stephen Moore, president, Club for Growth, e-mail communication to members, November 17, 2004.
31. It is important to note that Table 4.3 represents combined efforts for U.S. House and U.S. Senate elections in the state. In some categories, particularly for political party expenditures (as opposed to advocacy group expenditures), it is hard to disaggregate the ad-buy data to determine the number of spots and expenditures meant specifically for the Herseth–Diedrich race or Daschle–Thune race. Still, it is clear from a review of the independent groups participating in this election and our knowledge of what the groups' interests were and who the players were that the overwhelming support of non-candidate efforts went to the Thune campaign.
32. Glodt, interview, November 16, 2004.
33. Jason Schulte, executive director, South Dakota Democratic party, interview by Elizabeth T. Smith, Pierre, SD, November 17, 2004.
34. David Kranz, "Group: Voter Suit Not Political," *Sioux Falls Argus Leader,* June 30, 2004, p. 1B.
35. Chas Jewett, state director, Northern Plains Tribal Voter Education Project, Rural Ethnic Institute, telephone interview by Elizabeth T. Smith, October 31, 2004.
36. Geoff Earle, "Native American Votes Critical in S.D. Contest," *The Hill*, October 13, 2004, p. 1.
37. South Dakota Secretary of State, "United States Senator," www.sdsos.gov/electionsvoteregistration/pastelections_electioninfo04_GEsenate returns.sh (accessed December 15, 2004).
38. John J. Fialka, "Daschle Works to Get Out the Indian Vote," *Wall Street Journal*, November 1, 2004, p. A4.
39. Glodt, interview, November 16, 2004.
40. Earle, "Native American Votes Critical in S.D. Contest," p. 1; Glodt, interview, November 16, 2004.
41. Wadhams, interview, November 22, 2004.
42. Dirk Lammers, "GOP Makes Gains on Reservations, Vote Totals Show," *Sioux Falls Argus Leader*, November 12, 2004, p. B3.
43. Wadhams, interview, November 22, 2004.
44. Glodt, interview, November 16, 2004.
45. John J. Fialka, "Daschle Works to Get Out the Indian Vote," *Wall Street Journal*, November 1, 2004. p. A4.
46. See Chapter 1 in this volume.
47. Jason Schulte, executive director, South Dakota Democratic party, interview by Elizabeth T. Smith, Pierre, SD, November 17, 2004.

5

DÉJÀ VU ALL OVER AGAIN

THE 2004 KANSAS THIRD DISTRICT CONGRESSIONAL RACE

ALLAN J. CIGLER

University of Kansas

On November 2, 2004, three-term Democratic incumbent Dennis Moore defeated his Republican challenger, Kris Kobach, by a stunning 55 to 43 percent margin, winning by over 36,000 votes in a district with a substantial Republican registration advantage. To outside observers, the margin was especially surprising, considering that President Bush won the district by an overwhelming 61 percent of the vote. To those familiar with the political context, Kobach's defeat was not unanticipated; it simply represented the latest in a series of electoral debacles to befall the district's Republican congressional candidates due to cultural divisions within the party.

THE ELECTORAL CONTEXT

The Kansas Third District shares many of the characteristics typically associated with a "safe" Republican House constituency, including a party registration advantage greater than 15 percent.[1] The district is comprised of three counties in eastern Kansas, but it is dominated by one: Fast-growing Johnson County at its eastern end is a wealthy suburb of Kansas City, Missouri, where Republicans outnumber Democrats by more than 90,000. Two-thirds of all of the district's voters reside in Johnson County. Douglas County anchors the district's western boundary; nominally Republican in terms of registration, it is a liberal enclave, due in part to the presence of the University of Kansas. Wyandotte County, which comprises much of the northern and central portions of the district, is a working-class area with the state's largest minority population.

Until Moore defeated first-term incumbent Republican Vincent Snowbarger in a close 1998 election, Republicans had won all congressional elections rather easily for the previous 34 years.[2] From the New Deal until the late 1980s, Republicans throughout the state generally embodied fiscal rather than social conservatism. Snowbarger's 1996 victory resulted from an insurgent movement that enabled Christian Right elements to capture the state party organization as well as the county organization in the Third District.[3] The Christian Right takeover, however, sparked a counter-mobilization by the moderates, who recaptured the organization in 1998 after a bitter struggle.[4] Since then, Republicans have experienced a continuing internecine conflict that has altered the style and intensity of the state's electoral politics. Nowhere has the battle been as fierce as it has in the Kansas Third Congressional District.

Divisions within the party and the resulting selection of congressional candidates who emerged from their own primaries as representatives of only one wing enabled a moderate Democrat, Moore, to defeat the incumbent Snowbarger in 1998 and Republican challengers in the next two congressional elections. In each election, the conventional wisdom was that if Republicans could unite behind a candidate, they could defeat Moore. Registration figures appeared to be on the side of Republican optimists as well; Johnson County has been growing by over 10,000 persons a year over the past decade, and the Republican registration advantage over Democrats continues at a nearly two-to-one clip.[5] Early in 2004, it appeared that the congressional seat would be returned to its presumptive Republican home.

THE 2004 REPUBLICAN PRIMARY

One cannot fully understand the 2004 general election without understanding the dynamics of the Republican primary. Adam Taff, a physically attractive and articulate moderate, was all but anointed to be the nominee in 2004. Two years earlier, Taff, a former Navy pilot, had appeared as an unknown to win a close primary against a candidate endorsed and supported financially by the NRCC and backed by the district's social conservatives. Taff then went on to give Moore his closest contest, losing by just 7,000 votes.[6] Despite being outspent by Moore and having little national party support, Taff impressed party moderates and at least pacified most social conservatives by modifying his position on abortion to make it somewhat more restrictive. Taff announced he would run again in 2004, kept his campaign office open, and quickly received the preprimary endorsements of establishment Republicans.

However, Taff was challenged by two social conservatives in the primary. His most serious challenger was Kris Kobach, a constitutional law professor at the University of Missouri–Kansas City. Kobach, a Harvard graduate, had a law degree from Yale and a doctorate in political science from Oxford. At 38, his only previous elected public office was serving on a city council, but he had recently been part of the Bush administration, serving as an adviser to

Attorney General John Ashcroft. While in Washington, Kobach was credited with writing the sections of the Patriot Act dealing with registration and tracking of foreign visitors. Immigration and security were Kobach's major campaign issues early on, but it was his positions on moral issues that made the difference in the primary.

In the spring of 2004, the Kansas legislature had turned down an effort to place on the fall ballot a state constitutional amendment banning gay marriage. Evangelical ministers throughout the state were outraged; they organized to raise the political consciousness of social conservatives in order to defeat state legislators and candidates for other offices who did not share their views. The evangelical community in the Third District was especially energized and embraced Kobach in the congressional race, working to register members of evangelical churches, getting advanced voting ballots in members' hands, and educating them on the candidates' positions on the issues.[7] Kobach encouraged the relationship, and joint appearances by the candidate and evangelical ministers were commonplace. Kobach attacked Taff for being a liberal, accusing him of supporting the gay-rights agenda, easy access to abortion, and amnesty for illegal immigrants. One particularly hard-hitting, direct-mail ad late in the campaign depicted two plastic-figure men, arms locked, atop a wedding cake. The caption read, "I, John, take you, Larry . . . " At the bottom of the ad were the words, "Not in Kansas!" The back of the ad outlined Kobach's views on traditional marriage and his support for the president's call for an amendment to the Constitution on the matter. Taff opposed the measure. The ad both energized social conservatives for Kobach and incensed moderates against him.

Although a poll taken two weeks before the election gave Taff a healthy lead, the end result was still not settled on election day.[8] Provisional ballots had to be counted, and the outcome was unknown for six days. Low voter turn-out helped Kobach win the primary by only 207 votes.

THE CANDIDATES

The Moore campaign was caught off guard by Kobach's primary victory, but quickly recognized that it was a blessing in disguise. In all three previous campaigns, Moore's strategy was identical: make an intense effort to mobilize the district's Democrats, then appeal to moderate Republicans and independents by conveying an image of a bipartisan political moderate, more in tune with district values. This time it would be even easier. After three terms, Moore had developed a sophisticated constituency service operation, had a reputation as a strong pro-business advocate for district industries, was a member of the Blue Dog caucus in Congress, and was an initial supporter of President Bush's Iraq initiative and tax cuts. Claiming to be a moderate while portraying his opponent as an extreme social conservative would be relatively easy. Soon after the primary, national analyst Larry Sabato proclaimed that "the Republicans have severely damaged themselves again. Dennis Moore is the luckiest member of Congress."[9]

The Moore and Kobach campaign organizations, strategies, and financial resources could not have been more distinct from each other. The Kobach campaign conveyed the feeling of being an ideological movement rather than a party operation. There was no consultant hired to coordinate overall activities; decisions on hiring pollsters, media consultants, and fundraisers were made largely by Kobach and his campaign manager, Todd Abrajano, a 2002 graduate of Yale.[10] Volunteers were typically unpaid and were often recruited at rallies or church meetings.[11] The emphasis was on grassroots efforts to register and turn out evangelical voters.

The Moore campaign, in contrast, represented the model of the professional campaign organization.[12] Using the same consultants as in Moore's past elections, the campaign conducted extensive polling, including tracking and exit polls, and used focus groups to design commercials and direct-mail flyers. Volunteers were usually paid. State and local party connections were close, and together the two groups coordinated a massive GOTV effort directed at areas with a high concentration of known Democrats, large numbers of independents, and potential Republican defectors.

MONEY

Moore, who had faced no primary opposition, raised and spent a record amount for a Kansas congressional race. According to FEC data, the incumbent raised over $2.3 million and spent a like amount (see Table 5.1). Kobach,

TABLE 5.1 CANDIDATE RECEIPTS AND EXPENDITURES, KANSAS THIRD CONGRESSIONAL DISTRICT RACE, 2003 TO 2004

	DENNIS MOORE (D)	KRIS KOBACH (R)
From PACs	$1,062,968	$226,025
From individuals	1,211,737	868,105
From party	4,385	16,000
From candidate	0	62,470
Other contributions	33,500	112,991
Total receipts	2,312,590	1,285,591
Total expenditures	2,362,887	1,191,231
Cash on hand (as of 12/31/04)	26,276	94,351

Source: Federal Election Commission, "2003–04 U.S. House and U.S. Senate Candidate Info," December 31, 2004, www.fecinfo.com/cgi-win/x_candidate.exe?DoFn=&sYR=2004 (accessed February 11, 2005).

Note: Abbreviation: PAC, political action committee.

who had depleted much of his money in the primary, still did relatively well for a non-incumbent. He raised nearly $1.3 million and spent just under $1.2 million. When it became apparent late in the race that Kobach was going to lose, his campaign virtually stopped spending, and he repaid the $51,000 he had lent his campaign.[13]

The sources of both candidates' funds roughly paralleled what one would expect when an incumbent faces a challenger. Moore received over $1 million from PACs and a little over $1.2 million from individuals. The maximum individual PAC contributions of $10,000 came mostly from unions, contributed a total of nearly $190,000 to the Moore coffers, but business PACs contributed the largest aggregate amount of slightly over $418,000. Moore, a former district attorney, was generously supported by the trial lawyer community. Consistent with other 2004 contests, Moore also did well in raising money from individuals.

Kobach received 18 percent of his funds from PACs, the bulk of these contributions coming from ideological PACs, including those advocating immigration reform. Individuals who took their cues from a variety of ideological PACs were important contributors as well. Individual contributions to the Kobach campaign, the candidate's main source of funds, were largely the result of fundraisers. These were most successful when held in conjunction with visits of prominent Republicans to the district; one held in September featuring Vice President Dick Cheney raised over $200,000.[14] Another fundraiser brought former U.S. Representative J. C. Watts to town.

Both parties mounted substantial independent expenditure campaigns. As summarized in Table 5.2, the Democrats expended nearly $200,000 and the Republicans over $618,000. Both party committees reflect a mix of spending *for* their candidate and *against* the opponent.

TABLE 5.2   INDEPENDENT EXPENDITURES BY PARTY COMMITTEE, KANSAS THIRD CONGRESSIONAL DISTRICT RACE, 2003 TO 2004

PARTY COMMITTEE	CANDIDATE	INDEPENDENT EXPENDITURES FOR	INDEPENDENT EXPENDITURES AGAINST	TOTAL	PARTY TOTAL
DSCC					$694,017
	Kris Kobach	0	$324,900	$324,900	
	Dennis Moore	$369,117	0	369,117	
NRSC					618,259
	Kris Kobach	140,303	0	140,303	
	Dennis Moore	0	477,956	477,956	

Source: Federal Election Commission, ftp://ftp.fec.gov/FEC (accessed January 5, 2005).

Note: Abbreviations: DSCC, Democratic Senatorial Campaign Committee; NRSC, National Republican Senatorial Committee.

TABLE 5.3 THE AIR WAR: TELEVISION AND RADIO ADVERTISING EXPENDITURES, KANSAS THIRD CONGRESSIONAL DISTRICT RACE, 2004[a]

TYPE AND ORGANIZATION	TV	RADIO	TOTAL $ SPENT	CMAG TV
Democratic Allies[b]				
Candidates				
Dennis Moore for U.S. Congress	$719,034	$9,554	**$728,588**	$1,269,693
Political Parties				
DCCC	515,445	—	**515,445**	300,278
Republican Allies[b]				
Candidates				
Kobach for Congress	380,226	—	**380,226**	391,676
Political Parties				
NRCC	470,801	—	**470,801**	374,072
Interest Groups				
Progress for America Voter Fund	23,826	—	**23,826**	333,723
National Right to Work Committee				
PAC	5,810	—	**5,810**	—

[a]Please see Appendix A for a more detailed data explanation. The ad-buy data collected for this study may contain extraneous data because of the difficulty in determining the content of the ads. The parties or interest groups that purchased the ad buys possibly ran some ads promoting House, Senate, or presidential candidates or ballot propositions not in the study's sample but still within that media market. Unless the participating academics were able to determine the exact content of the ad buy from the limited information given by the station, the data may contain observations that do not pertain to the study's relevant House, Senate, or presidential battleground races. For comparison purposes the Campaign Media Analysis Group data are included in the table. Because of the sheer volume of television and radio stations and varying degrees of compliance in providing ad-buy information, data on spending by various groups might be incomplete. There data do not include every station in the state. This table is not intended to represent comprehensive organization spending or activity within the sample races. Television ads purchased from national cable stations that aired in this state are not reflected in this table. A more complete picture can be obtained by examining this table with Table 5.4.

[b]Certain organizations that maintained neutrality were categorized according to which candidates their ads supported or attacked or whether the organization was openly anti- or pro- conservative or liberal.

It appears that several of the television spots originally purchased by the Democratic Congressional Campaign Committee were canceled. This comes from looking at the total independent expenditures and Campaign Media Analysis Group data.

In blank cells, "—" only reflects the absence of collected data and does not imply the organization was inactive in that medium.

Source: Data compiled from David B. Magleby, J. Quin Monson, and Kelly D. Patterson, "2004 Campaign Communications Database," (Center for the Study of Elections and Democracy: Brigham Young University, 2005); and Campaign Media Analysis Group data.

Note: Abbreviations: DCCC, Democratic Congressional Campaign Committee; NRCC, National Republican Congressional Committee; PAC, political action committee.

The campaigns used their funds for both air war and ground war activities (see Table 5.3 and Table 5.4). Overall, Kobach for Congress sent out eight unique pieces of mail, ran five different television ads, and made five unique phone calls. Moore for Congress, with a financial advantage, was credited with 33 unique ads, including nine distinct television ads and seven different pieces of mail. The campaign also made 11 distinct phone calls. Both

TABLE 5.4 NUMBER OF UNIQUE CAMPAIGN COMMUNICATIONS BY ORGANIZATION, KANSAS THIRD CONGRESSIONAL DISTRICT RACE, 2004[a]

TYPE AND ORGANIZATION	*Type of Campaign Communication*						
	E-MAIL	MAIL	PERSONAL CONTACT	PHONE CALLS	RADIO ADS	TV ADS	TOTAL
Democratic Allies[b]							
Candidates							
Dennis Moore for U.S. Congress	1	7	3	1	11	9	32
Political Parties							
Kansas Democratic Party	—	8	—	—	3	—	11
Democratic Coordinated Campaign of Kansas	—	—	—	1	4	—	5
DCCC	—	—	—	—	—	2	2
Douglas County Democrats	—	—	—	—	1	—	1
Interest Groups							
Mainstream PAC	—	1	—	—	1	—	2
Human Rights Campaign	—	1	—	—	—	—	1
Kansas Democratic Victory Fund	—	1	—	—	—	—	1
Kansas Education Association	—	1	—	—	—	—	1
League of Conservation Voters	—	1	—	—	—	—	1
National Association of Home Builders	—	1	—	—	—	—	1
Sierra Club	—	1	—	—	—	—	1

Republican Allies[b]

Candidates						
Kobach for Congress	—	8	1	5	5	19
Political Parties						
NRCC	—	12	—	2	7	21
Republican Party of Kansas	—	1	—	—	—	1
Interest Groups						
Kansans for Life	1	2	—	—	—	3
National Right to Work Committee PAC	—	3	—	—	—	3
National Right to Life	—	1	—	1	—	2
National Pro-Life Alliance	—	1	—	—	—	1
NRA Political Victory Fund	—	1	—	—	—	1

Nonpartisan

Interest Groups						
AARP	—	1	—	—	—	1

[a]See Appendix A for a more detailed data explanation. Data represent the number of unique or distinct pieces or ads by the group and do not represent a count of total items sent or made. This table is not intended to portray comprehensive organization activity within the sample races. A more complete picture can be obtained by examining this table together with Table 5.3.

[b]Certain organizations that maintained neutrality were categorized according to which candidates their ads supported or attacked or whether the organization was openly anti- or pro- conservative or liberal.

In blank cells, "—" only reflects the absence of collected data and does not imply the organization was inactive in that medium.

Source: Data compiled from David B. Magleby, J. Quin Monson, and Kelly D. Patterson, "2004 Campaign Communications Database," (Center for the Study of Elections and Democracy: Brigham Young University, 2005).

Note: Abbreviations: DCCC, Democratic Congressional Campaign Committee; PAC, political action committee; NRCC, National Republican Congressional Committee; NRA, National Rifle Association; AARP, American Association of Retired Persons.

candidates spent nearly one-third of their total campaign budgets on television ads, but Moore's overall funding advantage enabled his campaign to outspend his competitor on ads by nearly $339,000. Radio advertising by both campaigns was little used.

The Kobach campaign started advertising on television a few days after the August primary. The ads were positive, and showed Kobach with his wife and family, conveying the importance he placed on marriage and family values, proclaiming his Kansas roots, and acquainting viewers with the candidate's resume. Glossy direct mailings from the campaign appeared in short order, emphasizing the campaign's theme of "A stronger Kansas. A safer America." Ads noted Kobach's support for the president's tax cuts, as well as his stance on "defending marriage and Kansas values" but emphasized the candidate's "priorities for a safer America," which included deploying 20,000 National Guard personnel to stop terrorists at the borders and "[return] the rule of law to immigration."

Kobach for Congress quickly turned to attack mode as the campaign attempted to link national security issues with the security of families in Kansas. Similar television and direct-mail ads accused Moore of having a "left-wing voting record." In one particularly hard-hitting ad entitled, "Why is Dennis Moore so . . . WORRIED?" Moore was chastised for failing to protect the country from terrorism, voting against using National Guard troops to protect the borders, voting to weaken the Patriot Act, and co-sponsoring legislation giving amnesty and in-state tuition to illegal aliens. Moore's opposition to tort reform and the Federal Marriage Amendment were also noted as secondary issues.

Moore's strategy in the early part of the campaign was to avoid being defensive by directly confronting the issues that Kobach was raising, but to nevertheless indicate that his record in the area of building a safe and secure nation and state was quite strong, both in terms of traditional physical security (e.g., more Homeland Security funds for local police) and matters of economic security, especially in protecting Social Security. Television ads and direct mailings boasted of Moore leading the fight to bring the AMBER Alert system, a plan designed to locate kidnapped children quickly, to Kansas City and supporting soldiers in Iraq and Afghanistan by sponsoring legislation that directed the Department of Defense to pay all of the travel costs associated with coming home for rest and recuperation. Television ads typically ended with Moore looking in the camera and proclaiming, "I never stopped working for families and never will." Moore stayed away from social issues in his ads, fearful of offending African American and Hispanic voters, a number of whom would not approve of his views on abortion and gay marriage.[15]

It was not until mid-September that the Moore campaign started doing its first "soft" negative ads, attacking Kobach's free-market positions on Social Security and Medicare and his emphasis on privatization. Soon the Moore campaign turned to attack ads that his opponents, and probably most who viewed the television and direct-mail ads, saw as attacking Kobach's character. The most devastating were designed to undercut Kobach's credibility on immigration by raising questions about his relationship to a number of anti-immigration groups.

Candidates of both parties usually avoid the issue of immigration. Republicans worry that supporting tougher immigration laws might anger their business allies that rely on cheap labor. Democrats typically do not want to remind voters that Democratic support of less-restrictive immigration laws may be related to a desire for minority groups' votes. Kobach's insistence on very restrictive immigration laws and tougher enforcement afforded Moore the opportunity to not-so-subtly label his opponent as an extremist at best and a racist at worst.

In television ads and direct mailings that hit the district in mid-October, the electorate was asked, "If you can judge a man by the company he keeps, what can we learn about a candidate who accepted seven contributions from groups with ties to white supremacists?" The ads pointed out that some groups who had contributed to Kobach were funded by what a *Wall Street Journal* writer had called "a white-supremacist outfit devoted to racial purity through eugenics."[16] The Federation for American Immigration Reform (FAIR), one Kobach contributor, is an organization that reputedly had received money from another organization that had financed research in eugenics, a controversial science "which seeks to improve the human race by selecting parents based on their hereditary traits."[17] Besides taking campaign funds from FAIR, Kobach was employed by the group during the election, on a retainer as their attorney in what other Moore ads called "a frivolous lawsuit" against the state of Kansas for granting in-state tuition to children of illegal aliens.[18] Kobach's connection to a radical fringe in the gun lobby had also been raised earlier.[19] The challenger had lost control of the agenda, and he became widely labeled as an extremist. A late mailing of the "I, John, take you, Larry . . . " ad, this time directed at Moore's opposition to the gay marriage amendment, probably just confirmed the label. A *Kansas City Star* poll conducted during the third week of October showed Kobach losing to Moore 50 percent to 38 percent with 11 percent of voters undecided. Eighteen percent of those Republicans polled said they supported Moore, as did 59 percent of independents.[20]

Phone banks were important in both of the candidates' campaigns. The Moore campaign made an estimated 400,000 calls.[21] Included were over 126,000 paid-persuasion calls and nearly 12,000 rapid-response calls. The campaign identified nearly 78,000 targets for a GOTV campaign and paid for nearly 78,000 GOTV live calls and a like number of GOTV auto-calls. It attempted to call each of the 78,000 likely Democratic voters on election day.

The Kobach campaign was not as systematically organized, but it did conduct a number of phone banks, most with the intent of both registering and persuading voters. The callers were typically unpaid volunteers; recipients of the calls were often targeted from lists of evangelicals, possibly gathered from church directories.[22] In trying to reach out to social conservatives, phone calls also targeted Catholic voters, focusing on the abortion issue.[23] On the Sunday before the election, volunteers put campaign flyers on car windows in church parking lots.

POLITICAL PARTIES

Both political parties were active in this race, though in different ways. With the state and local Republican party hampered by intra-party divisions and lack of funds, the advantage went to the fully mobilized Democrats.

DEMOCRATIC PARTY: GROUND WAR AND AIR WAR

In Moore's three previous victories, the state Democratic party's efforts were fundamental to his success, using the Kansas Coordinated Campaign (KCC) as a conduit.[24] The KCC is a quasi-independent political organization set up as an extension of the Kansas Democratic party and is reconstituted in election years as a statewide organization with a full-time director. In 2004, the KCC also had nine staff members in addition to the director. The staffers largely focused on the Third District: Four had primary responsibility for Wyandotte County, three for Douglas County, and two for Johnson County. With no other competitive congressional race in the state and few competitive state legislative races, almost all of their attention was directed toward supplementing the Moore campaign. The KCC also employed a variety of campaign service vendors and operated with a budget of "roughly $500,000."[25] The organization was largely funded by the campaigns it was to aid, with the aim of pooling resources to avoid duplication, especially on ground-war efforts.

Raising funds for the KCC was affected by BCRA. By law, Moore and his staff were forbidden from holding fundraisers and/or directly soliciting support for the party-coordinated campaign. Although those close to the campaign could and did encourage groups and individuals to independently contribute to the party effort, the lack of the celebrity presence of the congressman made fundraising more difficult. The Moore campaign was able, however, to transfer some of its own funds to the KCC, technically losing control of the money.[26] An indirect effect of BCRA was the rise of aggressive fundraising by various nationally oriented 527 committees in Kansas, creating a competition with the state party for limited donor money. Fundraisers were held by the state Democratic party, including ones where former Vice President Al Gore and former Texas Governor Ann Richards came to Kansas to raise funds designated for the KCC.

The KCC relied on sophisticated targeting efforts in order to run a precinct-level GOTV campaign. Using a Web-based program called Astro

2000, volunteers would either make targeted personal calls or go door-to-door to encourage likely Democratic voters to apply to register and/or advance vote.[27] Follow-up contacts were made within weeks if applications had not been received by the county clerk. Some potential voters were contacted three or four times. Volunteers were not only paid on an hourly basis, but were given an additional dollar "bounty" for every new Democrat registered and advance voting ballot turned in to the county clerk's office.

Although efforts concentrated on registering and turning out likely Democratic voters in Wyandotte and Douglas counties, 2004 was the first year in which KCC volunteers made forays into selected areas in Johnson County, passing out advanced voting applications and dropping off Moore campaign literature.[28] The effort focused only on areas where Moore had gotten at least 55 percent of the vote in the previous election. Efforts also targeted what volunteers referred to as "lazy Republicans," those who had voted just once in the last four elections, as well as independents. GOTV efforts were also extensive on election day; passenger vans filled with volunteers traveled to precincts that had been identified earlier in the day as "underperforming" in terms of Democratic turnout. These vans brought those who had not yet voted to the polls.[29]

The state Democratic party also supplemented Moore's direct-mail efforts by sending out eight unique campaign flyers and commissioning three unique phone calls. Most were highly critical of Kobach's stance on the immigration issue, while others slammed Kobach's consumption tax plan, claiming that the plan would "increase tax burdens on middle class families by 50 percent." Like the ads from the Moore campaign, the state party's ads also avoided social issues. These ads enabled Moore to run a largely positive direct-mail campaign touting his accomplishments, while others pounded home the image of Kobach as an extremist.

The DCCC was a factor in the race as well, with two unique television ads. One was designed to tout Moore's achievements, the other to discredit his challenger. With soft money banned by BCRA, the DCCC used the independent spending route, spending nearly $700,000 on the race (see Table 5.2), mostly for television ads. While the DCCC and the Moore campaign could not officially coordinate efforts, it was easy for the DCCC to monitor communications and design ads that complemented the local Democratic effort.

REPUBLICAN PARTY: AN AIR WAR, BUT NO GROUND WAR

State and local Republican party efforts on behalf of Kobach were virtually nonexistent. The state party had little in the way of funds and was controlled by moderates.[30] In Johnson County a number of moderates worked for both the Bush and Moore campaigns; yard signs for both candidates were prominently displayed in wealthy parts of the county. During the last week of the campaign, advertisements listing the names of Republicans for Moore appeared in the district's newspapers; some on the list were precinct committee chairs, and a few were elected Republican officials. Republicans had no GOTV organization like the KCC for ground-war activities. The only state-party mailing that even carried Kobach's name was generic, listing all Republican candidates as well.

The NRCC, however, aided Kobach with seven unique television ads costing well over half a million dollars and sent 12 direct-mail flyers. While a few of the flyers were targeted to specific categories of registered voters such as teachers, most were sent to all Republicans and independents in the district; some were even received by registered Democrats. According to FEC data on party independent expenditures, over $618,000 was spent by the NRCC, mostly on negative ads discrediting Moore (see Table 5.2). Since the president's position on immigration issues was contrary to Kobach's, the national Republican ads dealing with securing the nation's borders did not parallel the challenger's hard-line message. The gay marriage issue was only mentioned in passing. Instead, the focus was on standard Republican talking points dealing with the economy and tax cuts, eliminating business regulations, outlining the importance of local control of schools, and pointing out how liberals had undermined national morality. The ads condemned Moore for voting "to continue to allow the sale of violent and sexually explicit video games and movies to underage children" and to allow the "horrific practice of partial-birth abortion" and for thinking flag burning was permissible as merely "free speech." Positive Kobach flyers noted the challenger's commitment to unleashing "our great American companies to grow, flourish, and create jobs and prosperity here at home;" his desire as a fellow teacher to do "all that I can in Congress to strengthen our schools;" as well as his commitment to "reducing taxes for Kansas families and businesses at every opportunity."

INTEREST GROUP INFLUENCES

By traditional measures, interest groups were less active than usual in the race. The BCRA restrictions on broadcast communications and the fact that the race was not considered very competitive after the primary reduced the incentives to participate. Neighboring Missouri's swing-state status in the presidential race encouraged some Kansas groups, unions in particular, to send volunteers and resources across the state line where they perceived they might make a difference.[31] No 527 committees were active in Kansas.

Other than campaign contributions, most groups' election activity was largely confined to endorsements and perhaps a direct mailing or two (see Table 5.4). Negative ads were largely nonexistent; even groups like the NRA and anti-abortion groups on the Republican side and the LCV and the Sierra Club on the Democratic side relied more on voter guides than on attack ads. The NRA conducted a campaign workshop in the district but did not actively enter the fray.[32]

The Democratic effort, however, did receive substantial help in a variety of other forms. The International Brotherhood of Boilermakers, based in Kansas City, Kansas, let the KCC use part of its facilities as a base of operation.[33] The Sierra Club and the Human Rights Campaign, a gay rights organization, each "lent" Moore for Congress a staff member for the last two weeks of the campaign.[34] Various unions, the Kansas National Education Association (KNEA), and Farmland Industries made in-kind contributions in the form of providing facilities for phone bank operations.[35] In the case of Farmland Industries, a private business, the campaign took care to use only unpaid volunteers who were using facilities after working hours. The Mainstream Coalition, a local group organized to oppose the political activities of the Christian Right, ran its own phone bank in support of Moore.[36] The AFL-CIO, while not operating a separate GOTV operation, contributed financially to the campaign and to the KCC, where one of its members sat on the committee designing the KCC budget.[37] Unions, especially the United Automobile Workers (UAW), were quite responsive to calls for volunteers from both the KCC and Moore for Congress.[38]

On the Republican side, interest groups were even more crucial to the Kobach for Congress effort. However, some of the group connections had costs as well as benefits. To make up for an ineffective party, Kobach used the evangelical movement as his equivalent to the KCC; the movement became the driving force in his GOTV efforts with a strategy almost entirely directed toward activating his base. Unlike the broad public campaign, Kobach's GOTV efforts emphasized moral issues such as abortion and gay marriage. Evangelical churches, as they had been doing in the primary, actively registered parishioners, gave them advanced ballots, informed them about candidates' stances on issues, and encouraged them to vote in accordance with their values.

Connections to other groups repeatedly reinforced that Kobach was outside the political mainstream. For example, his focus on immigration rallied a number of group contributors to his campaign. Others did more: The Eagle Forum, which had endorsed Kobach and contributed $3,000 to his campaign, and Phylis Schlafly came to the district to discuss the immigration issue, appearing in a forum with Kobach.[39] Project America, a 501(c)(3) "educational" organization, designated the Third District race as one of five races where immigration was a main issue and put up three billboards in a part of the district where there was a concentration of Hispanic businesses.[40] The billboards discussed Moore's voting record on a number of immigration issues, including his position against a bill barring federal funding to any state or local government that did not share a person's immigration status with federal authorities. Yard signs supporting Kobach were placed nearby. The president of the local chapter of the League of United Latin American Citizens (LULAC) called the billboards "racist."[41] Kobach was asked to repudiate the ad, but he refused. The incident again caused the press to raise the issue of the kinds of groups that supported Kobach, such as Team America, which noted on its

Web site that if borders remain open, "our island of productivity and prosperity will soon disappear beneath a flood of Third-World squalor."[42]

CONCLUSION

As a practical matter, the general election was over once Kobach won the primary and continued his strategy designed to appeal to a relatively narrow base. His positions on virtually all issues put him on the extreme conservative fringe of a divided party. Whether it was taxes, immigration, or social issues like abortion and gay rights, Kobach alienated the kinds of moderates and independents he needed to upend Moore. Kobach's connections to the Christian Right were offensive to mainline Protestant and Jewish voters, raising serious questions about his views on church and state relations. For Moore to win, he had to get Republicans to join independents and Democrats in voting for him. Kobach's positions and supporters helped Moore with this objective.

Kobach's message difficulties should not overshadow what was an impressive Democratic operation. Despite being in a district with a substantial Republican registration advantage, after three terms in office Representative Moore had proved to be a strong incumbent with a sophisticated constituent service operation, an ability to raise funds both inside and outside of the district, and a voting record compatible with local interests. In the campaign, the combination of Moore for Congress, the DCCC, and the state party's coordinated campaign had the appearance of a well-oiled machine. The Democratic base was activated, and Moore was convincingly portrayed as a bipartisan moderate with values in tune with the district. The Kobach campaign was a much less professional operation, relying extensively on a loosely organized evangelical movement.

There were aspects of the 2004 campaign that reflected some of the changes brought about by BCRA. Probably because of the intense focus on the presidential race and a few Senate races, and because the groups sized up Kobach as a weak challenger, there was little broadcast electioneering by 527 groups in this race. The ban on national party soft money did not restrict party involvement; both parties engaged in relatively high levels of independent spending.[43] Ground war activities, especially direct mail by both the parties and the campaigns, appeared to be more important than in past years. Interest-group ground-war efforts, including union activity, were less than in earlier campaigns in the district.

NOTES

1. Thelma Helyar, ed. *Kansas Statistical Abstract 2000* (Lawrence, KS: Policy Research Institute, 2001); Michael Barone and Richard Cohen, *The Almanac of American Politics 2004* (Washington, D.C.: National Journal Group, 2004), pp. 651–58.

2. Allan J. Cigler. "The 1998 Kansas Third Congressional District Race," in *Outside Money: Soft Money and Issue Advocacy in the 1998 Congressional Elections*, ed. David B. Magleby (Lanham, MD: Rowman and Littlefield, 2000).
3. Allan J. Cigler and Burdett A. Loomis, "Kansas: The Christian Right and the New Mainstream of Republican Politics," in *God at the Grassroots, 1996: The Christian Right in American Elections*, eds. Mark J. Rozell and Clyde Wilcox (Lanham, MD: Rowman and Littlefield, 1997), pp. 207–22.
4. Allan J. Cigler and Burdett A. Loomis, "After the Flood: The Kansas Christian Right in Retreat," in *Prayers in the Precincts: The Christian Right in American Elections*, eds. John C. Green, Mark Rozell, and Clyde Wilcox (Washington, D.C.: Georgetown Univeristy Press, 2000), pp. 227–42.
5. For example, between January 2003 and October 2004, Republican registration in Johnson County increased by 14,700, Democratic registration increased by 7,186, and with 7,708 registered as independent. Kansas Secretary of State, Johnson County Election Office, www.jocoelection.org (accessed October 8, 2004).
6. Burdett A. Loomis, "Accentuating the Positive: Personality, Polling and Party in Kansas 3," in *Running on Empty? Political Discourse in Congressional Elections*, eds. L. Sanday Maisel and Darrell West (Lanham, MD: Rowman and Littlefield, 2004), pp. 15–26.
7. The close relationship between the Christian Right and candidates like Kobach sparked an effort by the Mainstream Coalition of Johnson County, a group made up mostly of Republican moderates concerned with the separation of church and state, to closely monitor evangelical church services in the weeks immediately preceding the primary election. The group sent nearly 100 volunteers to Sunday services throughout the district to see if clergy were adhering to federal tax code guidelines limiting political activity by nonprofit groups. See John Hanna, "K.C. Group on Lookout for Politics in Pulpits," *Lawrence Journal World*, July 18, 2004, p. B1.
8. Brad Cooper, "In Primary Field, Taff Leads GOP Rivals," *Kansas City Star*, July 21, 2004, p. A1.
9. Scott Rothschild, "Republicans 'Couldn't Get it Together,'" *Lawrence Journal World*, August 9, 2004, p. B1.
10. Todd Abrajano, campaign manager, Kobach for Congress, telephone interview by Allan J. Cigler, November 8, 2004.
11. Sean Hatfield, field volunteer, Kobach for Congress, telephone interview by Allan J. Cigler, November 16, 2004.
12. Julie Merz, campaign manager, Moore for Congress, telephone interview by Allan J. Cigler, December 8, 2004.
13. Brad Cooper, "In the Black," *Kansas City Star*, December 19, 2004, p. B1.
14. The Cheney breakfast gathering attracted 325 supporters who each paid $250 for the meal and an additional $2,000 if they wished to have their picture taken with the vice president. See Brad Cooper, "Cheney Lends a Hand to Kobach Campaign," *Kansas City Star*, August 25, 2004, p. B1.
15. Merz, interview, December 8, 2004.
16. Jason L. Riley, "GOP Nativists Tarnish Reagan's Shining City," *Wall Street Journal*, March 15, 2004, p. A17.
17. Brad Cooper, "Kobach Attacks His Rivals for Stance on Immigration," *Kansas City Star*, July 21, 2004, www.kansascity.com/mld/kansascity/news/local/9201880.htm (accessed January 29, 2005).
18. Kobach was representing Federation for American Immigration Reform in a lawsuit against the state of Kansas over a law that allowed undocumented immigrants to pay in-state tuition under certain situations. He said he was paid the standard retainer fee. Federation for American Immigration Reform was suing on behalf of out-of-state students who would be paying more for tuition than undocumented aliens. See Jim Sullinger, "Group Takes on Tuition Law," *Kansas City Star*, July 20, 2004, p. B1.
19. Brad Cooper, "Kobach Challenged on Campaign Gift," *Kansas City Star*, September 14, 2004. B3.
20. Brad Cooper, "Voters Prefer Moore, Poll Says," *Kansas City Star*, October 24, 2004, p. A1.
21. Merz, interview, December 8, 2004.
22. While there is no formal way to document this, one Kobach supporter volunteered that at a rally he was approached by a Kobach staff member. He was asked if he belonged to a

church and then asked if it was possible to get a list of church members and their addresses and phone numbers. He refused.

23. Some of the calls generated controversy. A number of recipients were Democrats, who wondered how a caller who identified herself as a "fellow Catholic" then pointed out that Dennis Moore "does not share our values" would have been able to obtain their phone number. Abrajano said the campaign bought the calling list from a company that sells databases. See David Ranney, "Kobach's Calls to Catholics Anger Some Voters," *Lawrence Journal World*, October 27, 2004, p. B1.

24. Information on the activities of the Kansas Coordinated Campaign was gathered in a variety of ways, including interviews with various party and campaign officials both before and after the election. The bulk of the specific information was provided by two main interviews conducted after the election: A.J. Carillo, director, Kansas Coordinated Campaign, interview by Allan J. Cigler, Lawrence, Kansas, November 19, 2004; Mark Simpson, executive director, Kansas Democratic Party, telephone interview by Allan J. Cigler, December 6, 2004.

25. Carillo interview, November 19, 2004.

26. Merz, interview, December 8, 2004.

27. Kansas has a procedure whereby voters may elect to cast their ballot starting 20 days prior to the election. It was estimated that about a third of the electorate had cast its vote prior to election day. See Melodee Hall Blobaum, "Advance Vote on Fast Tract to Hit 100,000," *Kansas City Star*, October 30, 2004, p. B1.

28. Brent Swenson, coordinator, Johnson County Kansas Coordinated Campaign, telephone interview by Allan J. Cigler, December 6, 2004.

29. Carillo, interview, November 19, 2004.

30. Prior to the August primary, the Republican Party, led by the state chair, pursued efforts to open the contests to unaffiliated voters. This was seen as an effort by moderates to diminish social conservative strength in the primaries. Republican opponents challenged the measure in court and prevailed. The court battle left the state party organization with little funds or credibility for the general election. See Scott Rothschild, "GOP to Ask Judge to OK Open Primary," *Lawrence Journal World*, July 25, 2004, p. A1.

31. Scott Rothschild, "Campaigns Drawing Kansas Out of State," *Lawrence Journal World*, October 27, 2004, p. A1.

32. Glen Caroline, director, Institute for Legislative Action Grassroots Division, National Rifle Association, interview by J. Quin Monson and Richard Hawkins, Fairfax, VA, November 10, 2004. Unconfirmed rumors suggested that the National Rifle Association had polled the district and found too many moderate ticket splitters (likely Bush-Moore voters) to get more involved in the race. See Kriswatch Blog, kriswatch.blogspot.com. (accessed September 21, 2004).

33. Merz, interview, December 8, 2004.

34. Ibid.

35. Ibid.

36. The phone calls were designed to inform recipients of Kobach's "extreme" views on immigration.

37. Merz, interview, December 8, 2004.

38. Ibid.

39. Loenard Zeskind, "Kris Kobach Loads Up with Anti-Immigration Ammo," *The Pitch* (a Kansas City area news and entertainment weekly), www.pitch.com/issues/2004-09-23/stline.html (accessed September 23, 2004).

40. Brad Cooper, "Latinos Object to Billboards Attacking Moore," *Kansas City Star*, October 14, 2004, p. B3.

41. Ibid.

42. Ibid.

43. The use of national-party independent spending was not without its problems. The Moore campaign noted that often its calls to the Democratic Congressional Campaign Committee's director of incumbent retention became bogged in legal compliance issues, creating communications problems. Merz, interview, December 8, 2004.

6

WHY CONTEXT MATTERS

THE PENNSYLVANIA THIRTEENTH CONGRESSIONAL DISTRICT RACE

ROBIN KOLODNY, SANDRA SUAREZ, AND JUSTIN GOLLOB

Temple University

National observers expected the contest for the open seat in Pennsylvania's Thirteenth Congressional District to be among the most competitive of the 35 or so competitive House races in 2004. In the end, Democrat Allyson Schwartz won the seat by a wide 56 percent to 41 percent margin over her Republican competitor Melissa Brown. The end result masks a fascinating story. This seat is in an area with one of the most moderate electorates in the nation. It was an important swing district in a presidential battleground state with a competitive U.S. Senate race and received a significant amount of attention from parties and interest groups. Both Schwartz and Brown weathered expensive and competitive primaries; interest-group activity proved critical in the primary and summer campaign season but less so in the fall. At the end of July Greenwood (R-PA 8), another comfortable incumbent member in the adjacent Eighth District, decided not to seek reelection, which significantly changed how Washington-based players viewed the race's importance of this race. This race serves as an example of how recent changes to campaign finance laws—in particular the elimination of soft money and the implementation of the Millionaire's Amendment through BCRA—can influence candidate decisions. In this race, the elimination of soft money had only a marginal effect on the outcome, while the Millionaire's Amendment played a significant role in Schwartz's victory.

THE ELECTORAL CONTEXT

The Thirteenth District is wealthier, more educated, older, more female, and more white than the overall U.S. population. It contains most of the northeast section of the city of Philadelphia and northern and eastern portions of

Montgomery County, the suburban area immediately west of Philadelphia. The district contains 200,377 registered Republicans and 206,429 registered Democrats.[1] Still, registration does not mean much in the Thirteenth District, where voters are fond of splitting their tickets.

Democrat Joe Hoeffel represented the Thirteenth District from 1998 to 2004. Hoeffel decided to seek election to the U.S. Senate against Republican incumbent Arlen Specter, creating an open seat. Even if Hoeffel had not vacated the seat, all eyes would have been on this race, as Hoeffel's margins had always been extremely thin (1998: 51.5 percent; 2000: 52.7 percent; 2002: 50.9 percent).[2] One reason for Hoeffel's bare margins was the historic Republican registration advantage in the district. After the 2000 election, the district underwent considerable change due to redistricting: Pennsylvania lost two congressional seats, and population shifts meant the Philadelphia area was destined to lose one seat. The new Thirteenth District now included a broader mix of urban and suburban voters, posing new challenges for congressional candidates.

THE CANDIDATES

The race featured two major party candidates, Allyson Schwartz and Melissa Brown, and two minor party candidates. Schwartz is a textbook liberal Democrat. She was elected to the state Senate in 1990 and is strongly associated with health care and child welfare issues: she was the driving force behind the state's Children's Health Insurance Program (CHIP). Schwartz is also pro-choice and Jewish, which made her very attractive for investment from national constituencies such as EMILY's List. In addition, Schwartz made a credible bid for the Democratic nomination for the U.S. Senate in 2000 and from that experience was well known to national party committees and groups. Schwartz's state senate incumbency and prior U.S. Senate bid gave her valuable experience in understanding how to run a congressional race. She had a large, well-funded, and well-directed electoral organization from early on in 2004, including five full-time fundraising paid staff and an average of 20 full-time paid canvassers from July to November.[3] Every single one of these employees received health care benefits from Schwartz. Although this might have been an expensive move, the result was a dedicated, motivated, and extremely professional operation that raised over $4.5 million, the third-highest amount among all U.S. House candidates and the most for any non-incumbent.[4]

Brown is a well-respected physician with deep roots in the district. She is a moderate Republican who is pro-choice, but the fact that she and her husband are both physicians gave her instant credibility and funding from a critical core constituency. Her profession also explains why the AMA got involved in this race. Having come close to beating Joseph Hoeffel in 2002—in part because she made a $915,000 donation to her own campaign—Brown seemed the obvious favorite in the Republican primary election. However, State Representative Ellen Bard and businessman Al Taubenberger entered the primary as well. Brown did not have an easy time gaining the nomination, as she thought she would, receiving only 38.8 percent of the vote compared to 34.8 percent for Bard and 26.4 percent for Taubenberger.

Once the primary was concluded, it was clear that Brown would face a very different race against Schwartz than she had against Hoeffel. Schwartz was prepared for a tough challenge from Brown, having learned from Hoeffel's experience in 2002. In addition, Brown's early decision not to invest her own money in the race as she had in 2002 lessened the energy of her 2004 campaign.

MONEY

CANDIDATES

While this race was expected to attract considerable spending from all sectors, the candidates' own spending was ultimately more significant than either party or interest group money. The early lead Schwartz managed over Brown and the other competitive races in the region explain this outcome.

The most important story behind the candidate fundraising in this race was Brown's personal wealth. Because she contributed $915,000 to her own race in 2002, the question was whether she would this time.[5] Obviously, the presence of any millionaire in a race draws attention from the opponent, but this would be the first cycle in which the Millionaire's Amendment in BCRA would apply. Under BCRA, if one candidate decides to use more than $350,000 in personal funds in a federal race, the opponent(s) are entitled to higher donation limits from individuals. Once a candidate files an intent to contribute personal funds beyond the $350,000 threshold, which must be filed with the FEC within 24 hours of such an expenditure, the opposing candidate(s) may accept individual contributions at three times the normal limit (raised from $2,000 to $6,000), and the national and state party committees may spend unlimited amounts of coordinated expenditures, provided that the total fundraising by the opponent, the Opposition Personal Funds Amount, does not exceed the total fundraising, including personal funds, of the millionaire candidate.[6]

There was wide-spread speculation about whether Brown would or would not invest her own resources in the 2004 campaign as she had in 2002. After the primary, Brown decided that she would not invest her own money; however, only top campaign intimates knew of her decision, making all sides uncertain until election day when a last-minute "surprise" investment could occur.[7] In the end Brown raised $1,956,061, which was $350,000 more than she did in 2002. She personally contributed only 9 percent of total receipts ($175,000) to her campaign, raised 52 percent from individuals, and

TABLE 6.1 CANDIDATE RECEIPTS AND EXPENDITURES, PENNSYLVANIA THIRTEENTH
CONGRESSIONAL DISTRICT RACE, 2003 TO 2004

	ALLYSON SCHWARTZ (D)	MELISSA BROWN (R)
From PACs	$687,224	$648,106
From individuals	3,908,881	1,014,596
From party	200	13,850
From candidate	0	175,000
Other contributions	727	104,509
Total receipts	4,597,032	1,956,061
Total expenditures	4,572,417	1,927,499
Cash on hand (as of 12/31/04)	24,616	32,666

Source: Federal Election Commission, "2003–04 U.S. House and U.S. Senate Candidate Info," December 31, 2004, www.fecinfo.com/cgi-win/x_candidate.exe?DoFn=&sYR=2004 (accessed February 11, 2005).
Note: Abbreviation: PAC, political action committee.

received 33 percent from PACs, with medical professional associations leading her donors (see Table 6.1). However, Brown spent nearly half of this money just getting through the primary and thus only had about $900,000 for the general election. By the end of October, the Brown campaign was so short of funds that it had nothing left to invest in TV advertisements and almost went "dark" the last two weeks before election day.[8]

The Schwartz campaign prepared for the Millionaire's Amendment in a variety of ways. First, the possibility of Brown's self-financing helped Schwartz persuade more donors up front. Since Brown was only required to give 24-hours notice of self-funding, Schwartz could credibly say to potential donors that she had to be ready far in advance of such a decision. Second, the finance staff became extremely familiar with the amendment and drafted fundraising appeals in case they were needed on short notice. The threat of Brown's spending contributed to Schwartz collecting $4,597,032. She raised 85 percent of this amount from individuals and 15 percent from PACs, personally loaning no money to her campaign.[9] Her fundraising success was so significant that she probably would not have qualified for the increased donor limits given the size of her Opposition Personal Funds. Still, the threat of Brown's investment explains why the DCCC and outside groups continued to invest in the race, even when September poll numbers were showing that the race was not tight.

POLITICAL PARTIES

Obviously, both parties were very aware of the uncertainty regarding Brown's personal wealth. However, the investment made by the parties depended heavily on other important political considerations in the Philadelphia area. Ultimately, the DCCC and NRCC both made coordinated expenditures and

TABLE 6.2   INDEPENDENT EXPENDITURES BY PARTY COMMITTEE, PENNSYLVANIA
THIRTEENTH CONGRESSIONAL DISTRICT RACE, 2003 TO 2004

PARTY COMMITTEE	CANDIDATE	INDEPENDENT EXPENDITURES FOR	INDEPENDENT EXPENDITURES AGAINST	TOTAL	PARTY TOTAL
DCCC					$795,643
	Melissa Brown	0	0	0	
	Allyson Schwartz	$795,643	0	$795,643	
NRCC					793,956
	Melissa Brown	484,422	0	484,422	
	Allyson Schwartz	0	$309,534	309,534	

Source: Federal Election Commission, ftp://ftp.fec.gov/FEC/ (accessed January 5, 2005).
Note: Abbreviations: DCCC, Democratic Congressional Campaign Committee; NRCC, National Republican Congressional Committee.

independent expenditures in this race (see Table 6.2), but this money included no television communications on the Democratic side and only a small buy on the Republican side.

Brown's campaign benefited from $40,322 of coordinated expenditures made by the NRCC and $793,956 of independent expenditures (see Table 6.2). The NRCC spent the vast majority of this money on direct mail, but some of it went to television ads and some may have gone to phone banks. The DCCC spent $36,236 in coordinated expenditures for Schwartz and $795,643 in independent expenditures.[10] According to Schwartz's finance director, the campaign believed that about a million dollars was spent by the NRCC against them and about a million dollars was spent for them from the DCCC. The Schwartz campaign was not aware of any television time purchased by the DCCC, and there was no evidence of television buys.[11] The DCCC did purchase radio time and sent mailers for Schwartz.

It is clear that the NRCC and the DCCC crafted different approaches to their air war in Pennsylvania's Thirteenth District. This was a response to two problems that both parties faced: the cost of media advertising in Philadelphia and the presence of two highly competitive House races bordering the Thirteenth District. The parties' media strategies differed because the means of their candidates differed. It was clear in October that Schwartz was favored to win, had a lot of cash on hand, and planned to use television advertising in the final two weeks of the race. Therefore, the DCCC chose to target narrower segments of the electorate in the Thirteenth District through radio advertisements, allowing them to use their finite resources for the more competitive adjoining districts. On the other hand, the Brown campaign was struggling, so the NRCC opted for a shotgun approach to target as many voters as possible by using network television. This exhausted the resources devoted to the Thirteenth District, which were diminished because other area races seemed more competitive, and it accounts for the NRCC's lack of spending on both radio and cable television.

As detailed in the following section, mail was the major weapon of choice for both party committees. As in the days of issue advocacy appeals, the NRCC made one important error in its mail, which may have hurt Brown.[12] The NRCC designed two negative mailers criticizing Schwartz for her views on abortion. One mailer asked, "Want to hear something scary? Allyson Schwartz has been called the '. . . abortion rights community's dream candidate . . .'"[13] The other chastised Schwartz for opposing parental notification requirements for minors saying "It's clear Allyson Schwartz doesn't value an unborn life, but why doesn't she value parents' rights? Allyson Schwartz— Wrong for Pennsylvania." The problem was that both candidates were pro-choice. When Planned Parenthood members received the mailing, the organization, which had endorsed both candidates, contacted the Brown campaign and threatened to withdraw its support. Once the Brown campaign convinced them that the NRCC, and not Brown, was responsible for the mail, Planned Parenthood kept the endorsement but made an additional PAC donation to Schwartz.[14]

INTEREST GROUPS

The number of interest groups involved in this race was fewer than in previous elections in this district. Notable absences included the Human Rights Campaign, which endorsed both candidates; Planned Parenthood with the exception of the PAC donation noted above; NARAL Pro-Choice America, the Sierra Club and to a lesser extent, AARP.[15] All these groups had previously spent significant funds for issue advocacy campaigns (both TV and direct mail) in the Thirteenth District, but in this cycle their contribution was trivial by comparison. Interest group involvement in the 2004 race was primarily a factor of Schwartz's record in the state senate, the salience of health and health care issues, and the presidential race. There were a total of twelve groups active on behalf of Schwartz, and only four groups on behalf of Brown. While it is difficult to generalize, the support that Schwartz received from groups suggests that they believed she had a greater chance of winning than Brown. Most interest group activity consisted of door-to-door canvassing, door hangers, polls, phone calls, mailings, and in-kind contributions. Though both candidates raised most of their funds from individual contributors, Brown was more dependent on PAC contributions than Schwartz. Brown received $648,106 (33 percent of total funds raised) mostly from health-related PACs. By contrast Schwartz received $687,224 (15 percent of total funds raised) from a variety of PACs, especially unions, followed by health, children, and education-related committees and trial lawyers.[16]

EMILY's List's Pennsylvania Women Vote! endorsed Schwartz and was one of the most visible groups during the general election campaign. The level of the group's involvement seems extreme because both candidates were pro-choice. However, EMILY's List's activities during the general campaign must be understood as part of a well-conceived, long-term strategy on behalf of Schwartz that began with the primary campaign. As EMILY's List political director Karen White indicated, the group got involved in the primary campaign after Hoeffel decided not to run because Schwartz was the only woman running in the Democratic primary, and the group's mission is to support pro-choice Democratic women. Schwartz was an especially attractive candidate because of her solid record during her 14 years in the state Senate, especially her pivotal role in enacting to provide health insurance for children and requiring child care providers to undergo criminal background checks.[17]

Because the high cost of the Philadelphia television market "would keep Schwartz off the air until late in the game"[18] and the largely inconsequential presidential primary could depress turnout in Schwartz's primary race against Joe Torsella, EMILY's List decided that door-to-door canvassing would be the best way to introduce Schwartz to the voters. They knocked on a total of 106,000 doors, sent 280,000 pieces of "targeted mail," made a voter identification canvas to find those who were sympathetic to Schwartz, and then made 69,000 phone calls. The group conducted two polls, one in January, which was a benchmark poll costing between $20,000 and $25,000, and a less expensive one in April, to make sure that the preferences of the targeted voters had not changed. Canvassing began on January 29 and ran through election day, involving about eighteen canvassers.[19] Newspaper reports suggested that EMILY's List's involvement during the primary was the main reason why Schwartz "outpaced" her Democratic primary challenger in fundraising. By April, Schwartz had outspent Torsella by $700,000. Of that, $358,000 reportedly came from EMILY's List donors.[20]

EMILY's List seemed to be less involved during the general election campaign because they decided they had "done enough to get the word out about Schwartz"[21] and that what she needed at this point was help with her fundraising. For this purpose, the group made use of people they call "finance trackers." These finance trackers are "not really working for the campaign" (i.e., they are not in-kind contributions to the candidate's campaign), but they "pop in and out of campaigns" and report back to the Washington office regarding the state of a candidate's finance, alerting the group of their candidate's needs for funds. The group also sent three pieces of mail highlighting Schwartz's work on behalf of children, crime prevention programs, and the Patient's Bill of Rights. The group estimates that it spent approximately $580,000 on behalf of Schwartz during both the primary and general campaigns.[22]

Other groups became involved in the campaign as a result of the relationship they had with Schwartz during her state Senate years. The LCV and Credit Union National Association (CUNA) are two such groups. According to the LCV, Schwartz "had a fantastic track record on state issues, when it came to environmental issues she was a leader."[23] Some group officials had a close relationship with the campaign; LCV's Pennsylvania Field Officer, as a private citizen, was a member of Schwartz's fundraising committee. The group's most important concern was the presidential campaign, but the Congressional race was appealing because it was an open seat and the LCV had a successful past record in the district. As Director Susan Gobreski explained, "money is limited, and you don't want a losing record so that your endorsement means nothing."[24] Thus, the group decided to support Schwartz as part of its strategy on behalf of Democratic presidential candidate John Kerry. Though the race seemed secure for Schwartz by October, the group nonetheless produced a door hanger on her behalf at a cost of $10,000.[25] The hanger's content attacked Brown by suggesting that she had engaged in fraudulent activities and by reminding voters that she had received a "Sleazy Award for her racially divisive campaign" from a *Philadelphia Inquirer* columnist. CUNA also got involved in the campaign because "Senator Schwartz was a supporter of credit unions during her years in Harrisburg." They sent out three pieces of mail at a cost of approximately $75,000. Two pieces highlighted Schwartz's work on behalf of children, and one detailed the ways she would help create jobs in Pennsylvania.[26]

The four groups involved in the race on behalf of Brown were the NFIB, the American Academy of Ophthalmology Political Action Committee (OPHTHPAC), the AMA, and the U.S. Chamber of Commerce. Early in the campaign, the NFIB sent out a questionnaire to both Brown and Schwartz. According to the group, "Brown's answers came closest to our interests." They presented this information to their members in the district, and Brown received a "solid endorsement."[27] The group's strategy on behalf of the candidate included a mailing to its members, a walking tour to introduce Brown to small business owners in the area, and a mailing to small business owners, both members and non-members. One of the mailings argued that Brown wanted to reform "unfair medical malpractice laws . . . which can be a major burden to small business." The second piece dealt with health insurance.[28] OPHTHPAC had an independent expenditure of $8,000.[29] It sent out one piece of mail pointing out that "hospitals across southeastern Pennsylvania are now limiting their services" due to runaway lawsuits, and since Melissa Brown is a physician, she would champion significant health care reforms. Finally, the AMA conducted a poll in mid-September that indicated that the race was neck and neck, that Brown's negatives were low, and her name recognition was at par with Schwartz's.

The AMA then decided to enter the race because of Brown's long-time support and her position on medical liability insurance. However, the Thirteenth District was the only race in which the group did not spend any money on television and radio because it felt that the cost of broadcast advertising in Pennsylvania was prohibitive and because "we are just talking about a House race."[30] They spent a total of $100,000 in this race with three mail pieces targeted to poll respondents who were swing voters and Brown supporters. The mailings dealt with the high cost of medical insurance in Pennsylvania.[31] The U.S. Chamber of Commerce sent three mailers and a door hanger, but the targeted area must have been small because no member of our network received them. Indeed, the Brown campaign seemed unaware of significant Chamber activity when asked about this point specifically. The mailers emphasized medical liability reform, health care, and economic growth and job creation. They were mostly pro-Brown, though some pieces contrasted the two candidates.

EFFECTS OF MONEY

The Thirteenth District story shows how political calculations by candidates, groups, and parties can shape the effectiveness of both ground and air wars in political campaigns. Overall, Brown's campaign suffered from a lack of money and support among key allies, both interest groups and parties, at critical times, lower financial resources compared to Schwartz, and a lack of momentum by Brown leading up to election day. Combined, these factors significantly hampered Brown's ability to conduct effective ground and air wars.

THE GROUND WAR

The most significant dimension of the ground war was the efficient, sizable, and consistent canvassing operation run by Schwartz. Although other groups hired canvassers at times to help her campaign, specifically EMILY's List and the LCV, these groups largely abandoned their efforts by mid-September since their sense of the race and polls showed Schwartz's lead was secure. Furthermore, groups believed that the adjacent congressional districts had more pressing needs. In contrast to Schwartz's campaign, Brown's canvassing operation was almost negligible. No other group appears to have done canvassing on her behalf.

The phones, at least in this contest, were relatively quiet, especially for Brown. It appears that there was only one unique call each from both Friends of Melissa Brown and the NRCC. Moreover, there does not appear to be any significant activity from outside groups for Brown. While the phone tended to be used more by Schwartz's Democratic allies, it still was not heavily used as measured by our reconnaissance network. As evidenced in Table 6.3, we recorded seven unique calls for Schwartz; all of these calls came from Democratic ally interest groups such as New House PAC (a PAC "dedicated to supporting Democratic House candidates"[32]) and EMILY's List.[33] Interestingly, there does not appear to be any significant phone activity by either Schwartz for Congress or the DCCC.

TABLE 6.3   NUMBER OF UNIQUE CAMPAIGN COMMUNICATIONS BY ORGANIZATION, PENNSYLVANIA THIRTEENTH CONGRESSIONAL DISTRICT RACE, 2004[a]

TYPE AND ORGANIZATION[b]	TYPE OF CAMPAIGN COMMUNICATION						
	E-MAIL	MAIL	PERSONAL CONTACT	PHONE CALL	RADIO ADS	TV ADS	TOTAL
Democratic Allies[c]							
Candidates							
Schwartz for Congress	15	3	5	—	—	4	27
Political Parties							
DCCC	—	10	—	—	1	—	11
Abington-Rockledge Democratic Committee	—	1	—	—	—	—	1
Interest Groups							
EMILY's List[d]	—	3	1	1	—	—	5
AFL–CIO	—	3	—	—	—	—	3
Credit Union Legislative Action Council of CUNA	—	3	—	—	—	—	3
ITC Research	—	3	—	—	—	—	3
New House PAC	—	—	—	2	—	—	2
American Federation of Teachers	—	—	—	2	—	—	2
Clean Water Action	—	1	—	—	—	—	1
League of Conservation Voters	—	—	1	—	—	—	1
National Organization for Women	—	1	—	—	—	—	1
Pennsylvania Gay and Lesbian Alliance	—	1	—	—	—	—	1
USA Public Opinion Group	—	—	—	1	—	—	1
We the People	—	—	—	1	—	—	1
Republican Allies[c]							
Candidates							
Friends of Melissa Brown	14	7	7	1	—	3	32

							Total
Political Parties							
NRCC	1	13	—	1	—	4	19
Lower Providence Republican Committee	—	1	—	—	—	—	1
Republican Federal Committee of Pennsylvania	—	1	—	—	—	—	1
Republican State Committee of Pennsylvania	—	1	—	—	—	—	1
Interest Groups							
U.S. Chamber of Commerce	—	3	—	1	—	—	4
American Medical Association	—	3e	—	—	—	—	3
National Federation of Independent Business	—	2	—	—	—	—	2
American Academy of Ophthalmology PAC	—	1	—	—	—	—	1
Nonpartisan							
Interest Groups							
Coalition for Peace Action	—	1	—	—	—	—	1

a See Appendix A for a more detailed data explanation. Data represent the number of unique or distinct pieces or ads by the group and do not represent a count of total items sent or made. This table is not intended to portray comprehensive organization activity within the sample races. A more complete picture can be obtained by examining this table together with Table 6.3.

b All state and local chapters or affiliates have been combined with their national affiliate to better render the picture of the organization's activity. For instance, Pennsylvania American Federation of Labor and Congress of Industrial Organizations data have been included in the American Federation of Labor and Congress of Industrial Organizations totals.

c Certain organizations that maintained neutrality were categorized according to which candidates their ads supported or attacked or whether the organization was openly anti- or pro-conservative or liberal.

d EMILY's List (also know as Pennsylvania Women Vote!) distributed three unique pieces of mail in the Thirteenth District. They also reported having a field program and doing phone calls in the district. Karen White, national political director, EMILY's List, interview by David B. Magleby and Richard Hawkins, Washington, D.C., November 8, 2004.

e Mike Cys, director of political and legislative grassroots, American Medical Association Political Action Committee, interview by David B. Magleby and Betsey Gimbel, Washington, D.C., December 14, 2004.

In blank cells, "—" only reflects the absence of collected data and does not imply the organization was inactive in that medium.

Source: Data compiled from David B. Magleby, J. Quin Monson, and Kelly D. Patterson, "2004 Campaign Communications Database," (Center for the Study of Elections and Democracy: Brigham Young University, 2005).

Note: Abbreviations: DCCC, Democratic Congressional Campaign Committee; AFL-CIO, American Federation of Labor and Congress of Industrial Organizations; CUNA, Credit Union National Association; PAC, Political Action Committee.

Despite the apparent lack of phone banking, there was quite a bit of mail activity from the Brown campaign and the NRCC. As evidenced in Table 6.3, a large amount of mail that was sent either by or for Brown came from the NRCC. Overall, we discovered 13 unique pieces of mail from the NRCC and seven unique pieces sent by Friends of Melissa Brown. The NRCC consistently claimed that Schwartz was "Wrong for Pennsylvania" and Pennsylvania families on the issues of taxes, crime, abortion, and health care. As previously discussed, other groups were involved in sending mail for Brown or against Schwartz, including the U.S. Chamber of Commerce (three unique pieces), the AMA (three unique pieces), the NFIB (two unique pieces), and the OPHTHPAC (one unique piece). There was other mail activity outside of these groups, but it was considerably less than that of the NRCC and the candidate.

Likewise, the DCCC made extensive use of mail to support Schwartz or attack Brown. Overall, we discovered 10 unique pieces of mail sent by the DCCC, but only three pieces from Allyson Schwartz for Congress. The DCCC mail linked Brown to the "Bush Agenda," highlighted Brown's involvement in an HMO "that was sued by the Pennsylvania Insurance Commissioner for fraud and conspiracy," and attacked her stance on prescription drug prices. Several interest groups sent mail, including the AFL-CIO (three pieces), the CUNA (three pieces), and Pennsylvania Women Vote! (three pieces). Other organizations were involved in GOTV and advocacy mail, but the majority of mail came from the DCCC and these interest groups. For a more detailed breakdown, see Table 6.3.

E-mail communications from both candidates tended to advertise events, seek financial and volunteer support, advertise their endorsements and accomplishments, and discuss policy positions. As evidenced in Table 6.3, Friends of Melissa Brown sent 14 unique e-mails between Labor Day and election day, while Schwartz sent 15 e-mails during the same period. Outside of one e-mail sent by the NRCC supporting Brown, the parties were all but absent in e-mail communications for the Thirteenth District.

THE AIR WAR

The two candidates and the NRCC were the only significant television presences in this race. This is not because Schwartz lacked support, but rather because she had sufficient funds to cover her own television buys, whereas Brown clearly did not. Still, Brown was unable to convince the NRCC to make a major investment in television. Indeed, the NRCC only bought a total of $331,180 in network television ads while Friends of Melissa Brown spent approximately $708,653 on television ads. In comparison Schwartz spent $1,161,925 on television while the DCCC did not spend any money on television ad buys for this race (see Table 6.4).

Interestingly, neither candidate nor the parties spent any money on cable television as measured by visits to two separate Comcast stations. This finding

TABLE 6.4 THE AIR WAR: TELEVISION AND RADIO ADVERTISING EXPENDITURES, PENNSYLVANIA THIRTEENTH CONGRESSIONAL DISTRICT RACE, 2004[a]

TYPE AND ORGANIZATION	TV	RADIO	TOTAL $ SPENT	CMAG TV
Democratic Allies[b]				
Candidates				
Schwartz for Congress	$1,161,925	—	**$1,161,925**	$2,541,145
Political Parties				
DCCC	—	104,100	**104,100**	—
Republican Allies[b]				
Candidates				
Friends of Melissa Brown	708,653	—	**708,653**	1,003,851
Political Parties				
NRCC	331,180	—	**331,180**	209,886

[a]Please see Appendix A for a more detailed data explanation. The ad-buy data collected for this study may contain extraneous data because of the difficulty in determining the content of the ads. The parties or interest groups that purchased the ad buys possibly ran some ads promoting House, Senate, or presidential candidates or ballot propositions not in the study's sample but still within that media market. Unless the participating academics were able to determine the exact content of the ad buy from the limited information given by the station, the data may contain observations that do not pertain to the study's relevant House, Senate, or presidential battleground races. For comparison purposes the Campaign Media Analysis Group data are included in the table. Because of the sheer volume of television and radio stations and varying degrees of compliance in providing ad-buy information, data on spending by various groups might be incomplete. There data do not include every station in the state. This table is not intended to represent comprehensive organization spending or activity within the sample races. Television ads purchased from national cable stations that aired in this state are not reflected in this table. A more complete picture can be obtained by examining this table with Table 6.4.

[b]Certain organizations that maintained neutrality were categorized according to which candidates their ads supported or attacked or whether the organization was openly anti- or pro- conservative or liberal. In blank cells, "—" only reflects the absence of collected data and does not imply the organization was inactive in that medium.

Source: Data compiled from David B. Magleby, J. Quin Monson, and Kelly D. Patterson, "2004 Campaign Communications Database," (Center for the Study of Elections and Democracy: Brigham Young University, 2005); and Campaign Media Analysis Group data.

Note: Abbreviations: DCCC, Democratic Congressional Campaign Committee; NRCC, National Republican Congressional Committee.

is interesting given the size and expense of advertising in the Philadelphia broadcast market.[34] As noted in the following paragraphs, the Philadelphia market was home to a number of competitive races including the presidential race, a U.S. Senate race, and seven competitive U.S. House races in Pennsylvania and New Jersey. Because of the high demand for airtime on broadcast television, it is a surprise that neither Brown nor Schwartz purchased cable airtime.

Instead of investing in television, the DCCC spent approximately $104,100 on radio ad buys. Outside of the DCCC, no candidate or group spent any money on radio. Brown made a significant radio purchase of approximately $27,000 to run from October 27 to November 2 but cancelled it shortly before the run date.[35] This supports the contention that Brown severely depleted her funds early in the campaign and failed to gain support from allies such as the NRCC to compensate for this shortcoming.

Taken as a whole, the ad-buy numbers are somewhat deceiving. By simply examining how much money was spent, one overlooks when the money was spent. The majority of Brown's television ad-buy money was spent early in the campaign, from late September to mid-October, leaving very little money for critical late October to early November ad buys. Overall, Brown spent roughly 5 percent of her total ad-buy money between October 24 and November 2, whereas Schwartz spent half of her total ad-buy money during the same period.[36] The NRCC did not spend any money on television for Brown between October 24 and November 2 and appears to have pulled out of the race by mid-October, opting to spend money in more competitive areas. For example, according to the data collected from public records and confirmed through conversations with a major Philadelphia network television station, the NRCC shifted an ad buy of about $192,000 for the Thirteenth District to the Pennsylvania Sixth Congressional District sometime between October 8 and 13.[37] Consequently, there was nearly a total absence of Brown commercials on television and radio leading up to the election.

This campaign was influenced by the dynamics in the two adjacent congressional districts. To the west the Thirteenth District is bordered by the Sixth District, which was newly drawn in 2001. Republican Jim Gerlach was elected to that seat in 2002 by a 51-percent margin, though the voter registration in that district favors Republicans by a larger margin.[38] In this cycle Gerlach was opposed by Lois Murphy, an attorney who formerly headed NARAL Pro-Choice Pennsylvania. The contrast between the two candidates was quite stark ideologically, and the incumbent seemed quite vulnerable in a district that was also considered important for the presidential race. Therefore, both parties and a wider spectrum of groups participated in this race, especially in buying television time. The NRCC spent $1,936,999 in independent expenditures, and the DCCC spent $1,432,496.[39]

To the east and north, the Thirteenth District is bordered by the Eighth District. This seat had been held by popular and moderate Republican incumbent Jim Greenwood since 1992. Greenwood was expected to win reelection easily in 2004, but on July 19, Greenwood announced his intention to retire at the end of the One hundred-eighth Congress.[40] His departure set off a fevered search for a Republican nominee and a close examination of the Democratic candidate Ginny Schrader. Thus, what was predicted to be a non-competitive, low-profile race became instantly competitive, especially since the eventual Republican nominee, Mike Fitzpatrick, was a conservative, pro-life Republican waging a campaign in a district that gave Al Gore its vote in 2000. The race became so competitive that the NRCC spent $2,270,296 in independent expenditures, and the DCCC spent $1,418,944.[41] As in the Sixth District, the Eighth District now had a pro-life Republican man facing a pro-choice Democratic woman, and groups who align on this issue focused their attention on these two districts, not the Thirteenth District.

According to the Brown campaign, the strategic retirement of Greenwood dealt them a mortal blow. Campaign money is not infinite, and if the NRCC felt it had to commit several million dollars to the Eighth District, it had to come out of somewhere. The Brown campaign indicated that the NRCC invests in incumbents first (i.e., Gerlach in the Sixth District), followed by open seats held by Republicans (the Eighth District), followed by open seats held by Democrats (the Thirteenth District), before considering promising Republican challengers.[42] Brown was also crippled by the high demand for scarce air time in the Philadelphia media market in 2004. Both the NRCC and DCCC were buying time in advance without indicating for which race it would be used because they were unsure in August which of the four races would be worthy of investment.[43] Both parties declined to spend much, if any, money on television ads in the Thirteenth District. The Brown campaign can plausibly contend that the presence of a newly competitive race deprived it of the opportunity for NRCC investment, stymied its own fundraising efforts, and eliminated any hope of buying more air time.

CONCLUSION

The Thirteenth District has long been competitive, but it may now have an incumbent who can solidify her constituency behind her. Schwartz was able to garner strong constituency support for several reasons. As an individual, Allyson Schwartz proved to be a prodigious fundraiser who received important early endorsements from key groups, invested early in a substantial field operation, stressed more positive issues, and proved capable of running a competitive race without the DCCC's help late in the game. Melissa Brown never seemed to get a significant fundraising operation going, did not develop an extensive field organization, ran a rather negative campaign, and could not convince the NRCC to invest in her campaign when other area races began to look more competitive. Because Schwartz's campaign organization was so strong, it was better able to maneuver in the new BCRA environment. Schwartz capitalized on the Millionaire's Amendment, while Brown was hurt by the ban on soft money because of dire financial needs late in her campaign. However, while Brown certainly could have been helped by soft money, it is unlikely that it would have made a difference in the outcome of the race. Brown was outmatched in this race, and it is unlikely that the NRCC would have invested soft money disproportionately into the Brown campaign when other competitive races were also at stake. Schwartz was also better able to conduct a consistent and comprehensive air war. Brown, on the other hand, seemed to have a scattered message and was all but absent from television leading up to election day. In conclusion, this race highlights that when studying elections, it is important to remember that context matters.

NOTES

1. Pennsylvania Department of State, Bureau of Elections, Voter Registration Statistics by Congressional Districts, 2004 General Election, (accessed April 17, 2006).
2. Calculated by author (Kolodny) from "Election Statistics" from the Clerk of the U.S. House of Representatives, clerk.house.gov/members/electionInfo (accessed January 11, 2005); see also Michael Barone and Richard E. Cohen, *Almanac of American Politics*, 2004 (Washington, D.C.: National Journal Group, 2004) and *CQ's Politics in America 2002* (Washington, D.C.: Congressional Quarterly Press, 2001).
3. Valerie Martin, finance director, Allyson Schwartz for Congress, telephone interview by Robin Kolodny, November 17, 2004.
4. See Federal Election Commission, "Congressional Candidates Spend $1.16 Billion During 2003–2004," press release, June 9, 2005, www.fec.gov/press/press2005/20050609candidate/20050609candidate.html (accessed July 7, 2005).
5. Center for Responsive Politics, "Total Raised and Spent, 2002 Race: Pennsylvania District 13," www.opensecrets.org/races/summary.asp?ID=PA13&Cycle=2002 (accessed December 13, 2004).
6. Federal Election Commission 2004, "Millionaire's Amendment," www.fec.gov/pages/brochures/millionaire.shtml#Introduction (accessed December 5, 2004).
7. Matthew Archbold, press secretary, Melissa Brown for Congress Campaign, telephone interview by Robin Kolodny, November 5, 2004.
8. Archbold interview, November 5, 2004.
9. Center for Responsive Politics, "Total Raised and Spent: 2004 Race – Pennsylvania District 13," www.opensecrets.org/races/summary.asp?=ID=PA13&cycle=2004 (accessed January 4, 2004); and Martin, interview, November 17, 2004.
10. Federal Election Commission, "Congressional Campaigns Spend $912 Million through Late November," press release, January 3, 2005, www.fec.gov/press/press2004/20050103canstat/20050103canstat.html (accessed January 4, 2005).
11. Martin, interview, November 17, 2004.
12. Anna Nibley Baker and David B. Magleby, "Interest Groups in the 2000 Congressional Elections," in *The Other Campaign: Soft Money and Issue Advocacy in the 2000 Congressional Elections*, ed. David B. Magleby (Lanham, MD: Rowman and Littlefield, 2003), p. 54.
13. Eichel, Larry, Op-Ed, Philadelphia Inquirer, 29 March 2000.
14. Archbold, interview, November 5, 2004.
15. Robin Kolodny and Sandra L. Suarez, "Air Wars versus Ground Wars: Pennsylvania's 13th District," in *Campaigns and Elections*, eds. Watson and Campbell (Boulder, CO: Lynne Rienner Publishers, 2003).
16. Federal Election Commission, "FEC Disclosure Database," www.fec.gov/finance/disclosure/norcansea.html (accessed December 31, 2004).
17. Karen White, national political director, EMILY's List, telephone interview by Sandra Suarez, November 18, 2004.
18. Ibid.
19. All figures obtained from White, interview, November 18, 2004.
20. Quoted in David Davies, "Schwartz-Torsella a Tough Choice for Democrats," *Philadelphia Daily News*, April 20, 2004; White, interview, November 18, 2004.
21. Karen White, National Political Director, EMILY's LIST, telephone interview, Sandra Suarez, November 18, 2004.
22. White, interview, November 18, 2004.
23. Susan Gobreski, Pennsylvania state director, League of Conservation Voters, telephone interview by Sandra Suarez, November 9, 2004.
24. Gobreski, interview, November 9, 2004.
25. Federal Election Commission, "FEC Disclosure Database," www.fec.gov/finance/disclosure/norcansea.html (accessed December 31, 2004).
26. Karen Kincer, political director, government affairs department, Credit Union National Association, telephone interview by Sandra Suarez, November 8, 2004.
27. Eric Rosedahl, regional political director, northeast region, National Federation of Independent Business, telephone interview by Sandra Suarez, November 8, 2004.
28. Rosedahl, interview, November 8, 2004.

29. Federal Election Commission, "FEC Disclosure Database," www.fec.gov/finance/disclosure/ norcansea.html (accessed December 31, 2004).

30. Mike Cys, director of political and legislative grassroots, American Medical Association Political Action Committee, telephone interview by Sandra Suarez, December 9, 2004.

31. Ibid.

32. Center for Responsive Politics, "The Major Player: Active Advocacy Groups in the 2004 Election Cycle." www.opensecrets.org/n275/527grps.asp, (accessed April 14, 2006).

33. Center for Responsive Politics, "New House PAC, 2004 Election Cycle," www.opensecrets. org/527s/527events.asp?orgid=18 (accessed December 14, 2004).

34. This information was gathered from the public political file from Comcast Montgomery County on September 23, 2004, and November 11, 2004, as well as Comcast Spotlight on November 15, 2004.

35. This information was gathered from the public political file from KYW News Radio 1060 AM on November 9, 2004.

36. These percentages are intended to highlight the approximate amount of money spent by the candidates during the late October/early November timeframe based on actual/contracted broadcast date ranges falling primarily between October 24 and November 2. Please note that the collected ad-buy data did not always fit neatly into the above date range, therefore these percentages represent approximations only.

37. This information was gathered from the public political file from WCAU NBC Channel 10, November 9, 2004, and December 9, 2004.

38. Leonard N. Fleming, "All Eyes are on House Races in PA," *The Philadelphia Inquirer*, October 30, 2004, p. A5.

39. Federal Election Commission, "Party Financial Activity Summarized for 2004 Election Cycle," press release, March 2, 2005, www.fec.gov/press/press2005/20050302party/Party2004final. html (accessed July 1, 2005).

40. Ben Pershing and Lauren W. Whittington, "Greenwood Set to Leave House: GOPer May Head Biotech Assoc.," *Roll Call,* July 20, 2004, www.rollcall.com/issues/50_9/news/6307-1. html (accessed January 28, 2005).

41. Federal Election Commission, "Congressional Campaigns Spend $912 Million through Late November," press release, January 3, 2005, www.fec.gov/press/press2004/20050103canstat/ 20050103canstat.html (accessed January 28, 2005).

42. The Brown campaign's assertion is well founded. See Robin Kolodny, *Pursuing Majorities: Congressional Campaign Committees in American Politics* (Norman, OK: University of Oklahoma Press, 1998).

43. Peter Cari, political director, Democratic Congressional Campaign Committee, telephone interview by J. Quin Monson and Betsey Gimbel, December 14, 2004.

7

A Texas Tussle

The Frost–Sessions Battle in the Thirty-Second District[1]

J. Matthew Wilson

Southern Methodist University

From the moment in January 2004 when Martin Frost announced his intention to abandon the newly redistricted Twenty-fourth District and challenge incumbent Republican Pete Sessions in the Thirty-second, observers both locally and nationally pointed to this race as the marquee congressional match-up of the 2004 electoral cycle.[2] It was one of only two races nationally, both of which were in Texas, that pitted incumbents against each other and as such promised to be bruising battles. During the spring and summer, the contest was widely predicted to be both expensive and close. In the end, the first of these predictions proved accurate; the two candidates together raised and spent more than $9 million, and the parties and interest groups added several million more, making this the most expensive House race of the electoral cycle, the costliest Texas had ever seen, and one of the three most expensive in U.S. history.[3] When all the votes were tallied, however, the contest was not much of a nail-biter. Sessions prevailed with 54 percent of the vote to Frost's 44 percent, a result consistent with the generally Republican character of the new district.

Given the intense national interest surrounding the race and the relative paucity of competitive House contests, one might have expected the candidates' own campaigns to be overwhelmed by outside money and activity. The two political parties and a variety of national interest groups clearly saw this contest as one of a handful in which they might be able to make a difference. Nevertheless, the two candidates exercised a high degree of message control, and their own strategic and advertising decisions, not those of outside forces, drove the race. The candidates' own ample war chests and an unusual pact disavowing outside interference combined to keep the focus of activity squarely in their own campaigns.

THE ELECTORAL CONTEXT

The Thirty-second Congressional District in Texas, as it was in 2004, was created as a result of a very controversial and bitterly partisan redistricting process in 2003. At different times, Democrats in the state House fled to Oklahoma and Democrats in the state Senate fled to New Mexico to break the legislative quorum and prevent votes on Republican-backed electoral maps.[4] In the end, however, Republicans in the legislature prevailed, engineering a districting plan that put seven incumbent Democrats at risk. The new arrangement, widely decried by Democrats as a partisan gerrymander orchestrated from Washington by House Majority Leader Tom DeLay, redrew Representative Martin Frost's Twenty-fourth District and made it strongly Republican.[5] The only competitive district left in the Dallas–Fort Worth area was the Thirty-second, where Frost promptly moved to launch an uphill battle against incumbent Republican Pete Sessions.

The Thirty-second District, as currently configured, is demographically diverse. Contained entirely within Dallas County, it combines affluent areas of northern Dallas and the suburb of Richardson with blue-collar, ethnically mixed sections of Irving and the heavily Hispanic Oak Cliff area of south Dallas. The district is right-leaning, but not dramatically so. Its urban character softens the conservatism, particularly on social issues, that characterizes more rural portions of the state. While the district was clearly drawn to create a Republican advantage (Republican candidates averaged 64 percent of the district's vote in recent statewide elections), its ethnic breakdown gave Democrats some reason for hope.[6] The district's voting-age population is 55 percent non-Hispanic white, 31 percent Hispanic, 8 percent black, and 6 percent "other" (mostly Asian). Moreover, the white population includes virtually all of Dallas's Jewish community, a traditional Democratic constituency estimated at 5 to 6 percent of the district.[7] Thus, Democrats faced a difficult, but not hopeless, battle in the Thirty-second District.

THE CANDIDATES

Many Democrats felt that Martin Frost had a fighting chance in the race. With 26 years of service in the House, Frost was the Dean of the Texas delegation and had represented much of the Dallas–Fort Worth area, including significant parts of the new Thirty-second District, at some time during his congressional career. He had developed a reputation as both a tough campaigner and a tireless worker for local interests,[8] and he had a more moderate voting record in many areas than most House Democrats.[9] Moreover, as former head of the DCCC, he had access to national fundraising networks that would be the envy of most candidates. Finally, as the only Jewish member of Congress in Texas history, Frost understandably enjoyed considerable support, both electoral and financial, from the district's significant Jewish population.

Pete Sessions, the son of former FBI director William Sessions, presented a contrasting profile in many ways. While also an incumbent member of Congress since 1996, Sessions had not sought leadership positions within the party and, unlike Frost, seldom talked about "pork-barrel" accomplishments. Instead, Sessions emphasized his conservative ideology, did not shy away from the label "extreme," and embraced an almost libertarian philosophy on economic questions.[10] While Sessions had faced some fairly close contests in the Fifth District, which he left after the 2000 election to run in the more compact and urban Thirty-second, Frost represented his first serious challenger in the new district.

MONEY

As mentioned previously, an extraordinary amount of money was raised and spent in this race, mostly by the candidates' campaigns. Aided by the higher contribution limits passed as part of BCRA, each candidate raised over $4.5 million, the clear majority of that coming from individual donations (see Table 7.1). While the national party organizations (see Table 7.2) and select interest groups also intervened, especially in the final days of the race, their combined broadcast expenditures of about $1.5 million were clearly secondary to those of the candidates (see Table 7.3). The fact that the candidates themselves were directly controlling the vast majority of the expenditures in this race allowed for fairly tight image and message control on both sides; the major arguments made on television, on the radio, and in

TABLE 7.1   CANDIDATE RECEIPTS AND EXPENDITURES, TEXAS THIRTY-SECOND
CONGRESSIONAL DISTRICT RACE, 2003 TO 2004

	MARTIN FROST (D)	PETE SESSIONS (R)
From PACs	$1,302,207	$1,692,242
From individuals	3,199,918	2,488,111
From party	10,000	27,150
From candidate	50	0
Other contributions	110,929	313,377
Total receipts	4,623,104	4,520,880
Total expenditures	4,761,288	4,512,464
Cash on hand (as of 12/31/04)	22,744	478,897

Source: Federal Election Commission, "2003–04 U.S. House and U.S. Senate Candidate Info," December 31, 2004, www.fecinfo.com/cgi-win/x_candidate.exe?DoFn=&sYR=2004 (accessed February 11, 2005).
Note: Abbreviations: PAC, political action committee.

TABLE 7.2 INDEPENDENT EXPENDITURES BY PARTY COMMITTEE, TEXAS THIRTY-SECOND CONGRESSIONAL DISTRICT RACE, 2003–2004

PARTY COMMITTEE	CANDIDATE	INDEPENDENT EXPENDITURES FOR	INDEPENDENT EXPENDITURES AGAINST	TOTAL	PARTY TOTAL
DCCC					$1,114,511
	Martin Frost	$671,126	0	$671,126	
	Pete Sessions	0	$443,385	443,385	
NRCC					747,483
	Martin Frost	0	663,833	663,833	
	Pete Session	83,650	0	83,650	

Source: Federal Election Commission, ftp://ftp.fec.gov/FEC (accessed January 5, 2005).
Note: Abbreviations: DCCC, Democratic Congressional Campaign Committee; NRCC, National Republican Congressional Committee.

direct mail had a remarkable, some might say mind-numbing, consistency. Anyone in the district even vaguely attentive to politics could not help but know, by campaign's end, that Frost was a "tax-and-spend liberal" and that Sessions was an "extremist" who supported a national sales tax. Neither candidate was dependent on outside efforts, largely because both were able to raise nearly unprecedented sums of money. Frost campaign spokesman Justin Kitsch repeatedly emphasized that "Martin Frost has all the money he needs to communicate with voters."[11] Likewise, Sessions' campaign manager Chris Homan insisted that their campaign always enjoyed an abundance of financial resources.[12] Thus, unlike some other competitive races around the country, the financial dynamics of this contest were overwhelmingly candidate-centered.

CANDIDATES

Both candidates enjoyed tremendous success with fundraising. Martin Frost's connections, including his seat on the House Rules Committee and prior leadership of the DCCC, gave him a national resource base on which to draw, as did his ties to the Dallas Jewish community.[13] In addition, resentment about perceived injustices in the redistricting process, even in the Republican-leaning district itself,[14] made the election to some extent a referendum on Tom DeLay and the whole re-map fight. This issue spurred contributions to Frost from incensed Democrats in Texas and nationally.[15] These factors, combined with the relative paucity of Democratic House opportunities around the country, served to funnel money into the Frost campaign.

All of these factors, though, were double-edged swords. Frost's national prominence and past political activity had earned him as many enemies as

TABLE 7.3   THE AIR WAR: TELEVISION AND RADIO ADVERTISING EXPENDITURES,
TEXAS THIRTY-SECOND CONGRESSIONAL DISTRICT RACE, 2004[a]

TYPE AND ORGANIZATION	TV	RADIO	TOTAL $ SPENT	CMAG TV
Democratic Allies[b]				
Candidates				
Martin Frost Campaign	$1,082,932	$152,150	**$1,235,082**	$1,995,692
Political Parties				
DCCC	879,410	11,500	**890,910**	927,502
Interest Groups				
Communication Workers of America	—	—	—	7,147
Stronger America Now	—	—	—	2,387
Republican Allies[b]				
Candidates				
Pete Sessions Campaign	1,546,557	231,084	**1,777,641**	2,137,955
Political Parties				
NRCC	657,250	—	**657,250**	—
Interest Groups				
Coalition for the Future American Worker	40,750	48,000	**88,750**	—
Nonpartisan				
Interest Groups				
AARP	—	—	—	300,203

[a]Please see Appendix A for a more detailed data explanation. The ad-buy data collected for this study may contain extraneous data because of the difficulty in determining the content of the ads. The parties or interest groups that purchased the ad buys possibly ran some ads promoting House, Senate, or presidential candidates or ballot propositions not in the study's sample but still within that media market. Unless the participating academics were able to determine the exact content of the ad buy from the limited information given by the station, the data may contain observations that do not pertain to the study's relevant House, Senate, or presidential battleground races. For comparison purposes the Campaign Media Analysis Group data are included in the table. Because of the sheer volume of television and radio stations and varying degrees of compliance in providing ad-buy information, data on spending by various groups might be incomplete. These data do not include every station in the state. This table is not intended to represent comprehensive organization spending or activity within the sample races. Television ads purchased from national cable stations that aired in this state are not reflected in this table. A more complete picture can be obtained by examining this table with Table 7.4.

[b]Certain organizations that maintained neutrality were categorized according to which candidates their ads supported or attacked or whether the organization was openly anti- or pro- conservative or liberal.

In blank cells, "—" only reflects the absence of collected data and does not imply the organization was inactive in that medium.

Source: Data compiled from David B. Magleby, J. Quin Monson, and Kelly D. Patterson, "2004 Campaign Communications Database," (Center for the Study of Elections and Democracy: Brigham Young University, 2005), and Campaign Media Analysis Group data.

Note: Abbreviations: DCCC, Democratic Congressional Campaign Committee; NRCC, National Republican Congressional Committee; AARP, American Association of Retired Persons.

friends. Amy Walter, U.S. House editor for the *Cook Political Report*, summed it up well: "The animosity that the Republicans have for Frost is unparalleled because Frost was able to long preserve what Republicans saw as an unfair redistricting advantage for Democrats."[16] This, combined with Frost's history as an aggressive partisan and bare-knuckled campaigner, made him the Republicans' top incumbent Democrat target nationwide.[17] The fervent desire among conservatives to "de-Frost Texas," as President Bush put it during an election-eve stop in the district, combined with Sessions' status as an incumbent member of the majority party, ensured a steady flow of campaign cash into his coffers.[18]

In the end, the Frost campaign slightly out-spent the Sessions campaign for the electoral cycle, spending $4.76 million to Sessions' $4.51 million. In a sense, though, these figures are misleading; Frost raised and spent almost $900,000 of that during 2003 to fight Republican redistricting proposals before he had even decided (or had been forced) to run in the Thirty-second District.[19] As a result, the Sessions campaign maintained a consistent cash-on-hand advantage throughout the race, particularly during the crucial final two weeks.[20]

The two campaigns were broadly similar in the sources of their funds, with a few interesting differences. Both raised the majority of their money from individuals, but Sessions drew a somewhat higher percentage than Frost from PACs, 37 percent versus 28 percent (see Table 7.1). This represented a major surge in individual donations from the previous cycle for both candidates; in 2002, Sessions drew 48 percent of his total funds from PACs and Frost a whopping 60 percent.[21] Based on the categories created by the Center for Responsive Politics, Frost drew the largest share of his contributions from "lawyers and lobbyists," while Sessions drew his largest share from "finance, insurance, and real estate," not surprising given the positions of the two men's political parties.[22]

Despite the Sessions cash advantage and the differential sources of money for the two campaigns, the real story here is the extraordinary amount of money raised by both candidates and the fact that both acknowledged that money did not play a significant role in the outcome. Each side had the resources to fill the airwaves and mailboxes in the district over the last month of the campaign and to communicate their major themes over and over again to voters. Since both sides had plenty of money to advertise heavily and to make their case, the outcome came down to campaign strategies and the partisan complexion of the district. Frost never found a way to make significant numbers of Republicans desert Sessions, and Sessions never made the sort of personal mistake or tactical blunder that would have allowed Frost a real opening.

POLITICAL PARTIES

While the national political parties and their allied interest groups did play some role in this race, it was sharply curtailed by a remarkable development early on in the campaign: a joint pledge by the candidates to discourage any outside intervention and to publicly disavow any advertising done by outside groups. This unusual commitment came in response to advertisements run in April on most of the major Dallas television stations by a group called the Coalition for the Future American Worker (CFAW), blasting Martin Frost's purported support for "bills encouraging mass immigration."[23] The ads featured grainy black-and-white images of Hispanics in the background and were immediately denounced by Frost and his supporters as racially inflammatory. While Sessions denied any knowledge of or involvement with the ads, he refused to specifically denounce them, preferring instead to ignore the controversy. This, in turn, prompted Frost to accuse Sessions of "hiding behind the white sheets of white supremacy," a charge the Sessions campaign angrily rejected.[24]

In response to the controversy over these ads, the two campaigns negotiated a pledge to try to curtail any outside interference in the race. Initially proposed by the Frost campaign[25] and signed by the two candidates in April, the pledge committed them to "publicly disavow any television, radio, direct mail, newspaper ad, e-mail, or telephone calls that are not specifically and publicly authorized by their campaigns; and publicly request the sponsors of any unauthorized communication to cease their communication to voters."[26] Since both campaigns knew that they would have substantial war chests at their disposal, they could make such a pledge without worrying that they would be inhibited in their efforts to disseminate their message. While the DCCC quickly agreed to abide by the candidates' request, the NRCC was noncommittal, and CFAW, the group whose efforts had spurred all of the uproar in the first place, professed their intention to ignore it.[27] Of course, the pledge was not legally binding; nonetheless, it served to sharply curtail the activities of outside groups.[28] There was virtually no party or interest group spending in the race until the very end. As late as October 7, party insiders said that they did not expect either the DCCC or the NRCC to run independent expenditure ads in the district.[29]

The party committees did buy some significant television advertising toward the end of the race, for a combined total of about $1.5 million, much less than what the candidates' own campaigns spent (see Table 7.3). While the party committees had initially planned only a limited presence in the Texas races and especially the Thirty-second District, given the candidates' ample campaign war chests, the DCCC decided in October to make a major push to save as many embattled incumbents as it could, borrowing $10 million to cover its expenditures in the races.[30] Thus, the DCCC began the influx of national party money, and the NRCC ultimately felt compelled to respond, generating a wave of back-and-forth attack ads during the final days that disproportionately favored the cash-strapped Frost campaign.[31] However, given that this race represented one of only a few hotly contested ones around the country, featured two incumbents, and played out in a major media market, both national parties' efforts must be viewed as modest. Whether driven by the candidates' disavowal of outside money, their ample war chests, or a combination of both, the national committees were content to play clearly secondary roles in this contest. In addition, the new BCRA requirement that parties spend "hard money" through independent expenditures made it even more difficult to justify the allocation of these scarce resources to a contest where the candidates had so much money at their disposal.

INTEREST GROUPS

Perhaps in response to the candidates' pledge, outside interest groups were even more limited in their activities. After the initial highly publicized advertisements of CFAW, only three other groups mounted any significant effort in the race: Planned Parenthood of North Texas on behalf of Frost and AJS and the Council for Citizens Against Government Waste on behalf of Sessions. In all three cases, the groups' activities were limited to targeted mailers attacking one of the candidates (see Table 7.4). While some other organizations, most notably labor unions and religious groups, contributed in ways other than advertising, such as canvassing and GOTV efforts, the overall national interest group effort was remarkably limited for a race of this magnitude.[32] Despite the race's intensity, importance, and relatively high national profile, it remained from start to finish a candidate-dominated contest.

THE EFFECTS OF MONEY

Because the Frost and Sessions campaigns directly controlled the great majority of the money spent in this race, they were able to achieve a high degree of message control in the advertising. From the outset, their respective strategies were relatively straightforward. Sessions adopted a fairly conventional game plan. He sought to portray Frost as a liberal, tie him to national Democratic figures like Senator John Kerry, and emphasize his own connections to President Bush.[33] Sessions touted his conservative ideology much more than his pork-barrel accomplishments. Early in the race, Sessions' chief of staff, Guy Harrison, admitted that "Pete is not out there waving the flag that he is the number one person on DART [Dallas Area Rapid Transit] or on bridges."[34] Frost, conversely, emphasized these sorts of local issues and projects, so much so that Sessions' campaign manager, Chris Homan, joked that he sounded like he was running for mayor.[35] This was part of Frost's strategy to de-emphasize national partisan conflict and make the race something other than a straight Democrat–Republican contest, which he would likely lose. From the outset, he faced two difficult tasks: He had to win very high margins in the Hispanic areas and increase turnout there to unprecedented

TABLE 7.4 Number of Unique Campaign Communications by Organization, Texas Thirty-Second Congressional District Race, 2004[a]

Type and Organization	Type of Campaign Communication						
	Mail	Newspaper/ Magazine	Personal Contact	Phone Call	Radio Ads	TV Ads	Total
Democratic Allies[b]							
Candidates							
Martin Frost Campaign	32	1	6	1	5	10	55
Congressman Martin Frost (taxpayer expense)	3	—	—	—	—	—	3
Political Parties							
DCCC	—	—	—	—	1	3	4
Interest Groups							
Action Fund—Planned Parenthood of North Texas, Inc.	2	—	—	—	—	—	2
Republican Allies[b]							
Candidates							
Pete Sessions Campaign	32	—	2	—	5	11	50
Congressman Pete Sessions (taxpayer expense)	4	—	—	—	—	—	4
Political Parties							
Texas Victory 2004—A Project of the Republican Party of Texas	5	—	2	—	—	—	7
NRCC	2	—	—	—	—	2	4

Interest Groups						
Americans for Job Security	2	—	—	—	—	2
Club for Growth	—	—	—	—	1[c]	1
Council for Citizens Against Government Waste	1	—	—	—	—	1
John Carona Campaign	1	—	—	1	—	1
U.S. Chamber of Commerce	—	—	—	1	—	1
Nonpartisan						
Interest Groups						
AARP	1	—	—	—	—	1

[a]See Appendix A for a more detailed data explanation. Data represent the number of unique or distinct pieces or ads by the group and do not represent a count of total items sent or made. This table is not intended to portray comprehensive organization activity within the sample races. A more complete picture can be obtained by examining this table together with Table 7.3.

[b]Certain organizations that maintained neutrality were categorized according to which candidates their ads supported or attacked or whether the organization was openly anti- or pro- conservative or liberal.

In blank cells, "—" only reflects the absence of collected data and does not imply the organization was inactive in that medium.

[c]Stephen Moore, president, Club for Growth, interview by David B. Magleby and Richard Hawkins, Washington, D.C., November 5, 2004.

Source: Data compiled from David B. Magleby, J. Quin Monson, and Kelly D. Patterson, "2004 Campaign Communications Database," (Center for the Study of Elections and Democracy: Brigham Young University, 2005).

Note: Abbreviations: DCCC, Democratic Congressional Campaign Committee; NRCC, National Republican Congressional Committee; AARP, American Association of Retired Persons.

levels, and he had to convince a significant minority of North Dallas Republicans to split their tickets and vote for Bush and Frost.[36] At the same time, he hoped to portray himself as an independent centrist and Sessions as a dangerous extremist whose ideology went well beyond being simply "conservative."[37] Both candidates' advertising clearly reflected these strategic objectives.

THE GROUND WAR

Both campaigns, as well as the few interest groups that chose to intervene in the race, saved their most aggressive attacks for direct mail. As reflected in Table 7.4, dozens of distinct mailers were produced and sent out during the course of the campaign. Given each side's substantial financial resources and the relatively low cost of direct mail, this form of campaigning was virtually unlimited in this race. Since direct mail can also be targeted more efficiently than either television or radio, it became the medium of choice for both sides to communicate their most incendiary attacks on each other. For example, two of the charges leveled at Sessions by Frost, that he was a streaker (he had been involved in a 1974 college mass nudity incident) and that he stole his opponent's yard signs (during his 2002 campaign), are encapsulated in one mailer headlined, "It's ten o'clock: Do you know where your Congressman is?" It concludes by asserting: "Pete Sessions admits indecent exposure as an 'immature' young man. But he's still lurking around in the dark, acting like one." In addition to a bevy of mailers hitting the key Frost campaign themes of air safety, job outsourcing, and opposition to a national sales tax, these attacks on Sessions' character comprised a large part of the Frost direct-mail campaign.

The Sessions campaign responded in kind. Seizing upon an incident earlier in the campaign in which Frost had invited Peter Yarrow of Peter, Paul, and Mary to perform at a campaign fundraiser, then later cancelled when it came to light that Yarrow was a convicted child molester, Sessions produced a mailer blasting Frost. The mailer, printed in English on one side and Spanish on the other, had "Martin Frost Child Molester" ("Martin Frost Molestador de Niños") in large gold block letters and surrounding words in smaller white typeface.[38] The full line read "Martin Frost Child Molester Timeline" and chronicled the Yarrow incident, but this was not apparent at first glance. Clearly, the negative tone of Frost's mailers was reflected in Sessions' direct-mail campaign as well, along with his standard campaign themes of conservative values and opposition to tax increases.

THE AIR WAR

After the initial salvo from CFAW, television advertising in this race became the exclusive province of the two campaigns and, to a lesser extent late in the contest, the national parties. In the summer and early fall, both sides ran a series of positive ads designed to introduce them to new constituents who might not be familiar with their records. In Frost's case, these emphasized his sponsorship of the AMBER Alert law and his successful dispute mediation during the American Airlines strike. Sessions' ads highlighted major national issues like job loss, rising healthcare costs, and taxes before outlining a "Pete Sessions solution" in each case.

As the campaign went on, however, the advertising became both more personal and more negative. Frost's ads, in keeping with his desire to blur ideological distinctions in the race, were both extremely creative and unusual for a Democrat: He sought to associate himself with popular conservatives like President Bush and Senator Hutchison while associating his opponent with liberal icons. Seizing on Sessions' opposition to a 2001 aviation security bill that passed 410 to 9 in the House, Frost denounced his opponent as soft on terror and out of step with President Bush on this important issue. Sessions made things worse for himself during the candidates' first debate by using Senator Ted Kennedy's security delays at Logan Airport in Boston as proof that air security had become unnecessarily tight.[39] A Frost television ad quickly followed on the topic of air safety, highlighting his support for tougher security measures and chiding Sessions for caring more about Ted Kennedy's travel schedule than passenger safety. The ad blurred partisan and ideological distinctions in the race, linking Frost with popular Republican measures and pairing Sessions with Ted Kennedy. Ultimately, though, Frost may have pressed this issue a bit too far. His campaign in mid-October aired a controversial advertisement on air safety that attacked Sessions' vote and showed black-and-white images of the twin towers' destruction. The ad was quickly denounced by former New York Mayor Rudy Giuliani, and by several victims' families. Indeed, Giuliani filmed an ad for Sessions the next week. The controversial nature of the ad may have cost Frost some of the advantage he had gained with the air safety issue.[40]

Sessions' ads were also primarily negative in the closing weeks of the campaign, seeking to paint Frost as a classic tax-and-spend liberal. Highlighting all of the areas in which Frost had previously supported tax increases, the ads argued that Texas could not afford "the cost of Frost." This theme was also emphasized in most of the late independent expenditures by the NRCC. These ads, while relatively standard fare in Republican congressional campaigns, proved highly effective in this race. By the end of the campaign, Sessions' polling showed that a clear majority of voters identified Frost as a "liberal," a huge albatross in a Republican-leaning district.[41] Ultimately, Sessions' ads did not need to be creative for him to win; if he could drive home the tax-and-spend message about Martin Frost, he would likely prevail on election day.

At the same time that messages about taxes and air safety dominated advertising in the mainstream media, the candidates were conducting a parallel campaign for Hispanic votes on *Telemundo* and *Univision*. Clearly, Frost's campaign efforts in the Hispanic community were more aggressive, and he knew that he would win the lion's share of their votes. Sessions, however, did not concede the group entirely to Frost, deploying his Mexican-American wife and a small army of volunteers wearing "Adelante con Pete Sessions" ("Forward with Pete Sessions") T-shirts in an effort to keep Frost from completely running away with the Oak Cliff precincts. For a time polls indicated that these efforts were paying some dividends, with 30 percent of Hispanics planning to vote for Sessions, until Frost aired a devastating ad on Spanish-language television. The ad began with footage from a 1996 interview in which Sessions said, of illegal immigrants, that "we run them down, and when we capture them, we do not process them—we put them on a military plane and fly them to the southernmost entry point in Mexico." This was interspersed with images of a Mexican-American family watching with consternation and was followed by their angry comments that "no somos lobos; no somos perros" ("we are not wolves; we are not dogs").[42] This, according to Sessions campaign manager, Chris Homan, was the most damaging advertisement that Frost ran during the entire campaign, in Spanish or in English. Within a week, Sessions' Hispanic vote share had dropped from over 30 percent to 15 percent.[43] While those numbers crept back up over 20 percent by election day, aided in part by rebuttal advertising featuring Sessions' wife, the ad's effect serves as testimony to the potential efficacy of targeted advertising in Spanish-language media.

CONCLUSION

In the end, after millions of dollars were spent, the redrawn Thirty-second District produced the outcome it was intended to deliver: a win for Sessions that was neither a landslide nor especially close. Both sides had plenty of money with which to pursue their campaign strategies, but Sessions was ultimately more successful. He managed to convince most voters in the district that Martin Frost was a liberal and that a vote for Sessions was an additional measure of support for President Bush. Frost, conversely, largely failed in his two key strategic objectives; registration and turnout in Hispanic precincts did not increase by nearly as much as he had hoped, and there was relatively little ticket splitting in North Dallas, where Sessions ran within 3 percent of Bush in most precincts.[44] This, in the end, produced a 10-point margin of victory for Sessions that will likely deter significant Democratic opposition in the near future. If Frost, with his tremendous financial resources and 26 years of experience in Congress, could not win more than 44 percent of the vote in the district, it is difficult to see another Democrat giving Sessions a run for his money any time soon.

This race provides some interesting lessons in terms of campaign finance. To begin with, it shows that national parties and interest groups do not *have* to be major players even in key, hotly contested races. The candidates' pledge, combined with their own impressive financial resources, succeeded in deterring outside intervention, especially from interest groups. As a result, both candidates were able to exercise strong message control, instead of being distracted and focusing on the issues important to outside groups, like the illegal immigration theme raised by CFAW. In addition, this race showcased the growing importance of Hispanic outreach in many districts and the utility of Spanish-language media for this purpose. Even though the end result was not quite as close as many predicted, the Frost–Sessions race in Texas's Thirty-second District provided great political theater and highlighted some key issues about money and campaigning in the current electoral climate.

NOTES

1. The author would like to thank Kristina Kiik for her excellent and invaluable work in collecting data for this chapter.
2. Bob Ray Sanders, "Republicans Must Endure Frost's Bite," *Fort Worth Star-Telegram,* January 18, 2004, p. B1.
3. Dave Levinthal, "Frost–Sessions Contest Was Year's Most Expensive Race for U.S. House," *Dallas Morning News,* December 4, 2004, p. B4.
4. Gromer Jeffers, Jr., "Democrats to Perry: Back Down; No More Special Sessions, Albuquerque Exiles Tell Governor," *Dallas Morning News,* August 26, 2003, p. A3.
5. Molly Ivins, "The Dirty Deal of Texas Redistricting," *Naples Daily News,* January 9, 2004, www.naplesnews.com/news/2004/jan/09/ndn_molly_ivins_the_dirty_deal_of_texas_redistric/(accessed December 14, 2004).
6. These data, from reports compiled as part of the Texas Legislative Council's redistricting analysis (www.tlc.state.tx.us/redist/congress.htm), overstate the Republican skew of the district somewhat, as they include some races where the Democrats fielded very weak, noncompetitive statewide candidates.
7. Martin Frost Campaign, "Fact Sheet: Martin Frost's TX-32 Re-election Campaign," press release, April 20, 2004, www.martinfrost.com/news/facts (accessed April 20, 2004).
8. Dave Levinthal, "Friend and Foe Alike Marvel at Resilience of Underdog Frost," *Dallas Morning News,* October 30, 2004, p. 1B. On the campaign trail, Frost repeatedly emphasized his role in securing federal funds for local transportation projects and his efforts on behalf of major local employers like American Airlines.
9. While Frost is not the consummate centrist that his campaign literature claims, his lifetime voting scores from both liberal and conservative interest groups—74 from Americans for Democratic Action (www.adaction.org [accessed January 7, 2005]) and 16 from The American Conservative Union (www.conservative.org [accessed January 7, 2005])—suggest that he is also far from his party's leftward fringe. To cite one specific example, Frost is a strong supporter of the war in Iraq and of President Bush's Middle East policy generally.
10. Dave Levinthal, "Sessions Pushes for Tax Changes and Doesn't Duck the Extreme," *Dallas Morning News,* October 31, 2004, p. B6. Sessions' interest group ratings—2 from Americans for Democratic Action and 97 from The American Conservative Union—reflect his consistently conservative philosophy.
11. Dave Levinthal, "Frost Leads Sessions in Cash Raised, Spent," *Dallas Morning News,* October 16, 2004, p. B7.
12. Chris Homan, campaign manager, Sessions for Congress, interview with Matthew Wilson, Dallas, TX, December 9, 2004. This financial security is underscored by the fact that the Sessions campaign ended the race with almost $500,000 unspent cash on hand (see Table 7.1).
13. Dave Levinthal, "Where the Cash Is Coming from for Sessions, Frost Race," *Dallas Morning News,* October 24, 2004, p. B1.

14. Dave Levinthal, "Voters Split Over New Lines; In Poll, Plurality Say Republican-friendly Boundaries Unfair," *Dallas Morning News*, October 12, 2004, p. 19A.

15. Dave Levinthal, "Heated Race between Frost, Sessions Gets Scorching," *Dallas Morning News*, September 11, 2004, p. A1.

16. Ibid.

17. Homan, interview, December 9, 2004.

18. Dave Levinthal, "Sessions Gets Boost from Bush during President's SMU Visit," *Dallas Morning News*, November 2, 2004, p. A10.

19. Todd Gillman, "Setting Up a Showdown; With Sessions–Frost Battle at Forefront, Fight for Congress Begins," *Dallas Morning News*, March 10, 2004, p. B1.

20. Homan, interview, December 9, 2004. This advantage is confirmed by Levinthal, "Where the Cash is Coming from for Sessions, Frost Race," p. B1.

21. Of course, two substantial variables had changed since 2002: The Bipartisan Campaign Reform Act had doubled the amount of money that an individual could give to a candidate from $1,000 to $2,000, and Frost and Sessions were now both facing a genuinely competitive and nationally visible election battle. Both of these factors likely drove up the level of individual contributions in the 2004 race.

22. Center for Responsive Politics, "2003–2004 Campaign Reports," www.opensecrets.org (accessed December 13, 2004).

23. The full text of this advertisement can be found at www.americanworker.org/dallasads.html (accessed January 7, 2005).

24. Dave Levinthal, "Frost Says Sessions Should Denounce Immigration Ads," *Dallas Morning News*, April 7, 2004, p. B8.

25. While Frost was first to suggest the pledge for no outside money, the Sessions campaign was happy to agree. As Sessions' campaign manager Chris Homan indicated, they expected all along to have a edge regarding cash on hand and, thus, were more than willing to limit any outside influences that might mitigate that advantage (Homan, interview, December 9, 2004).

26. Dave Levinthal, "Candidates Spar Over Clean Campaign Pledge," *Dallas Morning News*, October 19, 2004, p. B4.

27. Dave Levinthal, "Frost, Sessions Vow to Disavow 'Outside' Ads," *Dallas Morning News*, April 28, 2004, p. B12. Ironically, however, the Democratic Congressional Campaign Committee became the first outside group to significantly violate the pledge, and Frost refused to denounce their efforts on his behalf. The Coalition for the Future American Worker had attempted to run a second round of anti-immigration ads targeting Frost in August, but this time the effort was denounced by Sessions and rebuffed by all of the Dallas network affiliates. See Dave Levinthal, "Rivals Together on Immigrant Ads," *Dallas Morning News*, August 10, 2004, p. B10.

28. The actual inhibiting effects of the pledge were probably greater for interest groups than for the national party organizations. Peter Cari of the Democratic Congressional Campaign Committee suggested that his organization's relatively limited role in the Thirty-second District race, at least until the campaign's closing days, was more a function of the Frost campaign being flush with cash than of the non-intervention pledge; Peter Cari, political director, Democratic Congressional Campaign Committee, telephone interview by J. Quin Monson and Betsey Gimbel, December 14, 2004. Moreover, Frost himself indicated during the summer that the pledge was aimed more at "rogue" advocacy groups than at the party organizations; Martin Frost, Democratic candidate for U.S. House of Representatives, interview by Matthew Wilson, Coppell, TX, August 14, 2004.

29. "Veterans to Watch (24D, 18R)—Texas 32: Pull Out the Barf Bags, This One Is Getting Nasty," *House Race Hotline*, October 7, 2004. In the end this prediction proved incorrect.

30. "National Briefing—Battle for the House: TX-vestment," *House Race Hotline*, November 9, 2004.

31. Dave Levinthal, "National Parties Pour It On in Race," *Dallas Morning News*, October 27, 2004, p. B14.

32. Homan, interview, December 9, 2004.

33. Sessions was largely successful in these objectives. By the end of the race, his campaign's internal polling showed that a majority of voters in the district believed that the word "liberal" accurately characterized Martin Frost; Homan, interview, December 9, 2004.

34. Todd J. Gillman and Tony Hartzell, "DART Accusations open Congressional Campaign," *Dallas Morning News*, March 11, 2004, p. B1.
35. Homan, interview, December 9, 2004.
36. Frost, interview, August 14, 2004.
37. Ibid.
38. Dave Levinthal, "Frost Fires Back over 'Child Molester' Mailer," *Dallas Morning News*, October 21, 2004, p. B1.
39. Jennifer Arend, "Rivals Frost, Sessions Face off," *Dallas Morning News*, September 13, 2004, p. B1.
40. Dave Levinthal, "Use of Trade Center in Ads Stirs Debate," *Dallas Morning News*, October 19, 2004, p. B1.
41. Homan, interview, December 9, 2004.
42. "Frost Airs Ad on Sessions, Immigrants," *Al Día*, October 16, 2004, p. B3.
43. Homan, interview, December 9, 2004.
44. "Veterans to Watch (24D, 18R)—Texas 32: Back to Your Roots," *House Race Hotline*, October 1, 2004.

8

LOOKING BACK TO SEE WHERE
WE ARE GOING

DAVID B. MAGLEBY, J. QUIN MONSON,
AND KELLY D. PATTERSON

Brigham Young University

The case studies in this volume help to explain how candidates, parties, and interest groups have adapted to the BCRA campaign environment. Some of the adaptations appear to be very important, while others are seemingly inconsequential. History teaches that it often takes more than one election cycle for the electoral players—candidates, parties, interest groups, and individual donors—to adapt to new rules. Therefore, it is important to wait at least one more election cycle to see which practices may endure.

Even more than is normally the case, the 2004 presidential election overshadowed the other contests on the ballot, including contests for the U.S. Senate and U.S. House. "The Senate is important," said Harold Ickes, "but taking down a sitting president is a monumental task."[1] This focus on the presidential race was true not only in media attention but also in terms of candidate, party, and interest group expenditures. The NRA, for example, decided not to invest in the Oklahoma Senate race, although the organization would have allocated resources to this race in previous years.[2]

There were several highly contested Senate races in 2004, but these were typically not in presidential battleground states, excepting Florida, Pennsylvania, and for a time Colorado. Competitive U.S. Senate races in 2004 were either in states that had gone heavily to Bush in 2000 and were considered safe for Bush in 2004, or in states that had been competitive in 2000. None of the competitive U.S. Senate races in 2004 were in states that had gone substantially to Gore in 2000 or were seen as safe for Kerry in 2004. The red-state nature of most competitive U.S. Senate races in 2004 had important implications. Bush carried Oklahoma by 32 percent, Alaska by 27 percent, South Dakota by 21 percent, South Carolina by 17 percent, and North

Carolina by 12 percent. Political professionals from both parties frequently commented to us on how difficult it is for a Senate candidate to overcome that kind of advantage at the top of the ticket. Benjamin Jones, speaking of the red-state nature of the map said, "at some point you can build the best team in the world but you can't make up that margin."[3]

The surge in spending on the 2004 presidential race is well documented, but less frequently observed is the record campaign spending in several 2004 US Senate races. In four of the races we monitored in 2004—Alaska, Colorado, Oklahoma, and South Dakota—new records were spent by the candidates in money raised and spent. Candidates, as we have demonstrated, exploited the higher individual contribution limits allowed under BCRA and in at least one case the Millionaire's Amendment, which allows a candidate opposing a self-financed millionaire spending substantial amounts of personal fund to have higher individual contribution limits. In Colorado Senate, Democrat Ken Salazar raised $750,000 in this way in his contest against millionaire Republican Pete Coors.

The number of competitive Senate races in 2004 was typical of recent election years. However, the number of competitive U.S. House races in 2004 dwindled to historical lows. Figure 8.1 plots the number of competitive contests for the U.S. House over the last seven elections. The final number would have been even smaller without the unusual redistricting of Texas congressional districts enacted by the Texas legislature in 2003. This partisan gerrymandering changed the partisan composition of Texas districts to benefit

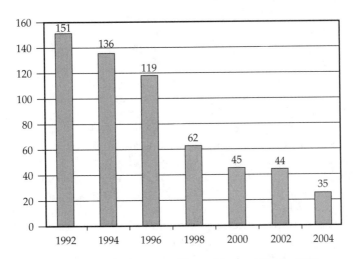

FIGURE 8.1   COMPETITIVE HOUSE RACES, 1992 TO 2004

Source: Charlie Cook, "National Overview," *Cook Political Report,* October 4, 2002, p. 6; "2004 Races at a Glance," *Cook Political Report,* October 15, 2004, www.cookpolitical.com (accessed May 25, 2006).

Note: Competitive races are those classified by Cook as "toss ups" or leaning toward one party.

Republicans and forced Democratic incumbents to run against Republican incumbents. The net effect of the redistricting, a retirement, and an incumbent switching parties were a gain for the GOP of six seats in the Texas delegation. Roughly 12 percent of competitive House races in 2004 were the result of this single act of redistricting. In the Texas Thirty-second District race (see Chapter 7), Texas Democrat Martin Frost lost a difficult campaign to Republican incumbent Pete Sessions. Nick Lampson, Max Sandlin, and Charles Stenholm were also casualties of redistricting.[4]

The small number of competitive races in both the House and Senate in 2004 meant that groups and parties concentrated their efforts and spending on a relatively small number of races, as they have in the past. This concentration of efforts continues the trend of groups and parties seeking to maximize their impact by spending on those races where their resources have the best chance of swinging a race their way. It also meant that safe-seat incumbents were pressed to contribute excess funds in their campaign accounts to their respective party congressional campaign committees. The South Dakota At-Large district candidate Stephanie Herseth (D) received $179,000 from other candidate committees, the most out of all races for the U.S. House. Republican House members also invested in this race, giving $105,500 to Herseth's opponent, Larry Diedrich, the tenth highest amount from other candidate committees.[5]

The small number of competitive races and the importance attached to the presidential race led some interest groups to alter their normal practices. Many groups that had previously concentrated their resources on congressional races devoted most of their resources to the presidential race in 2004. The LCV and NARAL Pro-Choice America both saw their presidential expenditures grow to unprecedented levels. Mark Longabaugh, senior vice president of political affairs at the LCV, called his organization's focus on the presidential election a "historic shift."[6] One major exception to the LCV focus on the presidential races was its heavy investment in the Colorado U.S. Senate race. As summarized in the Colorado Senate case study, the LCV spent $1.1 million on mail, GOTV, and television ads, trying to speak to voters who were concerned about the environment.[7] The LCV branded Coors "Polluter Pete" in their mail and television campaign, which not only captured national attention but also resonated with Coloradan voters.[8]

Another factor that reinforced the presidency-centered nature of 2004 is the relatively small number of gubernatorial contests on the 2004 ballot. Over time, states have shifted gubernatorial elections to mid-term or off years. Only eleven states elected governors in 2004.[9] Of these, only six were competitive, and, among those six, only New Hampshire was considered a true presidential battleground state in the end. All these factors combined suggest that it is necessary to wait at least one more election cycle to accurately gauge the extent to which changes in interest group and party behavior have more to do with a competitive presidential cycle than changes in the campaign finance law. With the president-centered nature of the cycle clearly in our mind, we look at some patterns that may emerge in subsequent cycles.

LOOKING BACK TO LOOK AHEAD[10]

Several patterns emerge from our examination of the individual races. First, congressional candidates, party committees, and interest groups in competitive 2004 elections continued to rely heavily on personal contact, mail, telephone, and e-mail—what we have called the "ground war"—to communicate with voters. In the competitive races monitored in 2004 by the CSED project, U.S. House candidates and Democratic U.S. Senate candidates sent an average of about 10 pieces of general election mail (see Table 8.1). The number for Republican U.S. Senate candidates was about six per contest. In addition, the parties and interest groups had extensive mail campaigns, with the NRSC sending more Senate mail than the DSCC. Groups for which we gathered at least 10 unique pieces of mail across our sample of contests included, on the Democratic side, CSS, the AFL-CIO, the Sierra Club, the LCV, and the National Education Association (NEA). Similarly visible Republican-leaning direct-mail campaigns came from the U.S. Chamber of Commerce, the NRA, the NAR, National Right to Life, the United Seniors Association, the NFIB, and the Seniors Coalition. The U.S. Chamber of Commerce had the most aggressive mail campaign in our contests in 2004, with 56 unique mail pieces. Democratic candidates in our sample races had more active phone contacting, but candidates in both parties made extensive use of the phone, as did the state parties. Consistent with the Bush campaign's greater use of radio in 2004, Republican Senate candidates ran more unique radio ads than did Democratic Senate candidates.[11] Democratic Senate and House candidates had more unique television ads than their Republican opponents, but the NRCC and NRSC produced more ads than the DCCC and DSCC.

Comparing the ground war across cycles in congressional elections is subject to the vagaries of sampling, size of state, and so on, but there appears to have been substantially less mail or phone bank activity from the state party committees in 2004 than in 2000 or 2002. This is not surprising given the loss of soft money, which was previously the primary source of funds for such mail and phone banks. Interest groups that also appeared to scale back their direct-mail operations in congressional races included the AFL-CIO, the Sierra Club, the NEA, and NARAL Pro-Choice America. As noted, many of these organizations consciously decided to give less emphasis to congressional races in 2004. On the Republican side, however, we see evidence of more mail in congressional races in 2004 than previously by the Chamber of Commerce and the NAR. Other major Republican allies were near parity with past cycles.[12] Electioneering by parties and interest groups in 2004

TABLE 8.1 NUMBER OF UNIQUE CAMPAIGN COMMUNICATIONS BY ORGANIZATION, SAMPLE CONGRESSIONAL RACES, 2004[a]

Type and Organization	E-mail	Mail	Newspaper/ Magazine	Personal Contact	Phone Call	Radio	TV	Total Unique Ads
Democratic allies								
Candidates								
Democratic Senatorial Candidates	105	51	27	5	29	37	151	405
Democratic Congressional Candidates	29	86	7	14	28	20	78	262
Political parties								
State Democratic Parties	2	57	—	4	14	—	4	81
DCCC	—	47	—	—	1	3	29	80
DSCC	—	18	—	—	—	2	33	53
Local Democratic Parties	—	4	1	—	1	—	—	6
Interest groups								
Citizens for a Strong Senate	—	13	—	—	1	—	9	23
AFL-CIO	4	13	—	—	2	—	—	19
Sierra Club	2	10	—	—	7	—	—	19
League of Conservation Voters	—	10	1	1	1	1	3	17
National Education Association	—	13	—	—	3	—	—	16
EMILY's List	8	5	—	1	1	—	—	15
America Coming Together	4	7	1	1	—	—	—	13
Focus South Dakota	—	5	8	—	—	—	—	13
NARAL Pro-Choice America	4	8	—	—	—	—	—	12
New House PAC	—	—	—	—	9	—	—	9
We the People	—	—	—	—	7	—	—	7
New Democrat Network	—	—	—	—	—	—	6	6
American Federation of Teachers	—	5	—	—	—	—	—	5
Issues Matter	—	—	—	—	2	2	1	5
AFSCME	—	4	—	—	—	—	—	4
Human Rights Campaign	1	3	—	—	—	—	—	4

Association of Trial Lawyers of America	—	2	—	—	—	—	1	3
Credit Union Legislative Action Council of CUNA	—	3	—	—	—	—	—	3
Florida Women Vote	—	3	—	—	—	—	—	3
ITC Research	—	—	—	—	3	—	—	3
Moving America Forward	—	3	—	—	1	—	—	3
NC Association of Educators	—	2	—	—	—	—	—	3
Oklahomans for Sound Leadership	—	3	—	—	—	—	—	3
Planned Parenthood Action Fund	—	3	—	—	1	—	—	3
Alaska State Employees Association	—	1	—	—	—	—	—	2
American Family Voices	—	—	—	—	—	—	2	2
Clean Water Action	—	2	—	—	—	—	—	2
Democracy for America	2	—	—	—	—	—	—	2
Individual Donors	—	—	—	—	—	2	—	2
NM Federation of Education Employees	—	2	—	—	—	—	—	2
People for the American Way	1	1	—	—	—	—	—	2
USA Public Opinion Group	—	—	—	—	2	—	—	2
Republican allies								
Candidates								
Republican Senatorial Candidates	59	30	37	3	10	53	123	315
Republican Congressional Candidates	23	99	6	8	18	21	69	244
Political parties								
State Republican Parties	21	158	—	5	17	1	2	204
NRCC	1	51	1	—	13	—	38	103
NRSC	—	29	1	—	7	5	52	94
Local Republican Parties	1	2	1	—	—	—	—	4

(continued)

TABLE 8.1 NUMBER OF UNIQUE CAMPAIGN COMMUNICATIONS BY ORGANIZATION, SAMPLE CONGRESSIONAL RACES, 2004 *(continued)*

Interest groups							
U.S. Chamber of Commerce	—	56	2	12	1	—	1	72
National Rifle Association	—	17	6	—	—	3	7	33
National Association of Realtors	—	25	1	—	—	—	1	27
National Right to Life	—	16	—	—	2	4	—	22
United Seniors Association	—	13	2	—	—	1	5	21
Americans for Job Security	—	6	2	—	2	1	7	18
American Medical Association	—	—	10	—	—	2	5	17
NFIB	—	12	—	—	—	2	—	14
The Seniors Coalition	—	12	1	—	—	—	—	13
Club for Growth	1	—	2	—	—	—	7	10
Focus on the Family Action	—	6	1	—	—	—	—	7
Associated Builders and Contractors	—	6	—	—	—	—	—	6
National Association of Home Builders	—	6	—	—	—	—	—	6
National Right to Work Committee	—	6	—	—	—	—	—	6
Susan B. Anthony List	—	1	—	—	4	—	—	5
Individual Donors	—	—	4	—	—	—	—	4
You're Fired	—	—	—	—	—	2	2	4
American Democracy Project	—	3	—	—	—	—	—	3
Council For Government Reform	—	3	—	—	—	—	—	3
Freedom Works	1	—	—	1	1	—	—	3
Hispanos Unidos	—	3	—	—	—	—	—	3
Kansans for Life	—	2	1	—	—	—	—	3
Thanksgiving 2004 Committee	—	—	3	—	—	—	—	3
60 Plus	—	2	—	—	—	—	—	2
Americans for Tax Reform	—	1	—	—	—	—	1	2

Americans United to Preserve Marriage	—	—	—	—	—	—	—	2	2
Ave Maria List	—	1	—	1	—	—	—	—	2
National Pro-Life Alliance	—	2	—	—	—	—	—	—	2
Nonpartisan									
Interest groups									
JustGoVote.org	—	14	—	4	—	—	—	—	18
AARP	1	7	—	1	—	—	—	—	9
True Majority.org	4	—	—	—	—	—	—	—	4
Southwest Voter Registration Education Project	—	1	—	2	—	—	—	—	3
Americans for Better Government	—	1	—	1	—	—	—	—	2
Mainsteam PAC	—	1	—	1	—	—	—	—	2
Puerto Rico Federal Affairs Admin.	1	2	—	—	—	—	—	—	2
Rock the Vote	—	—	—	1	—	—	—	—	2
Women's Voices. Women Vote.	—	2	—	—	—	—	—	—	2

[a]Data represent the number of unique or distinct pieces or ads by the group and do not represent a count of total items sent or made. This table is not intended to portray comprehensive organization activity within the sample races.

[b]All state and local chapters or affiliates have been combined with their national affiliate to better render the picture of the organization's activity. For instance, National Rifle Association Institute for Legislative Action and National Rifle Association Political Victory Fund data have been included in the National Rifle Association totals.

[c]Certain organizations that maintained neutrality were categorized according to which candidates their ads supported or attacked or whether the organization was openly anti- or pro- conservative or liberal.

In blank cells, "—" only reflects the absence of collected data and does not imply the organization was inactive in that medium.

Source: Data compiled from David B. Magleby, J. Quin Monson, and Kelly D. Patterson, "2004 Campaign Communications Database," (Center for the Study of Elections and Democracy: Brigham Young University, 2005).

Note: Abbreviations: DCCC, Democratic Congressional Campaign Committee; DSCC, Democratic Senatorial Campaign Committee; AFL-CIO, American Federation of Labor and Congress of Industrial Organizations; NARAL, National Abortion and Reproductive Rights Action League; PAC, political action committee; AFCSME, American Federation of State, County and Municipal Employees; CUNA, Credit Union National Association; NRCC, National Republican Congressional Committee; NRSC, National Republican Senatorial Committee; NFIB, National Federation for Independent Business; AARP, American Association of Retired Person.

again included a mix of television and radio but had an even greater emphasis on mail, phone calls, personal contact, and GOTV.

In several of the congressional races, the groups and parties did more contacting through mail and phone than the candidates, sometimes with dramatic success. For example, outside group expenditures seem to have kept Tony Knowles (D) competitive in the Alaska U.S. Senate race.[13] In the Colorado Senate race, the Democrats outperformed the Republicans. The opposite was the case in North Carolina.[14]

Second, while groups and parties seemed to rely on modes of communication developed in previous cycles, new organizations, in both the presidential and congressional races, cropped up to disseminate those messages. The 2004 cycle saw growth in interest group activity through 527 and 501(c) organizations. The most visible and well funded of these operated nearly exclusively in presidential battlegrounds, and the content of the ads focused on the presidential race. However, these ads may have had some spillover on congressional elections like the Florida and Colorado Senate races and competitive House races in Pennsylvania. Especially important in the presidential race were the ads run by Democratic allies in the March to August period when Bush was aggressively seeking to knock Kerry from the race. These ads run by the Media Fund and others helped keep Kerry competitive. Towards the end of the race two pro-Bush groups emerged whose ads helped reinforced key Bush themes. The Swift Boat Veterans for Truth attacked Kerry's record as a war hero and his ability to lead the country; and another group, Progress for America, ran an effective positive ad that told the story of President Bush showing compassion to the daughter of a victim of the terrorist attacks of September 11, 2001. Outside groups on the Democratic side were also heavily involved in voter mobilization through a Section 527 group named the America Votes Coalition and especially by the well-funded America Coming Together.[15]

This is not to say that interest groups were unimportant to U.S. Senate races. In South Dakota, an array of interest groups were important contributors to the defeat of Tom Daschle. The U.S. Chamber of Commerce alone sent 14 different mailers in the South Dakota race.[16] In Ken Salazar's (D) victory in Colorado, interest groups were important on the air and on the ground, especially liberal interest groups who "were considerably more active on the ground than conservative groups."[17] In North Carolina, AJS, the NAR, and the NRA were important to the Burr victory.[18] One group, the Club for Growth, boasted, "We carried Tom Coburn on our back" in the Oklahoma Senate race.[19]

Without the competition from an intense and competitive presidential election, it is not unreasonable to expect that additional groups will form in the future to affect congressional elections or that existing groups will spend more money on House and Senate contests than they did in 2004. Early in the 2004 cycle, some 527 organizations were formed with an exclusive emphasis on congressional elections. Such 527s included the New House PAC and the Democratic Senate Majority Fund on the Democratic side and the National Committee for a Responsible Senate and the Leadership Forum on the Republican side.[20] These early Congressional 527 committees, however, were initially deemed a failure for many reasons. The concept behind congressional 527s was hard to explain to donors, and there was little initial excitement over the House and Senate contests. "The polarization of this [presidential] race is so high," claimed one pollster, "but it just isn't moving over to the Congress."[21] The congressional 527 organizations also proved to be "bureaucratically unmanageable."[22] In addition, prolonged uncertainty regarding the outcome of *McConnell* v. *FEC* and the consistent flow of funds towards the presidential contest crippled the fundraising efforts of these more nascent 527 organizations.[23] Finally, corporations did not play a significant role in financing 527 organizations. Instead, corporate money principally flowed to business trade organizations, also known as 501(c)(6) organizations, who could communicate with their members without the usual campaign finance restrictions.[24]

A second generation of congressional 527s emerged later in the summer and thrived, having resolved many of the problems that plagued its predecessors. The LCV, for example, made the Colorado Senate race a major priority, spending nearly $500,000.[25] The CSS, which spent $1.2 million favoring Democrat Erskine Bowles in North Carolina, spent nearly $750,000 for Democrat Ken Salazar in Colorado, over $400,000 for Democrat Brad Carson in Oklahoma, and over $300,000 for Democrat Tony Knowles in Alaska. The Club for Growth spent nearly $2 million against Arlen Specter in the Pennsylvania primary[26] and almost $900,000 for Tom Coburn in the Oklahoma Senate race.[27]

A possible harbinger of 527 and 501(c) group activity in 2006 and beyond is the formation of groups operating in only one contest. For example, in the Colorado Republican primary, one 527 group, Colorado Conservative Voters, spent nearly $1 million against Coors and for Bob Schafer.[28] Another single-contest 527 was "You're Fired," a group founded by Robin Arkley, which ran ads in the South Dakota Senate race against Tom Daschle.[29]

Finally, the increase in the amount of money that individuals can contribute may enhance the effect of bundling, a process where a group solicits contributions for a candidate and then delivers these checks together in a bundle demonstrating the collective contribution of the members of the group. Some groups have long bundled individual contributions. ALIGNPAC, a political action committee of independent insurance agents, for instance, collected $250,000 from insurance agents and in 1986 presented the donation to Senator Robert Packwood, then chair of the Senate Finance Committee.[30] The most important interest groups in terms of bundling in 2004 were EMILY's List, the Club for Growth, and MoveOn.

CONCLUSION

Our focus in this book has been on how competitive congressional elections are financed. It is important to underscore that the vast majority of congressional contests are not competitive. In these contests the challengers are poorly funded and largely invisible. The number of competitive contests has declined since 1996 at the same time that the margin of party control in the House and Senate as become narrow. This has meant that individuals, groups, and party committees concentrate their attention and interest on those few races that have the potential to determine party control.

While competitive races are different in terms of level of funding, attention from outside groups, and so on, they also demonstrate some key regularities of congressional elections generally. First, incumbency matters. In both House and Senate races, the incumbent often had advantages that could be exploited. Lisa Murkowski, even though her incumbency was the result of a gubernatorial appointment, benefited from her visible support of allowing drilling for oil in the Arctic National Wildlife Refuge (ANWR). In the House races we monitored, such as Utah 2, New Mexico 1, and Kansas 3, the incumbents were able to point to their record in office as a positive element of their campaign.

Even with the large investments by party committees, outside groups, individual donors, and the candidates themselves it is important to remember that candidates matter. Voters evaluate strengths and weaknesses and what they like and dislike about candidates, and this appeal or lack of it becomes important. Examples of candidates who were found wanting by voters were Pete Coors in the Colorado Senate race, Dave Thomas in the Colorado 7 House race and Kris Kobach in the Kansas 3 House race. As Kyle Saunders and Robert Duffy observe, "Any hopes Thomas might have had about running on the issues were dashed in mid-September with the release of a grand jury report about the 1999 Columbine High School shootings. Media coverage centered on Thomas' rule in a private meeting held a few days after the shooting, focusing on charges that Thomas might have helped cover up the existence of an affidavit that might have allowed the sheriff to obtain a search warrant for one of the killer's homes. The Beauprez campaign and the NRCC immediately seized on the report to launch an offensive from which Thomas never recovered."[31] Sometimes candidates self-destruct late in the race; others do it earlier. One race we anticipated studying in 2004 was the Illinois Senate race, but Republican front-runner Jack Ryan had to withdraw from the race after the primary because of a personal scandal.

Second, ideological interest groups, such as the Christian Right, will remain active in congressional contests but will also continue to face the tension between backing a candidate who shares their values or who has a chance of winning the general election. Sometimes groups are not forced to face such a trade off. However, in the Kansas 3 race, the Christian Right was instrumental in selecting a Republican nominee who could not win the votes of moderate Republicans in the district. In the Colorado Senate race, the Christian Right's preferred candidate did not prevail in the primary. The result led to lackluster support from the Christian Right for Pete Coors, costing him precious votes in his unsuccessful electoral bid. Much has been written about the influence of the Christian Right and other ideological groups in congressional elections. The examples in this volume seem to indicate that the ideology of these groups can be both a blessing and a curse. The commitments of the groups make it possible to mobilize resources on behalf of candidates. Yet the commitment sometimes precludes the opportunity to back candidates who do not share all of the group's values. Consequently, these groups often lose opportunities to put candidates in office who would be more sympathetic to their causes.

Another characteristic present in several of the congressional races we examined is that local issues and local leaders matter, despite the national attention brought by outside money and outside groups. The heavy involvement of Alaska Senator Ted Stevens campaigning for Lisa Murkowski helped reelect Murkowski. The tobacco buyout enacted by Congress helped Republican Brad Miller demonstrate he could deliver on a crop that continues to be very important to North Carolina. Another regularity we saw in 2004 was that coattails from a candidate of the predominant party in the state matter. President Bush and the Republican advantage in registration helped elect Republicans in competitive races in such red states as Alaska, North Carolina, Oklahoma, and South Dakota.

Finally, divisive intraparty primaries often hurt the chances of the candidate who emerges from that contest. This was true in three of our contests. The battle for the nomination in Colorado Senate among the Republicans left the more conservative base of the party disaffected when their preferred candidate, Bob Schafer, lost the primary to the better known and better funded Pete Coors. Similar divisive primaries in Kansas 3 and Pennsylvania 13 among the Republicans hurt their candidates in the general election.

Competitive congressional elections in 2004, as has been the case in recent election cycles, saw a major infusion of "outside money." This spending by parties and groups was important. In 2004, that money came into the race via party and other independent expenditures and spending by Section 527 organizations. As with the expenditure of soft money in the recent past, much of this money was spent on candidate-specific advertising and was largely negative in tone. The success of Swift Boat Veterans for Truth in the presidential race will likely reinforce the sense that attacks by 527 organizations can be consequential. Outside group and political party activity was important to several of the races we monitored.

Two major trends that may continue in 2006 are the presence of contest-specific section 527 organizations, some that engaged in heavy activity even in primary elections. Second, the nature of House elections is now such that there are very few arenas in which groups and party committees compete. That, plus the gradually expanding GOP majority in the House, probably means the focus in 2006 will remain more on the Senate than on the House.

Notes

1. Harold Ickes, founder, Media Fund, interview by David B. Magleby and Betsey Gimbel, Washington, D.C., September 16, 2004.
2. Charles Cunningham, director of Federal Affairs, National Rifle Association, interview by David B. Magleby and Kristina Gale, Washington, D.C., November 5, 2004.
3. Benjamin Jones, research director, Democratic Senatorial Campaign Committee, interview by David B. Magleby and J. Quin Monson, Washington, D.C., November 10, 2004.
4. Staff, "Redistricting Pays Off for GOP," *Houston Chronicle*, November 3, 2004, p. 5.
5. For PAC citation, see Center for Responsive Politics, "Candidate to Candidate Giving: Leadership PACs," www.opensecrets.org/overview/cand2cand.asp?Cycle=2004&Display = leadpacs (accessed May 16, 2005). For candidate committee data, see Center for Responsive Politics, "Candidate to Candidate Giving: Candidate Committees," www.opensecrets.org/bigpicture/cand2cand.asp?Cycle=2004&Display=cmtes (accessed May 16, 2005).
6. Mark Longabaugh, political affairs senior vice president, League of Conservation Voters, interview by David B. Magleby, Betsey Gimbel, and Joe Hadfield, Washington, D.C., July 24, 2004.
7. See Chapter 2 in this volume.
8. Ibid.
9. CNN.com, "Election Results," www.cnn.com/ELECTION/2004/pages/results/governor (accessed January 27, 2005).
10. J. Quin Monson, "Get On TeleVision vs. Get On The Van: GOTV and the Ground War in 2002," *The Last Hurrah?: Soft Money and Issue Advocacy in the 2002 Congressional Elections*, eds. David B. Magleby and J. Quin Monson (Washington, D.C.: Brookings Institution Press, 2004), pp. 90–91.
11. David B. Magleby, J. Quin Monson, and Kelly D. Patterson, *Dancing Without Partners: How Candidates, Parties and Interest Groups Interact in the Presidential Campaign*, (Lanham, MD: Rowman and Littlefield, forthcoming); David B. Magleby, "Change and Continuity in the Financing of Federal Elections," *Financing the 2004 Election*, eds. Anthony Corrado, David B. Magleby, and Kelly D. Patterson, (Washington, D.C. Brookings Institution Press, forthcoming).
12. See David B. Magleby, ed., "Overview," in *Election Advocacy: Soft Money and Issue Advocacy in the 2000 Congressional Elections*, A report of a grant funded by the Pew Charitable Trust (Brigham Young University, Center for the Study of Elections and Democracy, 2001), p. 37; see also David B. Magleby and J. Quin Monson, "The Last Hurrah?: Soft Money and Issue Advocacy in the 2002 Congressional Elections," in *The Last Hurrah?: Soft Money and Issue Advocacy in the 2002 Congressional Elections*, eds. David B. Magleby and J. Quin Monson, A report of a grant funded by the Pew Charitable Trusts (Brigham Young University, Center for the Study of Elections and Democracy, February 3, 2003), pp. 41–42.
13. See Carl Shepro and Clive Thomas, "The 2004 Alaska U.S. Senate Race," in *Dancing Without Partners: How Candidates, Parties, and Interest Groups Interact in the New Campaign Finance Environment*, eds. Magleby, Monson, and Patterson. A report of a grant funded by the Pew Charitable Trusts (Brigham Young University, Center for the Study of Elections and Democracy, 2005), p. 165.
14. See Chapter 2 in this volume.
15. *Financing the 2004 Election*, eds. Corrado, Magleby, and Patterson; *Dancing Without Partners: How Candidates, Parties and Interest Groups Interact in the Presidential Campaign*, eds. Magleby, Monson, and Patterson.
16. See Chapter 3 in this volume.
17. See Chapter 2 in this volume.

18. See Chapter 3 in this volume.
19. Stephen Moore, president, Club for Growth, interview by David B. Magleby and Richard Hawkins, Washington, D.C., November 5, 2004.
20. Chris Cillizza, "Leaders Fill PAC Coffers," *Roll Call*, October 27, 2003; Ben Pershing, "House Administration Sets Hearing on 527s," *Roll Call*, November 13, 2003.
21. Ed Goeas, president, The Tarrance Group, interview by David B. Magleby and Betsey Gimbel, Arlington, VA, June 3, 2004.
22. Andy Grossman, director of research and technology, America Coming Together, interview by David B. Magleby, Betsey Gimbel, and Joe Hadfield, Washington, D.C., June 24, 2004.
23. Chris Cillizza, "Congressional 527s Are a Flop," *Roll Call*, April 26, 2004, pp. 1, 3.
24. Kent Cooper, vice president, PoliticalMoneyLine, interview by David B. Magleby and Kristina Gale, Washington, D.C., November 9, 2004.
25. See Chapter 2 in this volume.
26. Pamela M. Prah, "Anti-tax Groups Post Mixed Record in Nov. 2 Elections," Stateline.org, December 22, 2004, www.stateline.org/live/viewpage.action?sitenodel=136&languageid= 1&contentid=15881 (accessed January 26, 2005).
27. See Ronald Keith Gaddie, and others. "The 2004 Oklahoma U.S. Senate Race," in *Dancing Without Partners*, eds. Magleby, Monson, and Patterson, p. 222.
28. See Chapter 2 in this volume.
29. See Chapter 4 in this volume.
30. David B. Magleby and Candice J. Nelson, *The Money Chase: Congressional Campaign Finance Reform* (Washington, D.C.: Brookings Institution Press, 1990), p. 20.
31. Saunders, Kyle and Robert Duffy, "The 2004 Colorado 7th Congressional District Race," in *Dancing Without Partners: How Candidates, Parties, and Interest Groups Interact in the New Campaign Finance Environment.*

APPENDIX A: INTERVIEWS BY CSED RESEARCHERS

NAME	TITLE	ORGANIZATION	DATE(S)
Martin Burns	Manager, State Communications Office; Internal Communications	AARP	11/5/04, 06/02/04
Beth Berendson	Organizer	ACORN Ohio	10/27/04
Andy Grossman	Director of Research and Technology	ACT	11/12/04, 06/24/04, 02/12/04
Jess Goode	Ohio State Communications Director	ACT	10/27/04
Karin Johanson	State Director Florida	ACT	7/24/04, 11/19/04
Larry Gold	Legal Counsel	ACT	12/17/04
Steve Rosenthal	CEO	ACT	12/17/04
Tait Sye	Florida State Communications Director	ACT	07/24/04
Matt Tomey	New York State Volunteer Coordinator	ACT	08/24/04
Norm Ornstein	Resident Scholar	AEI	12/18/03
David Boundy	Deputy Director, Political Department	AFL-CIO	12/16/04
Keith Goodman	Research Analyst, Political Department	AFL-CIO	12/16/04, 07/08/04
Mike Podhorzer	Assistant Director, Political Department	AFL-CIO	12/16/04, 07/08/04
Dave Kolbe	Political Director, Community Services and Legislation	AFL-CIO Ohio	10/27/04
Pierrette "Petee" Talley	Secretary-Treasurer	AFL-CIO Ohio	10/27/04
Kim Alfano Doyle	President and CEO	Alfano Leonardo Communications	06/24/04
Jim Kawka	Regional Political Director, Division of Political and Legislative Grassroots	AMA PAC	12/16/04

Name	Title	Organization	Date(s)
Mike Cys	Director, Division of Political and Legislative Grassroots	AMA PAC	12/16/04
Steve Rosenthal	CEO	America Coming Together	12/17/04
Cathy Duvall	National Field Director	America Votes	08/18/04
Cecile Richards	President	America Votes	12/28/04
Jim Jordan	Communications Consultant	America Votes	07/06/04
Parag Mehta	Deputy Political Director	America Votes	07/06/04
Angela Manso	Deputy Director and Chief of Staff	America's Families United	08/17/04
Peter Valcarce	Political Consultant	Arena Communications	11/05/04
Ned Monroe	Director of Political Affairs	Associated Builders and Contractors	11/8/04, 08/19/04
Linda Lipson	Legislative Liaison	Association of Trial Lawyers of America	12/17/04, 06/03/04
Whit Ayres	President	Ayres, McHenry, and Associates	09/16/04
Kristina Wilfore	Executive Director	Ballot Initiative Strategy Center	11/18/04, 08/17/04
Lauren McClintock	Campaign Director	Ballot Initiative Strategy Center	11/18/04
Bernadette Budde	Senior Vice President	BIPAC	11/4/04, 06/22/04, 02/02/04
Tom Mann	Senior Fellow in Governance Studies	Brookings Institute	09/17/04, 06/21/04
Tony Corrado	Visiting Fellow	Brookings Institute	09/17/04, 09/24/04
Michael Ellis	Research Analyst	Bush/Cheney '04	11/18/04, 06/03/04
Nathan Hollifield	Tampa Bay Field Director	Bush/Cheney '04	07/24/04
Sara Taylor	Deputy to the Chief Strategist	Bush/Cheney '04	11/18/04, 06/03/04
Terry Nelson	Political Director	Bush/Cheney '04	01/05/05
Michael Alvarez	Professor of Political Science	California Institute of Technology	05/20/04
Marianne Holt Viray	Managing Director	Campaign Legal Center	09/17/04, 11/11/03
David Donnelly	Director	Campaign Money Watch	08/19/04
Trevor Potter	Campaigns and Election lawyer	Caplin and Drysdale	10/28/04, 04/27/04
Michael Malbin	Executive Director	CFI	03/10/04
Robert G. Boatright	Research Analyst	CFI	03/10/04
Rob Jordan	National Director of Federal and State Campaigns	Citizens for Sound Economy	11/11/04, 08/20/04
David Keating	Executive Director	Club for Growth	06/22/04
Stephen Moore	President	Club for Growth	11/05/04, 02/13/04

Name	Title	Organization	Date(s)
Michael Petro	Chief of Staff and Vice President, Business and Government Relations	Committee for Economic Development	11/19/04
Curtis Gans	Director	Committee for the Study of the American Electorate	10/29/04
Chellie Pingree	President	Common Cause	03/10/04
Ed Davis	Research Director	Common Cause	12/17/04
Matt Schaffer	Research Analyst	Common Cause	12/17/04
Matt Angle	Chief of Staff	Congressman Martin Frost	06/01/04
Aron Pilhofer	Database editor	CPI	10/28/04, 06/03/04, 02/02/04
Kori Bernards	Communications Director	DCCC	03/09/04
Peter Cari	Political Director	DCCC	12/14/04, 04/28/04
Kay Oshel	Chief, Division of Interpretations and Standards	Department of Labor	07/08/04
Larry Yud	Head of the Enforcement Division	Department of Labor	07/08/04
Amy Pritchard	Political Director	DNC	01/13/05, 02/02/04
Ellen Moran	Director, Independent Expenditure Unit	DNC	12/16/04, 08/19/04
Gail Stoltz	Former Political Director	DNC	02/02/04
Josh Wachs	COO	DNC	01/11/05
Lina Brunton	Voter Contact Director	DNC	08/18/04, 06/24/04
Marie Terese Dominguez	Independent Consultant on Hispanic Outreach	DNC	12/17/04
Benjamin Jones	Research Director	DSCC	11/10/04
Brad Woodhouse	Communications Director	DSCC	11/11/03
David Hamrick	National Field Director	DSCC	12/16/04
David Rudd	Executive Director	DSCC	03/10/04
Paul Tewes	Political Director	DSCC	02/20/04
Karen White	Political Director	EMILY's List	11/08/04, 08/17/04
Sheila O'Connell	Senior Advisor	EMILY's List	02/21/04
Chris Murray	Political Director	Environment 2004	08/16/04
Bob Biersack	Deputy Press Officer	FEC	10/29/04
Michael Toner	Commissioner	FEC	10/29/04
Paul Clark	Disclosure Systems Analyst	FEC	06/02/04
Laurie Moskowitz	Partner	FieldWorks	06/02/04
Tom Minnery	Vice President, Public Policy	Focus on the Family	12/16/04
Eddie Mahe	Strategic Communications Counsel	Foley and Lardner LLP	07/07/04
Fred Yang	Partner	Garin, Hart, and Yang Research Group	11/10/04

NAME	TITLE	ORGANIZATION	DATE(S)
J. Toscano	Senior Vice President	GMMmb	08/17/04
Pamela Mantis	Vice-President for Communications	GOPAC	07/07/04
Ed Brookover	Chairman of the Political Practice	Greener and Hook	03/09/04
Judith Kindell	Attorney	IRS	11/11/03
Martin Hamburger	Media Consultant	Laguens Hamburger Strategies	06/02/04
Celinda Lake	President	Lake, Snell, Perry, and Associates Inc.	06/22/04
Andy Schultheiss	Southwest Regional Director	LCV	07/16/04
Chuck Porcari	Communications Director	LCV	04/27/04
Mark Longabaugh	Senior Vice President, Political Affairs	LCV	11/10/04, 06/24/04
Lloyd Leonard	Legislative Director	League of Women Voters	03/09/04
Michael Matthews	Principal	LSG strategies	06/01/04
Erik Smith	Executive Director	The Media Fund	11/10/04, 06/02/04
Harold Ickes	President	The Media Fund	11/11/04, 09/16/04
John Hutchins	Owner	Media Strategies and Research	07/16/04
Wes Boyd	Co-founder	MoveOn.org	12/14/04, 09/10/04
Claude Foster	National Field Director	NAACP Voter Fund	12/15/04
Elizabeth Shipp	Political Director	NARAL Pro-Choice America	11/09/04, 03/09/04
Tiffany Adams	Vice President, Public Affairs	National Association of Manufacturers	11/05/04, 04/27/04
David Rehr	President	National Beer Wholesalers Association	11/05/04, 08/20/04
Linda Auglis	Political Affairs Director	National Beer Wholesalers Association	11/05/04, 08/20/04
Dennis Friel	East Field Manager Campaign 2004	NEA	11/04/04, 06/02/04
Lily Eskelson	Secretary-Treasurer	NEA	06/02/04
Simon Rosenberg	President	New Democrat Network	12/16/04, 07/06/04
Ivan Frishberg	Director	New Voter Project	11/11/04
Andrew Fimka	Coordinator, Political Programs	NFIB	12/15/04
Sharon Wolff Sussin	National Political Director	NFIB	12/15/04, 03/10/04
Chuck Cunningham	Federal Affairs Director	NRA	11/05/04, 02/02/04

NAME	TITLE	ORGANIZATION	DATE(S)
Glen Caroline	Director, NRA-ILA Grassroots Division	NRA	11/10/04
Jim Landry	Research Analyst	NRSC	11/11/03
Patrick Davis	Political Director	NRSC	11/11/04, 08/19/04, 11/11/03
Ben Ginsberg	Election Lawyer	Patton Boggs	11/10/04, 06/23/04
Kimberly Robson	Deputy Field Director for Legislative Election Programs	People for the American Way	11/05/04, 07/07/04
Mary Jean Collins	Vice President and National Field Director	People for the American Way	12/13/04
Bob Bauer	Election lawyer	Perkins Coie	11/11/04, 06/03/04
Ken Bowler	Vice President—Federal Government Relations	Pfizer	03/11/04
David Williams	Political Director	Planned Parenthood	11/08/04, 04/28/04
Kent Cooper	Co-founder	Political Money Line	11/09/04, 04/27/04
Tony Raymond	Co-founder	Political Money Line	04/27/04
Mike Lux	President	Progressive Strategies	11/12/04, 02/13/04
Bill McInturff	Partner and Co-Founder	Public Opinion Strategies	09/17/04
Blaise Hazelwood	Political Director	RNC	09/08/04, 12/20/04
Charles Spies	Deputy Counsel	RNC	12/15/04
Dan Gurley	Deputy Political Director	RNC	06/01/04
Noe Garcia	Director of Coalitions and Grassroots Outreach	RNC	03/08/04
Raul Damas	National Grassroots Director	RNC	12/13/04, 08/18/04
Jim Innocenzi	Media Consultant	Sandler and Innocenzi	07/07/04
Andy Stern	President	SEIU	11/08/04
Jack Polidori	Political Director	SEIU	02/19/04
Greg Haegele	Political Director	The Sierra Club	11/11/04, 06/01/04
Michael Vachon	Communications Director	Soros Political Director	11/08/04
April Schiff	President	Strategic Solutions	07/24/04
Jennifer Bingham	Executive Director	Susan B. Anthony List	09/16/04
Chris LaCivita	Senior Advisor	Swift Boat Veterans for Truth	11/17/04, 6/22/04, 02/02/04
Dan Hazelwood	President	Targeted Creative Communications	11/09/04, 06/02/04
Alexander Gage	President	TargetPoint Consulting	12/16/04
Brent Seaborn	Vice President	TargetPoint Consulting	12/16/04

Name	Title	Organization	Date(s)
Michael Myers	Vice President	TargetPoint Consulting	12/16/04
Curt Anderson	Independent Consultant; NRSC	The Anderson Group	12/15/04
Derek Willis	Data Specialist	The Center for Public Integrity	06/03/04, 02/12/04, 11/11/03
Larry Noble	Executive Director	The Center for Responsive Politics	12/18/03
Sheila Krumholz	Research Director	The Center for Responsive Politics	4/27/04, 12/18/03
Steve Weiss	Communications Director and Editor	The Center for Responsive Politics	12/18/03
Wally Clinton	Chairman	The Clinton Group	06/21/04
Susan Hirshmann	President	The Leadership Forum	11/18/04
Doug Usher	Vice President	The Mellman Group	08/16/04
Mark Mellman	President and CEO	The Mellman Group	11/12/04
Ed Goeas	President, CEO	The Terrance Group	11/05/04, 06/30/04
Evan Tracey	CEO	TNS Media Intelligence/CMAG	10/28/04, 04/28/04
Monica Franklin	Assistant General Counsel	Turner Broadcasting	09/17/04
Bill Miller	Vice President, Public Affairs and National Political Director	U.S. Chamber of Commerce	11/09/04, 06/24/04, 02/01/04
Bob Bennett	U.S. Senator	U.S. Senate, Utah	11/05/04
Rob Bishop	U.S. Representative	U.S. House, Utah	09/15/04
Arlene Holt Baker	President	Voices for Working Families	11/18/04, 08/17/04
Kate Snyder	Women's Program Director	Voices for Working Families	11/18/04
Kenny Diggs	National Field Director	Voices for Working Families	11/18/04
John Guzik	Vice President	Williams & Mullen Strategies	12/19/03
Heather Booth	Independent Consultant		11/18/04, 06/23/04

Note: Abbreviations: AARP, American Association of Retired Persons; ACORN, Association of Community Organizations for Reform Now; ACT, America Coming Together; AEI, American Enterprise Institute; AFL-CIO, American Federation of Labor and Congress of Industrial Organizations; AMA PAC, American Medical Association Political Action Committee; BIPAC, Business Industry Political Action Committee; CFI, Campaign Finance Institute; CPI, Center for Public Integrity; DCCC, Democratic Congressional Campaign Committee; DNC, Democratic National Committee; DSCC, Democratic Senatorial Campaign Committee; FEC, Federal Election Commission; GMMB, Greer, Margolis, Mitchell, Burns; GOPAC, GOP PAC; IRS, Internal Revenue Service; LCV, League of Conservation Voters; NAACP, National Association for the Advancement of Colored Persons; NARAL, National Abortion and Reproductive Rights Action League; NEA, National Education Association; NFIB, National Federation of Independent Business; NRA, National Rifle Association; NRA-ILA, National Rifle Association Institute for Legislative Action; NRSC, National Republican Senatorial Committee; RNC, Republican National Committee; SEIU, Service Employees International Union; CMAG, Campaign Media Analysis Group.

INDEX